Berk

Infants, Children, and Adolescents,

Fourth Edition

JoDe Paladino and Laura E. Berk,
Illinois State University

Allyn and Bacon
Boston ▸ London ▸ Toronto ▸ Sydney ▸ Tokyo ▸ Singapore

Copyright © 2002 by Allyn & Bacon
A Pearson Education Company
75 Arlington Street
Boston, MA 02116

Internet: www.ablongman.com

ISBN 0-205-33609-4

Printed in the United States of America

10 9 8 7   04 03 02

Table of Contents

Table of Contents

Preface

As you embark on the fascinating journey of studying child development, it is our hope that this Study Guide will help you master the material in your text, *Infants, Children, and Adolescents (4e)*. Our intention in preparing the Study Guide is to provide you with active practice in learning the content of your textbook, thought-provoking questions that help you think critically about the material, and pleasurable exercises that assist you in mastering the basic vocabulary of the field. But to get the most out of the Study Guide, you must approach your reading assignments and classroom experiences with good study habits. In the following sections, we offer some basic study tips, which, if followed carefully, will improve your learning in any college course. Then we show how you can use this Study Guide to enhance your mastery of child development.

STUDY TIPS

Learning any new subject is a challenging and effortful task. Organizing your time, creating a climate for learning, previewing the material, reading actively, reviewing effectively, and using effective classroom learning techniques are essential parts of any successful study plan.

1. **Organizing Your Time.** Map out your study hours ahead of time to guarantee that you have enough time to study well. Purchase a study plan book covering the school year in which the days of the week are divided into time periods with sufficient space to write in a weekly schedule. Set aside at least two hours of study time for each class meeting. At the beginning of each week, write in what you intend to do during each study period. Then stick to your plan, checking off each item listed as you complete it. At the end of each week, evaluate how well your study schedule worked, and modify the next week's plan in light of your conclusions.

   Following a schedule eases the work of studying because it does away with the energy-consuming, conflict-ridden tasks of making decisions like these: "Should I study now or later?" "If I study now, what should I do first and what next?" In addition, your schedule will probably show that you have more time than you thought for activities you want to do — especially if you maintain your study schedule and use your time wisely.

2. **Creating a Climate for Learning.** Choose a place to study that is relatively free of distractions, both visual and auditory. If your desk is cluttered with photos and mementos, clear it so that you will not be tempted to focus on those items instead of your course assignments. To mask distracting sounds, some students find it helpful to play soft music while studying. If you do so, try to choose music that is not attention-grabbing itself. Make sure your study area is well lighted and that study implements (pens, pencils, and paper) are nearby so that you do not have to interrupt your work to get them. Finally, if you study regularly in a special place set aside for that purpose, you will save time because entering that space will trigger a "mental set" for getting down to work quickly.

3. **Previewing the Material.** Begin mastering a chapter by previewing the material. Look ahead and identify the highlights of the assignment by reading the introduction, major headings, and summaries. Previewing permits you to grasp the structure of the information in the assignment. When you know the layout of what you are about to learn, you are better able to organize the information meaningfully and remember it. Previewing has been shown to reduce the amount of study time needed while increasing learning.

4. **Reading Actively.** Read carefully, searching for main points. Underline them in your textbook, and write them down in your notebook. Keep in mind that studying is different from just reading. When you study, your mind is constantly active, and you are always searching for important ideas. If you approach your assignment passively, by

reading without grappling with the material, you will retain very little.

5. **Reviewing Effectively.** After you finish the assignment, review what you have read. Once again, read the chapter introduction, major headings, and summaries. However, keep in mind that reviewing is not limited to rereading. It involves trying to recall what you have read. Jot down key ideas associated with each major heading. Make up questions about the material and answer them, checking your answers against the content of your text. As you test yourself, you will be anticipating questions that your instructor will ask on examinations. Since you will have answered them in advance, exams will be that much easier when you take them.

6. **Applying Effective Classroom Learning Techniques.** Effective classroom learning requires good listening and note-taking skills. In class, exercise the utmost concentration and discipline in holding your mind on the track of your instructor. As you listen, become actively engaged with the subject matter. Try to anticipate the next point, summarize what has been said in your own words, and imagine the test questions that might be asked about the material. Offer comments about content related to your own knowledge and experience, and ask your instructor about statements that are unclear. The more involved you are in class, the easier it will be to remember the information.

Just as you listen actively, take notes energetically. The format of your notes is critically important. Put the date of the lecture and its subject at the top of the page. Write your notes toward the right-hand side, leaving a generous left-hand margin. Listen for key ideas, and write them down in an organized fashion; do not try to capture every word. As soon after the lecture as possible, read your notes and fill in the gaps. Use the left-hand margin to highlight major points and add more detail.

7. **Before, During, and After an Examination.** If you follow the suggestions in the preceding sections, you will avoid the frantic, last-minute cramming that results in disorganized thinking, poor retention, and fear of the test-taking situation. Instead, since you have learned the material gradually and methodically, you will be in a good position to approach the examination confidently—as an opportunity to show your instructor the extent of your knowledge. Get a good night's sleep beforehand, and review your notes one more time the day of the test.

When you get the examination, look it over to get an idea of how quickly you will need to work. Then budget your time accordingly. If the test is in objective format (such as multiple choice and true-false), read each question carefully and entirely, making sure that you notice all qualifying words, such as *usually, always, most, never,* and *some*. At the same time, refrain from reading into questions information that is not there. If the test is in essay format, it requires that you organize your thoughts and express them clearly to do well. Write a brief outline of major points in the margin of your paper, thinking carefully about the arrangement of ideas. As your write, be sure you stick closely to the subject of the question. Include examples, important facts, and explanations to document your generalizations; avoid empty padding of the answer. Reserve 5 to 10 minutes of the period to check your paper before you turn it in.

After the exam has been graded, look over your errors carefully, checking incorrect and omitted answers against the textbook and lecture notes. View the test results as an opportunity to find out what your weaknesses are and to take steps to overcome them. By analyzing the reasons for your mistakes, you will greatly reduce the chances of repeating them on the next text.

This Study Guide is designed to help you create an effective study system for mastering child development. Each of its chapters is organized into the following parts:

CHAPTER SUMMARY

We begin with a brief summary of the chapter, mentioning major topics and general principles in text discussion. Each text chapter includes three additional summaries: (1) an informal summary at the beginning of each chapter, (2) a structured summary at the end of the chapter, and (3) a series of brief reviews, or interim summaries, placed at critical points in the text narrative. Thus, the summary in the Study Guide will be your fourth review of the information in the chapter and should be read before beginning the remaining activities in the guide.

LEARNING OBJECTIVES

The learning objectives describe what you should be able to do once you have mastered the material in each section of the chapter. Look over these objectives before you begin to read, as part of previewing. Then take notes on information relevant to each objective as you move through the chapter. When you finish reading, try to answer each objective in a few sentences or short paragraphs as you review. Once you have completed this exercise, you will have generated your own summary of chapter content. Because it will be written in your own words, it should serve as an especially useful chapter overview that can be referred to as you prepare for examinations.

STUDY QUESTIONS

The main body of each Study Guide chapter consists of study questions, organized according to major headings in the textbook, that will assist you in identifying main ideas and grasping essential concepts. You can use the study questions in several different ways. You may find it helpful to answer each question as you read the chapter, as part of your effort to read actively. Alternatively, try reading one or more sections and testing yourself by answering the relevant study questions. Finally, use the study question section as a device to review for examinations. If you work through it methodically, your retention of chapter material will be greatly improved.

ASK YOURSELF . . .

In each chapter, critical thinking questions that appear at the end of each section of material in your textbook are listed, with space to answer each of them. Answering these questions will help you analyze important theoretical concepts and research findings. Many questions require that you apply what you have learned to problematic situations faced by parents, teachers, and children. In this way, they will help you think deeply about the material and inspire new insights. Each question is page-referenced to chapter material that will help you formulate a response.

TERM REVIEW PUZZLES

To help you master the central vocabulary of the field, we have provided crossword puzzles that test your knowledge of important terms and concepts. Answers can be found at the back of the Study Guide. If you cannot think of the term that matches a clue in the puzzles, your knowledge of information related to the term may be insecure. Reread the material in the text chapter related to each item that you miss. Also, try a more demanding approach to term mastery: After you have completed each puzzle, cover the clues and write your own definition of each term.

SELF-TESTS

Once you have thoroughly studied each chapter, test your knowledge by taking the 25-item self-test. Then check your answers using the key at the back of the Study Guide. Each item is page-referenced to chapter content so that you can conveniently return to textbook sections related to questions that you missed. If you answered more than a few items incorrectly, spend extra time rereading the chapter, writing responses to learning objectives, and reviewing the study question section of this guide.

SUGGESTED READINGS

We hope that as a result of studying child development, you will be motivated to extend your knowledge. In each Study Guide chapter, you will find from three to five suggested readings, which have been carefully chosen to build on chapter content and to be accessible to students who are new to the field of child development. Each suggested reading is accompanied by a brief description of its content.

Now that you understand how this Study Guide is organized, you are ready to begin using it to master *Infants, Children, and Adolescents (4e)*. We wish you a rewarding and enjoyable course of study.

JoDe Paladino and Laura E. Berk

CHAPTER 1

HISTORY, THEORY, AND RESEARCH STRATEGIES

Chapter Summary

Child development is the study of all aspects of human growth and change from conception through adolescence. Researchers often segment the first two decades of life into five age periods. In addition, development is often divided into three broad domains — physical development, cognitive development, and emotional and social development. These divisions make the vast, interdisciplinary study of human constancy more orderly and convenient.

Theories lend structure and meaning to the scientific study of children. This chapter provides an overview of philosophical and theoretical approaches to child study from medieval to modern times. It also reviews major research strategies used to study child behavior and development. When compared and contrasted, historical philosophies and contemporary theories raise three basic issues about what children are like and how they develop: **(1)** Is development continuous or discontinuous? **(2)** Is there one course of development or many? **(3)** Is nature or nurture more important in development? Theories also differ in the degree to which they emphasize stability versus potential for change. Many theories, especially modern ones, take a balanced point of view and recognize the merits of both sides of these issues.

Research methods commonly used to study children include systematic observation, self-reports, psychophysiological methods, the clinical, or case study, method, and ethnography. Investigators of child development generally choose either a correlational or an experimental research design. To study how their participants change over time, they use special developmental research strategies — longitudinal, cross-sectional, longitudinal-sequential, and microgenetic designs. Each method and design has both strengths and limitations.

Conducting research with children also poses special ethical dilemmas. Ethical guidelines for research and special committees determine if the benefits of research outweigh the risks and ensure that children's rights are protected.

1

LEARNING OBJECTIVES

After reading this chapter, you should be able to:

1.1 Explain the importance of the terms *interdisciplinary* and *applied* as they help to define the field of child development. (4-5)

1.2 Explain the role of theories in understanding child development, and describe the three basic issues on which major theories take a stand. (6-9)

1.3 Trace historical influences on modern theories of child development, from medieval times through the early twentieth century. (11-15)

1.4 Describe the theoretical perspectives that influenced child development research in the mid–twentieth century, and cite the contributions and limitations of each. (15-22)

1.5 Describe five recent theoretical perspectives of child development, noting the contributions of major theorists. (23-30)

1.6 Identify the stand that each modern theory takes on the three basic issues of child development presented earlier in this chapter. (32)

1.7 Describe the methods commonly used to study children, and cite the strengths and limitations of each. (34)

1.8 Contrast correlational and experimental research designs, and cite the strengths and limitations of each. (40-41)

1.9 Describe four research designs used to study development, noting the strengths and limitations of each. (43)

1.10 Discuss the unique ethical concerns which arise when conducting research on children. (46-48)

STUDY QUESTIONS

1. Child development is devoted to the study of _all aspects of human growth and change from ~~birth~~ conception to adolescence._

    It is encompassed in a larger discipline known as _developmental psychology_

    _____.

    (4)

The Field of Child Development

1. Child development is an *interdisciplinary* field. Explain what this means. (5)

    Information about CD was obtained from many fields, including sociology, pyscho, anthropology and biology, and various applied fields (education, medicine, family studies)

2. List the five age periods used to segment the first two decades of life. (5)

    A. _Prenatal_

    B. _Infancy/Toddlerhood_

    Age Span: _Conception to 2 yrs_

    C. _Early Childhood_

    Age Span: _2 - 6 years_

D. _Middle childhood_

Age Span: _6-11 years_

E. _Adolescence_

Age Span: _11-20 years_

3. List and describe the three domains of development. (5-6)

   A. _physical - changes in size, shape, appearance, brain development, perceptual and motor capacities, physical health_

   B. _cognitive - thought processes, intellect, attention, memory, imagination, problem solving, language_

   C. _social/emotional - em. communication, self understanding, interpersonal skills, moral reasoning, behavior_

Basic Issues

1. What are the three elements of a good theory? (6)

   A. _definition_   B. _explanation_

   C. _effects on future_

2. Cite two reasons that theories are important to the study of child development. (6)

   A. _Theories provide a set of expectations for observations/meaning_

   B. _" " " provide a basis for action_

3. (True) or False: Theories differ from opinion and belief in that they are subject to scientific verification. (7)

4. Match each theoretical approach with the appropriate description: (7-9)

   _2_ Considers development to be universal across children and across cultures

   _3_ Views development as a process of gradually building upon pre-existing skills

   _6_ Regards environment as the most important influence in development

   _1_ Considers child development in light of distinct contexts

   _4_ Views development as a progression through a series of qualitatively distinct stages

   _5_ Views heredity as the most important influence in development

   1. Multiple courses of development
   2. Single course of development
   3. Continuous
   4. Discontinuous
   5. Nature
   6. Nurture

5. True or False: Most modern theories of development take a strong position on controversial issues such as the nature-nurture debate. (9)

Biology and Environment: Resilient Children

1. _____ refers to the ability to spring back from adversity (10).

2. Briefly list and describe the three broad factors that appear to offer protection from the damaging effects of stressful life events. (10)

A. _____

_____

B. _____

_____

C. _____

_____

Historical Foundations

1. Preformationism, a medieval view of development, regards children as

_____.

(11)

2. True or False: The Puritans placed a high value on the development of reasoning in children. (12)

3. During the Enlightenment, the British philosopher John Locke regarded the child as a *tabula rasa*, which means _____
Briefly explain his view. (12)

_____

_____

_____

4. Jean Jacques Rousseau, a French philosopher during the Enlightenment, introduced the notion of children as noble savages. Explain what he meant by this term. (13)

_____

_____

_____

5. Describe some of the key differences in the theories put forth by John Locke and Jean Jacques Rousseau. (12-13)

_____

_____

_____

6. What are the two principles emphasized in Darwin's theory of evolution? (13)

   A. _____ B. _____

7. What technique did scientists in the late nineteenth and early twentieth centuries use to develop the baby biographies, and what are the limitations of using this type of technique to study child development? (15-16)

_____

_____

_____

_____

_____

8. _____ is generally regarded as the founder of the child study movement. (14)

9. The _____ approach to child development uses age-related averages to represent typical development. (14)

10. _____ constructed the first successful intelligence test. (14)

11. Why did this test succeed, while previous efforts to create a useful intelligence test had failed? (15)

_____

_____

12. A translated version of this test was developed for use with American children. What is the name of this instrument? (15)

_____

Mid-Twentieth-Century Theories

1. True or False: The psychoanalytic perspective emphasizes understanding the unique developmental history of each child. (16)

2. Freud's theory of development is known as _Psychosexual stages_ . (16)

3. Name and briefly describe the three components of personality outlined in Freud's theory. (16-17)

   A. Id – _____

   _____

   B. ego _____

   _____

   C. super ego _____

   _____

4. List the five developmental stages that comprise Freud's psychosexual theory. (16)

   A. oral _____   D. latency _____

   B. anal _____   E. genetal _____

   C. phallic _____

5. Discuss some of the criticisms of Freud's theory. (17)

   _____

   _____

   _____

   _____

6. In what way did Erikson build upon and improve Freud's theory? (17)

   _____

   _____

   _____

7. Match each of Erikson's stages with the appropriate description: (18)

_6_ Successful resolution of this stage depends on the adult's success at caring for other people and productive work.

_4_ The primary task of this stage is the development of a sense of self and a sense of one's place in society.

_5_ Successful resolution of this stage depends on a warm, loving relationship with the caregiver.

_7_ In this stage, children experiment with adults roles make-believe play.

_2_ Successful resolution of this stage depends on parents granting the child reasonable opportunities for free choice.

_8_ In this stage, successful resolution involves reflecting on life's accomplishments.

_3_ The development of close relationships with others helps ensure successful resolution of this stage.

_1_ Children who develop the capacity for cooperation and productive work resolve this stage successfully.

1. Industry vs. inferiority
2. Autonomy vs. shame and doubt
3. Intimacy vs. isolation
4. Identity vs. identity diffusion
5. Basic trust vs. mistrust
6. Generativity vs. stagnation
7. Initiative vs. guilt
8. Ego integrity vs. despair

8. Discuss two contributions and two limitations of psychoanalytic theory. (17-18)

Contributions: _____

_____

Limitations: _____

_____

9. True or False: Behaviorism focuses on the inner workings of the mind. (18)

10. Watson's study of little Albert, a 9-month-old baby who was taught to fear a white rat by associating it with a loud noise, supported Pavlov's concept of _classical conditioning_. (19)

11. Distinguish between primary drives and secondary drives, as discussed in Clark Hull's Drive Reduction Theory. (19)

Primary drives: _____

_____

Secondary drives: _____

_____

12. B. F. Skinner, who proposed _Operant conditioning_ theory, believed that behaviors could be increased by following them with _reinforcement_ and decreased by following them with _punishment_. (19)

13. Describe the concept of observational learning, as elaborated in Bandura's social learning theory. (19)

_____

_____

_____

14. Bandura's theory has been revised to include the importance of _____. Based upon this change, the theory is now referred to as a _____ approach rather than a social learning approach. (20)

15. According to the social-cognitive perspective, children develop _____ and a sense of _____ based upon selective observations of others and direct feedback about the worth of their own behaviors. (20)

16. What is meant by the term _applied behavior analysis_? (20)

Procedures that combine reinforcement and modeling to eliminate undesirable behaviors and increase desirable responses

17. Discuss two limitations of behaviorism and social learning theory. (20)

_____

_____

_____

18. Define Piaget's notion of *adaptation*. (21) _a biological concept that the mind structures of develop to better represent the external world._

19. Match each of Piaget's stages with the appropriate description: (22)

_2_ During this stage thought becomes more complex, and children develop the capacity for abstract reasoning.

_1_ This stage is characterized by the use of eyes, ears, and hands to explore the environment.

_4_ During this stage children develop the capacity for abstract thought.

_3_ This stage is marked by the development of logical, organized reasoning skills.

1. Sensorimotor
2. Preoperational
3. Concrete Operational
4. Formal Operational

20. Piaget used the _____ as his chief method for studying child and adolescent thought. (21)

21. Describe two major contributions of Piaget's theory. (22)

A. _Convinced psych field that children are active learners_

B. _Encouraged the development of discovery learning._

22. Describe two recent challenges to Piaget's theory. (22)

A. _He underestimated the competencies of toddlers infants & preschoolers_

B. _Studies show performance can be improved w/ instruction, challenging discovery learning as the best way to learn._

Recent Theoretical Perspectives

1. Briefly describe the information-processing view of child development. (23)

The human mind is viewed as a symbol manipulating system through which information flows — regarded as a continuous process

2. How are flow charts used by information-processing researchers? (23)

_____

_____

3. In what basic way are information processing and Piaget's theory alike? In what basic way are they different? (24)

    A. _____

    B. _____

4. Cite one strength and two limitations of the information-processing approach. (24)

Strength: _____

Limitation: _____

Limitation: _____

5. _____ is concerned with the adaptive value of behavior and its evolutionary history. (25)

6. Compare and contrast the concept of a critical period with that of a sensitive period. (25)

_____

_____

_____

7. Explain how John Bowlby used the principles of ethology to understand the infant-caregiver relationship. (26)

_____

_____

_____

8. Discuss the roles of biology and environment as they relate to child development based on ethological theory. (26)

_____

_____

_____

10

9. Describe the benefits of cross-cultural research. (26)

_____

_____

10. Explain the importance of social interaction according to Vygotsky's sociocultural theory. (26-27)

_____

_____

_____

11. True or False: Piaget and Vygotsky both viewed cognitive development as a socially mediated process. (27)

12. Compare and contrast the theories of Piaget and Vygotsky. (27)

_____

_____

_____

_____

_____

13. True or False: Because cultures select tasks for children's learning, children in every culture develop unique strengths not present in others. (27)

14. Vygotsky's emphasis on culture and social experience led him to neglect _____ contributions to development. (27)

15. What is the defining feature of ecological systems theory? In other words, what makes it unique from other theories? (27)

_____

_____

16. Match each level of ecological systems theory with the appropriate description or example: (28-29)

_____ Relationship between the child's home and school

_____ The influence of cultural values

_____ The parent's workplace

_____ The child's interaction with parents

1. Exosystem
2. Microsystem
3. Mesosystem
4. Macrosystem

17. Provide examples of factors in each system that can enhance development. (28-29)

Microsystem: _____

Mesosystem: _____

Exosystem: _____

Macrosystem: _____

18. Bronfenbrenner's _____-system refers to temporal changes that affect development, such as the timing of the birth of a sibling. (29)

19. True or False: In ecological systems theory, development is controlled neither by environmental circumstances nor by inner dispositions, but rather by the interaction of the two. (29)

20. A new perspective on child development emphasizes that the child's mind, body, and physical and social worlds form an integrated system that guides mastery of new skills. This approach is known as

_____ . (29)

12

Comparing Child Development Theories

1. Identify the stand that the following modern theories take on the three basic issues of childhood and child development: (31)

Theory	One Course of Development versus Many Courses of Development	Continuous versus Discontinuous Development	Nature versus Nurture
Psychoanalystic theory	one	disc	both
Behaviroism and social learning	many	cont	nature
Piaget's cognitive-developmental theory	one	disc	both
Information processing	one	cont	both
Ethology	one	both	both
Vygotsky's sociocultural perspective	many	cont	both
Dynamic systems theory	many	both	both

Studying the Child

1. Research usually begins with a _____, or a prediction about behavior drawn from a theory. (31)

2. Compare and contrast the techniques used in naturalistic and structured observations, noting strengths and limitations of each approach. (34)

    _____

    _____

    _____

3. How do structured interviews differ from clinical interviews, and what are the benefits of each technique? (34)

    _____

    _____

    _____

    _____

4. _____ methods measure the relationship between physiological processes and behavior. (36)

5. List some physiological measures commonly used to infer psychological state. (36)

_____

_____

6. What are some of the concerns with using psychophysiological methods? (36)

_____

_____

_____

7. What is the primary goal of the clinical method? (37)

_____

8. What are the drawbacks of using the clinical method? (37)

_____

_____

_____

9. Under what circumstances might a researcher employ the clinical method despite its limitations? (37)

_____

_____

_____

10. How is ethnographic research similar to the clinical method? How is it different? (38)

Similar: _____

Different: _____

11. Describe the ethnographic method and discuss its limitations. (39)

_____

_____

_____

12. Explain the basic features of the correlational design. (40)

_____

_____

_____

13. True or False: A correlational design does not permit researchers to determine cause-and-effect relationships between the variables. Explain your answer. (40)

_____

_____

_____

14. A correlation coefficient can range from _____ to _____. The magnitude of the number shows the _____ of the relationship between the two variables, whereas the sign of the number indicates the _____ of the relationship. (40)

15. A researcher determines that the correlation between warm, consistent parenting and delinquency is .18. Explain what this indicates about the relationship between the two variables. (40)

_____

_____

_____

16. If the same researcher (in question 15 above) had found a correlation coefficient of +.45, what would this have indicated about the relationship between warm, consistent parenting and delinquency? (40)

_____

_____

_____

17. What is the difference between a correlation of +1.00 and a correlation of –1.00? (40)

_____

_____

18. What is the primary distinction between a correlational design and an experimental design? (41)

_____

19. Describe the difference between an *independent* and a *dependent* variable. (41)

_____

_____

20. What is the feature of an experimental design that enables researchers to infer a cause-and-effect relationship between the variables? (41)

_____

_____

21. _____ is a procedure which allows researchers to control for unknown characteristics of the participants which could reduce the accuracy of the findings. (42)

_____

_____

_____

22. Discuss the difference between field experiments and natural experiments. (44)

_____

_____

_____

23. Why might a researcher opt to use either a field experiment or a natural experiment rather than conducting a laboratory experiment? (42)

_____

_____

_____

24. True or False: Experiments conducted in the field are typically just as well controlled and rigorous as laboratory experiments. (41)

25. In a _____ design, the same participants are studied repeatedly at different ages and changes are noted. Alternatively, in a _____ design, separate groups of participants differing in age are studied at the same point in time. (42,44)

26. Discuss the advantages and drawbacks of longitudinal studies and cross-sectional studies. (42-44)

Longitudinal studies: _____

_____

_____

Cross-sectional studies: _____

_____

_____

27. _____ refer to the influence of cultural-historical change on the accuracy of longitudinal research findings. (44)

28. The _____ design combines the techniques used in longitudinal research with those used in cross-sectional research. (44)

29. Describe the microgenetic design. (45)

_____

_____

_____

30. Discuss some of the ethical concerns of conducting research on children. (46-48)

_____

_____

_____

_____

Cultural Influences: Immigrant Youths

1. True or False: Immigrant youths tend to fare poorly in school compared to native children, and they also tend to exhibit higher rates of delinquent behavior. (38-39)

ASK YOURSELF . . .

REVIEW: Why are there many theories of how children develop? Cite three basic issues on which almost all theories take a stand.

_____

_____

_____

_____

APPLY: A school counselor advises a parent, "Don't worry about your teenager's argumentative behavior. It shows she understands the world differently than she did as a young child." What stance is the counselor taking on the issue of *continuous* or *discontinuous* development? Explain.

_____

_____

_____

_____

CONNECT: Provide an example of how one domain of development (physical, cognitive, or emotional/social) can affect development in another domain.

_____

_____

_____

_____

REFLECT: Cite an aspect of your development that differs from a parent's or grandparent's when he or she was your age. How might *contexts* explain this difference?

_____

_____

_____

_____

REVIEW: Suppose we could arrange a debate team between John Locke and Jean Jacques Rousseau on the nature–nurture controversy. Summarize the argument that each historical figure is likely to present.

_____

_____

_____

_____

REFLECT: Find out if your parents read Gesell, Spock, or other parenting-advice books when you were growing up. What questions about child rearing most concerned them? Do you think today's parents of young children have concerns that are different from those of your parents? Explain.

_____

_____

_____

_____

REVIEW: New theories often become prominent because they overcome the limitations of existing theories. What aspects of behaviorism made it attractive to critics of psychoanalytic theory? How does Piaget's theory respond to a major limitation of behaviorism?

_____

_____

_____

_____

APPLY: A 4-year-old becomes frightened of the dark and refuses to go to sleep at night. How would a psychoanalyst and a behaviorist differ in their views of how this problem developed?

_____

_____

_____

_____

CONNECT: Although social learning theory focuses on social development and Piaget's theory on cognitive development, they have enhanced our understanding of other domains as well. Mention an additional domain of development addressed by each theory.

_____

_____

_____

_____

REVIEW: What features of Vygotsky's sociocultural theory distinguish it from Piaget's cognitive-developmental theory?

_____

_____

_____

_____

APPLY: Return to the Biology and Environment box on page 10. How does the story of John and Gary illustrate bidirectional influences within the microsystem, as described in ecological systems theory?

_____

_____

_____

_____

REFLECT: To illustrate the chronosystem in ecological systems theory, select an influential event from your childhood, such as a move to a new neighborhood, an inspiring teacher, or parental divorce or remarriage. How did the event affect you? How might its impact have differed had you been 5 years younger? How about 5 years older?

_____

_____

_____

_____

REVIEW: What strengths and limitations do the clinical method and ethnography have in common?

_____

_____

_____

_____

APPLY: A researcher wants to study the thoughts and feelings of children who experienced their parents' divorce. Which method is best suited for investigating this question? Why?

_____

_____

_____

_____

CONNECT: Refer to the Cultural Influences box on pages 38-39. What explains the close link between academic success and positive psychological adjustment among first- and second- generation immigrant youths?

_____

_____

_____

_____

REVIEW: Explain how cohort effects can distort the findings of both longitudinal and cross-sectional studies.

_____

_____

_____

_____

APPLY: A researcher compares children who went to summer leadership camps with children who attended athletic camps. She finds that those who attended leadership camps are friendlier. Should the investigator tell parents that sending children to leadership camps will cause them to be more sociable? Why or why not?

_____

_____

_____

_____

CONNECT: Can researchers enhance children's cognitive, emotional, and social development by fully explaining research activities and rights to them, in language they can understand? Explain.

_____

_____

_____

_____

REFLECT: Suppose a researcher asks you to enroll your baby in a ten-year long longitudinal study. What factors would lead you to agree and stay involved? Do your answers shed light on why longitudinal studies often have biased samples? Explain.

_____

_____

_____

_____

SUGGESTED STUDENT READINGS

Goldhaber, D. (2000). *Theories of human development: Integrative perspectives.* Mountain View, CA: Mayfield Publishing Co. Presents an extensive review and critique of the most influential developmental theories, including coverage of classic theories and contemporary theories. The author also pays careful attention to the methodology for studying human development and how research methods contribute to and enhance our overall knowledge of the developmental process.

Greig, P. & Taylor, J. (1999). *Doing research with children.* London: Sage Publications Ltd. Reviews the various techniques and approaches, including the unique ethical and legal concerns, that are associated with child development research. This book provides a framework for studying children which can be utilized by students, researchers, practitioners, educators, and others working in the field of child development.

Moen, P., Elder, G. H., Jr., & Luscher, K. (Eds.). (1995). *Examining lives in context: Perspectives on the ecology of human development.* Washington, DC: American Psychological Association. Extends Bronfenbrenner's perspective, illustrating how ecological systems theory can be applied to a number of real-life problems. Explores how multiple contextual factors influence individuals, families, and communities across the lifespan.

Richardson, K. (1999). *The origins of human potential: Evolution, development, and psychology.* New York: Routledge. Presents a refreshing perspective on the development of cognitive competence. The author uses a dynamic systems approach in an attempt to illustrate the complexity of genetic and environmental factors and how these interactions contribute to cognitive development.

PUZZLE TERM REVIEW

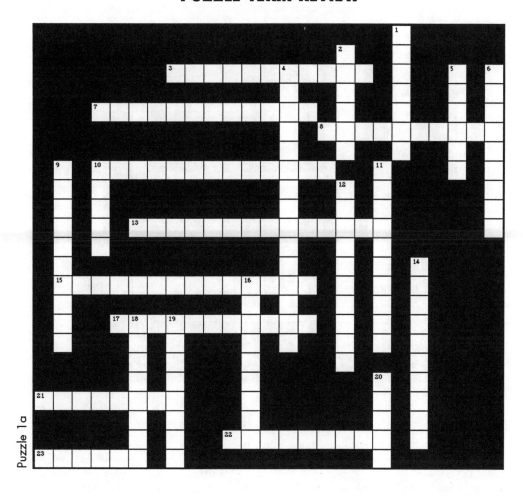

23

Across

3. Baby _____: day-to-day descriptions and impressions of a child's behavior
7. Rousseau viewed children as _____ _____ naturally endowed with an innate plan for orderly, healthy growth. (2 words)
8. Genetically determined, naturally unfolding course of growth
10. _____ theory: focuses on how social interaction contributes to development
13. Piagetian stage characterized by symbolic but illogical thinking
15. _____ _____ theory (two words): emphasizes the role of observational learning in the development of behavior
17. The approach that emphasizes the study of directly observable events
21. Vygotsky viewed development as a _____ mediated process.
22. _____ period: a time that is optimal for certain capacities to emerge
23. Describes, explains, and predicts behavior

Down

1. The nature-_____ controversy
2. Psycho_____ theory: Freud's theory focusing on early sexual and aggressive drives
4. Medieval view of children as miniature adults
5. Psycho_____ theory: Erikson's stage theory of development entailing resolution of psychological conflicts
6. Piaget's _____ developmental theory suggests that children actively construct knowledge as they manipulate and explore their world.
9. Information-_____ approach: views the human mind as a symbol-manipulating machine
10. A qualitative change characterizing a particular time period of development
11. _____ systems theory: views the child as developing within a complex system of relationships
12. View of development as gradually adding on more of the same types of skills that were there to begin with
14. View of the child as a blank slate (2 words)
16. _____ approach: age-related averages computed to represent typical development
18. Theory concerned with the adaptive value of behavior
19. Psycho_____ perspective: emphasizes the unique developmental history of each child
20. Constructed the first successful intelligence test

PUZZLE TERM REVIEW

Puzzle 1b

Across

1. Variable manipulated by the researcher
5. _____ design: permits inferences about cause and effect
8. _____ assignment helps researchers control for characteristics of participants that could reduce the accuracy of their findings.
9. _____ design: researchers present children with a novel task and follow mastery over a series of closely spaced meetings
11. _____ design: researchers gather information without altering the participants' experience
12. In ecological systems theory, the term _____ refers to temporal changes in a child's environment.
15. _____ observation: researchers go into a natural environment to observe a behavior of interest
16. The clinical method or _____ study approach
20. A number describing how two variables are related is called a correlation _____.
22. _____ design: the same participants are studied repeatedly at different ages
23. _____ design: groups of people differing in age are studied at the same point in time

Down

2. _____ systems perspective: the child's mind, body, and physical and social worlds form an integrated system
3. _____ experiments: researchers gather data on pre-existing groups (e.g.,families)
4. Variable expected to be influenced by the experimental manipulations
6. _____ methods: measure the relationship between physiological processes and behavior
7. _____ effects are the effects of cultural historical change on the accuracy of findings
10. In a structured _____, each participant is asked the same questions in the same way.
12. Informed _____ is an ethical principle that requires special interpretation when research participants are children.
13. In a _____ interview, the researcher uses a flexible, conversational style to probe for a participant's point of view.
14. A prediction
17. Participant observation of a culture
18. In ecological systems theory, the _____-system consists of connections between the child's immediate settings (e.g., home, school, etc.)
19. In _____ observations, the researcher sets up a situation that evokes a behavior of interest and then observes that behavior in a laboratory setting
21. In _____ experiments, researchers randomly assign people to treatment conditions in natural settings.

24

SELF-TEST

1. Our knowledge of child development is interdisciplinary. What does this mean? (5)

   a. Our knowledge of child development is based exclusively on research conducted by people in the field of child development.
   b. Child development is not recognized as a distinct field of study.
   c. Individuals from diverse fields have contributed to our knowledge of child development.
   d. Child development is part of a larger discipline known as developmental psychology.

2. Which of the following is NOT a characteristic of a good theory? (6)

   a. predicts behavior
   b. describes behavior
   c. modifies behavior
   d. explains behavior

3. How do theories differ from opinion? (7)

   a. Theories are based on scientific research.
   b. Theories must be scientifically confirmed.
   c. Theories offer a more complete picture of behavior.
   d. Theories and opinions do not differ.

4. Stage theories conform to which of the following perspectives of development? (8)

   a. nature
   b. discontinuous
   c. continuous
   d. nurture

5. In medieval times: (11)

   a. childhood was not recognized as a separate phase of the lifecycle.
   b. children were regarded as evil and stubborn.
   c. childhood experiences were regarded as crucial for healthy development.
   d. toys and games were designed to amuse children.

6. Which of the following terms reflects John Locke's view of children as blank slates? (12)

   a. noble savage
   b. environmental determinism
   c. tabula rasa
   d. preformationism

7. Which of the following is NOT true of the normative approach to child study? (14)

   a. It emphasizes objective measurement techniques (e.g., questionnaires).
   b. It requires behavioral measurements of large numbers of children in order to develop a picture of age-related changes in typical development.
   c. It was developed in response to the limitations of the baby biographies.
   d. It is narrowly focused on only a couple of areas of development.

8. The first successful intelligence test, created by Alfred Binet represented an improvement over previous tests primarily because: (15)

   a. it was able to reduce intelligence to its simplest elements.
   b. it measured abilities indirectly.
   c. it was culturally unbiased.
   d. it was based on a well-developed theory.

9. Which of the following theories is noted for its focus on the unique developmental history of each child? (16)

   a. behaviorism
   b. social learning theory
   c. psychoanalytic theory
   d. information processing

10. According to Freud's theory, which of the following is the conscious, rational part of personality which redirects biological impulses so that they are expressed in socially acceptable ways? (16)

    a. id
    b. ego
    c. superego
    d. conscience

11. Behaviorism focuses on the study of: (18)

    a. unconscious motives for behavior.
    b. imitation as a mechanism for learning new behaviors.
    c. cognitive reasoning underlying behavior.
    d. directly observable events.

12. According to Piaget's theory, each of the four stages of development is characterized by: (21)

    a. advances in motor development.
    b. increased capacity to process information.
    c. a distinct psychosocial crisis.
    d. qualitatively distinct ways of thinking.

13. New evidence challenging Piaget's theory suggests that he: (22)

    a. overestimated the competencies of young children.
    b. underestimated the competencies of young children.
    c. overlooked several important areas of cognitive development.
    d. used overly simplified measures in his studies of cognitive development.

14. Which of the following techniques is used by information-processing theorists to map the precise steps that individuals use to solve problems and complete tasks? (23)

    a. cognitive maps
    b. schematic representation
    c. flowcharts
    d. mental operations charts

26

15. Which theory is concerned with the adaptive value of behavior and its evolutionary significance? (25)

    a. ethology
    b. ecological systems theory
    c. sociocultural theory
    d. behaviorism

16. According to _____, cognitive development is a socially mediated process. (26)

    a. Piaget
    b. Vygotsky
    c. Bronfenbrenner
    d. Hull

17. Which of the following is NOT consistent with Bronfenbrenner's ecological systems theory? (27-29)

    a. The timing of an environmental change, such as a parental divorce, affects its impact on the child.
    b. Heredity and environment are both instrumental in shaping development.
    c. Children are passive beings who are acted upon by their environment.
    d. Child development is viewed within a complex system of relationships which are affected by the surrounding environment.

18. Dynamic systems theory focuses on: (30)

    a. the impact of changes occurring in the child's mind, body, and physical and social worlds.
    b. describing universal features of development.
    c. children's ability to learn through modeling.
    d. consistencies across various systems, or domains, of development.

19. A researcher interested in the development of aggression in young children goes to a preschool to observe classroom behavior. She keeps a record of all aggressive acts occurring during her observation. This is an example of a(n): (33)

    a. structured observation.
    b. naturalistic observation.
    c. ethnographic observation.
    d. field experiment.

20. Ethnography aims to understand a culture or distinct social group through: (39)

    a. participant observation.
    b. clinical interviews with members of the group.
    c. case study reports.
    d. structured observation.

21. What is the major limitation of correlational research? (40)

    a. It does not provide information about the strength of the relationship between the variables of interest.
    b. Correlational studies are typically conducted in a laboratory setting, and, therefore, give us little information about natural life circumstances.
    c. It does not allow us to infer cause and effect.
    d. It does not indicate the direction of the relationship between the variables.

22. An experimental design permits inferences about cause and effect because: (41)

    a   experimental studies are conducted in natural settings rather than in a laboratory.
    b. the researcher controls changes in the independent variable.
    c. the researcher controls changes in the dependent variable.
    d. the researcher systematically assigns participants to specific treatment conditions based upon their known characteristics.

23. A researcher is interested in studying peer relationships. He recruits a sample of kindergarten children and examines changes in their relationships with peers over the next ten years. This is an example of a: (42)

    a. cross-sectional design.
    b. longitudinal-sequential design.
    c. microgenetic design.
    d. longitudinal design.

24 Imagine that a researcher finds that 5-year-olds in the 1950's learned more slowly than do the 5-year-olds of today. Which of the following poses a threat to the accuracy of such a finding? (44)

    a. biased sampling
    b. investigator bias
    c. cohort effects
    d. age effects

25. Which of the following is NOT one of children's research rights? (47)

    a. privacy
    b. informed consent
    c. knowledge of the results
    d. knowledge of possible deception prior to research participation

CHAPTER 2

BIOLOGICAL AND ENVIRONMENTAL FOUNDATIONS

Chapter Summary

T his chapter examines the complex contributions of heredity and environment to development. Principles of genetic transmission determine the characteristics that make us human and contribute to individual differences in appearance and behavior. Inheritance of harmful recessive genes and abnormalities of the chromosomes are major causes of serious developmental problems. Genetic counseling and prenatal diagnosis help people at risk for transmitting hereditary disorders assess their chances of giving birth to a healthy baby.

Environmental influences on development are equally as complex as hereditary factors. The family has an especially powerful impact, operating as a complex and dynamic social system in which members exert direct, indirect, and third-party effects on one another. Socioeconomic status influences child-rearing practices, and poverty and homelessness undermine effective family functioning and children's well-being. The quality of community life, from neighborhoods and schools to small towns and cities, also affects children's development. Cultural values, laws, and government programs shape experiences in all of these contexts.

Child development specialists view the relationship between genetic and environmental factors in different ways. Some believe that it is useful and possible to answer the question of "how much" each contributes to behavior. Others think that heredity and environment cannot be divided into separate influences. They want to discover "how" these two major determinants of development work together in a complex, dynamic interplay.

LEARNING OBJECTIVES

After reading this chapter, you should be able to:

2.1 Describe the relationship between phenotypes and genotypes. (54)

2.2 Describe the structure of the DNA molecule, and explain the process of mitosis. (55)

2.3 Explain the process of meiosis. (55-57)

2.4 Explain how the sex of the new individual is determined. (57)

2.5 Identify two types of twins, and explain how each is created. (57)

2.6 Explain how alleles influence the inheritance of traits, such as through dominant-recessive inheritance, codominance, X-linked inheritance, and genetic imprinting. (58-63)

2.7 Describe chromosomal abnormalities, including Down Syndrome and abnormalities of the sex chromosomes. (63-64)

2.8 Discuss reproductive options available to prospective parents. (68-72)

2.9 Describe the role of family in child development, noting direct and indirect family influences, as well as the adaptable nature of the family system. (74-76)

2.10 Discuss the impact of socioeconomic status and poverty on family functioning. (76-78)

2.11 Summarize the role of neighborhoods, schools, towns, and cities in the lives of children. (78-80)

2.12 Discuss how cultural values and public policies influence the well-being of children. (80-84)

2.13 Describe several conceptions of the relationship between heredity and environment in influencing development, and explain the methods commonly used to study these variables. (85-91)

STUDY QUESTIONS

1. _____Traits_____ are directly observable characteristics which depend in part on the ____genes____, the complex blend of genetic information transmitted from one generation to the next. (54)

Genetic Foundations

1. Rodlike structures in the nuclei of cells which store and transmit genetic information are called ____chromsomes____. (54)

2. Chromosomes are made up of a chemical substance called ____DNA____. It looks like a _____ and is composed of segments called _____. (55)

3. The process through which DNA duplicates itself so that each new body cell contains the same number of chromosomes is called ____mitosis____. (55)

4. Sex cells, or ____meiosis____, are formed through the process of ____gametes____. These special cells contain only __23__ chromosomes, half as many as a regular body cell. (55)

5. True or False: The crossing over of chromosomes during meiosis creates new hereditary combinations unique to the individual. (55)

6. The twenty-two matching pairs of chromosomes are called _____. (57)

7. The twenty-third pair of chromosomes, also called the _____, determine the sex of the child. In females, this pair is called __XX__, whereas in males it is called __XY__. (57)

8. Match each of the following terms with the appropriate description: (57)

_2_ The most common type of multiple birth

_1_ The cause of this type of twinning is unknown

_1_ Older maternal age and use of fertility drugs are major causes of this type of twinning

_2_ These twins are genetically no more alike than ordinary siblings

_1_ These twins share the same genetic makeup

1. Identical, or monozygotic, twins
2. Fraternal, or dizygotic, twins

9. Explain why children of single births are often healthier and develop more rapidly than twins. (57)

_____

_____

_____

10. Each of two forms of a gene located at the same place on the autosome is called a(n) ___allele___. (58)

11. If the alleles from both parents are alike, the child is _homozygous_ and will display the inherited trait. If the alleles inherited from the mother and father are different, then the child is _heterozygous_, and the relationship between the alleles will determine the trait that will appear. (58)

12. Explain the nature of dominant–recessive inheritance. (58)

_____

_____

_____

_____

13. Provide one example of a recessive disorder and one example of a dominant disorder. (60-61)

Recessive: _____

Dominant: _____

14. True or False: Serious diseases typically result from dominant alleles. (59)

15. A pattern of inheritance in which both alleles influence the person's characteristics is referred to as __*CO*_____. (59)

16. True or False: Males are more likely to be affected by X-linked inheritance than are females. (61)

17. Name two X-linked conditions or disorders. (62)

    A. _hemophelia_____ B. _C_____

18. _____ occurs when alleles are chemically marked in such a way that one pair member is activated, regardless of its makeup. (62)

19. Explain how harmful genes are created. (63)

    _____

    _____

20. Describe polygenic inheritance, and give an example of a trait that is determined by this pattern of inheritance. (63)

    _____

    _____

    _____

21. _____, the most common chromosomal disorder, is often due to a defect in the _____ chromosome. For this reason, the disorder is sometimes called _____. (63)

22. List the physical and behavioral characteristics of Down syndrome. (64)

    Physical: _____

    _____

    Behavioral: _____

    _____

23. True or False: The occurrence of Down syndrome rises with maternal age. (64)

24. True or False: Disorders of the sex chromosomes have more serious consequences for development than do disorders of the autosomes. (64)

32

Reproductive Choices

1. What is the purpose of genetic counseling, and who is most likely to seek this service? (66)

   _____

   _____

   _____

2. _____ are medical procedures that permit detection of developmental problems before birth. (67)

3. True or False: The techniques used in fetal medicine rarely result in complications such as premature labor or miscarriage. (67)

4. The risk of adoption failure is greatest for what two groups of children? (71)

   _____

5. True or False: Adopted children have more learning and emotional difficulties than do children in the general population. (71)

Social Issues: Health — The Pros and Cons of Reproductive Technologies

1. Discuss some of the concerns surrounding the use of donor insemination and in vitro fertilization. (68)

   _____

   _____

   _____

   _____

2. Describe some of the risks involved with surrogate motherhood. (68)

   _____

   _____

   _____

3. True or False: The United States has laws strictly regulating reproductive technologies. (69)

Biology and Environment: The Human Genome Project

1. The Human Genome Project is an international research program aimed at deciphering the chemical makeup of _____ _____ _____and identifying all 50,000 to 100,000 human genes. (70)

2. Describe the main goals of this project. (70-71)

_____

_____

_____

Environmental Contexts for Development

1. Discuss the differences between direct and indirect familial influences. (74-75)

_____

_____

_____

_____

2. Discuss some of the ways in which the family system must adapt over time. (75-76)

_____

_____

_____

_____

3. Describe the influence of SES on parenting practices and parent-child interaction. (76)

_____

_____

_____

_____

4. True or False: Higher-SES children show more advances in cognitive development and tend to perform better in school than do lower-SES children. (77)

5. Discuss the impact of poverty on family functioning. (77)

_____

_____

_____

_____

_____

6. Describe the developmental risks associated with homelessness in children. (78)

_____

_____

_____

_____

_____

7. True or False: Dissatisfaction with one's community is associated with increased child abuse and neglect. (78)

8. Explain why neighborhood resources have a greater impact in disadvantaged neighborhoods than in well-to-do neighborhoods. (78)

_____

_____

9. What are some features of the school environment which impact developmental outcomes among students? (79)

_____

_____

_____

10. Why are higher-SES parents more likely to have regular contact with teachers than are lower-SES parents? (79)

_____

_____

11. True or False: Children living in small towns are more actively involved in the community than are children living in larger towns and cities. (80)

12. In _____ societies, people think of themselves as part of a group and stress group goals over individual goals. In _____ societies, on the other hand, people think of themselves as separate entities and are largely concerned with their own personal needs. (82)

13. True or False: Among developed nations, the United States has served as a forerunner in the development of public policies to safeguard children. (82)

14. List some of the areas in which American public policy regarding children is deficient. (82)

_____

_____

_____

15. The _____ is the international treaty which commits each cooperating country to work toward guaranteeing environments that foster children's development, protect them from harm, and enhance their community participation and self-determination. The United States (is/is not) one of the few countries in the world that has not yet ratified this treaty. (83)

Cultural Influences: The African-American Extended Family

1   Describe some of the ways in which extended-family relationships benefit African-American families. (81)

_____

_____

_____

_____

Understanding the Relationship Between Heredity and Environment

1. _____ is a field devoted to uncovering the contribu-
   tions of nature and nurture as they relate to individual differences in human traits
   and abilities. (85)

2. What are two methods used by behavioral geneticists to infer the role of heredity
   in human characteristics? (85)

   A. _____ B. _____

3. In measuring the extent to which individual differences in various traits are due to
   genetic factors, researchers often obtain estimates based on
   _____, which compare the characteristics of
   family members. (86)

4. True or False: Heritability estimates for intelligence and personality are approximately .50, indicating that genetic makeup can explain half of the variance in these
   traits. (86)

5. What is a concordance rate? (86)

   _____

   _____

6. What do concordance rates of 0 and of 100 mean? (86)

   0: _____

   100: _____

7. When a concordance rate is much higher for (identical/fraternal) twins, then
   heredity is believed to play a major role. (86)

8. Discuss some of the limitations of heritability estimates and concordance rates. (87)

   _____

   _____

   _____

9. _____ emphasizes that each person responds to
   the environment in a unique way because of his or her genetic makeup. (88)

10. Define the term *canalization*. (88)

_____

_____

_____

11. True or False: A recent expansion of the concept of canalization indicates that both heredity and environment can limit development. (89)

12. The concept of _____ suggests that an individual's genetic makeup influences the environments to which that person is exposed. (89)

13. Describe passive, evocative, and active genetic–environmental correlations. (89-90)

Passive: _____

_____

Evocative: _____

_____

Active: _____

_____

14. The tendency to choose environments that complement our own heredity is called _____. (91)

15. _____ refers to the development of the individual resulting from ongoing, bidirectional exchanges between heredity and the environment. (91)

Biology and Environment: Uncoupling Genetic Environmental Correlations for Mental Illness and Antisocial Behavior

1. True or False: Adopted children whose biological mothers have psychological disorders are more likely to develop mental illness when reared in maladaptive homes than when reared in healthy homes. (90)

REVIEW: Explain the genetic origins of PKU and Down syndrome. Cite evidence indicating that heredity and environment contribute to the development of children with these disorders.

_____

_____

_____

_____

APPLY: Gilbert and Jan are planning to have children. Gilbert's genetic makeup is homozygous for dark hair. Jan's is homozygous for blond hair. What proportion of their children are likely to be dark haired? Explain.

_____

_____

_____

_____

39

CONNECT: Parents of children with genetic disorders, such as Down syndrome, often face increased stress. Referring back to our discussion of ecological systems theory in Chapter 1 (see pages 27-29), explain why this is so. What factors, within and beyond the family, can help such parents support their child's development?

_____

_____

_____

_____

REVIEW: Describe the ethical pros and cons of fetal surgery, surrogate motherhood, postmenopausal-assisted childbearing, and detection of abnormal genes resulting from the Human Genome Project.

Fetal surgery:

_____

_____

_____

_____

Surrogate motherhood:

_____

_____

_____

_____

Postmenopausal-assisted childbearing:

_____

_____

_____

_____

Detection of abnormal genes:

_____

_____

_____

_____

APPLY: A woman over the age of 35 has just learned that she is pregnant. Although she would like to find out as soon as possible whether her child has a chromosomal disorder, she wants to minimize the risk of injury to the developing organism. Which prenatal diagnostic method is she likely to choose?

_____

_____

_____

_____

REFLECT: Put yourself in the place of a woman who is the carrier of fragile X syndrome but who wants to have children. Would you become pregnant, adopt, use a surrogate mother, or give up your desire for parenthood? Explain. If you became pregnant, would you opt for prenatal diagnosis? Why or why not?

_____

_____

_____

_____

REVIEW: Links between family and community are essential for children's well-being. Provide examples and research findings from our discussion that support this idea.

_____

_____

_____

_____

APPLY: Check your local newspaper for a week and one or two national news magazines to see how many and what kind of articles appear on the condition of children and families. Why is it important for researchers to communicate with the general public about children's needs?

_____

_____

_____

_____

CONNECT: How does poverty affect functioning of the family system, thereby risking children's development in all domains?

_____

_____

_____

_____

REFLECT: Do you agree with the widespread American sentiment that government should not intrude in family life? Explain.

_____

_____

_____

_____

REVIEW: Why did one group of experts conclude that heritability estimates have too many problems to yield firm conclusions about the relative strength of genetic and environmental influences on development?

_____

_____

_____

_____

APPLY: Bianca's parents are both accomplished musicians. Bianca began taking piano lessons when she was 4 years old and was accompanying her school choir by age 10. When she reached adolescence, she asked her parents if she could attend a special music high school. Explain how genetic-environmental correlation promoted Bianca's talent.

_____

_____

_____

_____

CONNECT: The discussion of range of reaction on page 88 illustrates genetic-environmental interaction for intelligence that unique blends of heredity and environment lead to both similarities and differences in behavior. How do the findings shown in Figure 2.10 in the Biology and Environment box on page 90 depict this idea for anti-social behavior?

_____

_____

_____

_____

REFLECT: What aspects of your own adolescent and adult development — for example, interests, hobbies, college major, and vocational choice — are probably due to niche-picking? Explain.

_____

_____

_____

_____

SUGGESTED STUDENT READINGS

Baker, D. L., Schuette, J. L., & Uhlmann, W. R. (Eds.), (1998). *A guide to genetic counseling.* New York: Wiley-Liss. A detailed presentation of the components, theoretical framework, goals, and unique approaches used in genetic counseling.

Children's Defense Fund (2000). *The state of America's children*, 2000. Washington, DC: Author. Provides a comprehensive analysis of the current condition of children in the United States, government-sponsored programs serving them, and proposals for improving child and family programs.

Jargowsky, P. A. (1997). *Poverty and place: Ghettos, barrios, and the American city.* New York: Russell Sage Foundation. Discusses the impact of growing up in impoverished inner city neighborhoods on a variety of developmental outcomes. Illustrates the notion of context as a powerful influence on child development.

Johnson-Powell, G., Yamamoto, J., Wyatt, G. E., & Arroyo, W. (Eds.), (1997). *Transcultural child development: Psychological assessment and treatment.* New York: John Wiley & Sons, Inc. Written primarily for professionals working with children from other cultures, this book focuses on the impact of culture on child development with a particular emphasis on the development of psychological disorders.

Lamb, M. E. (Ed.), (1999). *Parenting and child development in "nontraditional" families.* Mahwah, NJ: Lawrence Erlbaum Associates, Inc., Publishers. A collection of chapters that examines how nontraditional patterns of child care affects development. Topics include dual-earner families, single parenthood, poverty, adoption, parents with gay or lesbian sexual orientations, and nonparental child care.

Segal, N. L. (1999). *Entwined lives: Twins and what they tell us about behavior.* New York: Dutton/Penguin Books. Presents a compelling account of the unique behavioral and physical development of twins. The author covers topics such as the unusual language patterns of twins, the role of fertility treatments in twin conceptions, the loss of a twin through death, and how conjoined twins interact on a daily basis.

PUZZLE TERM REVIEW

Puzzle 2a

Across

2. _____ status is an index of a family's social position and economic well-being.
5. _____ inheritance: The recessive gene is carried on the X chromosome
6. Fraternal, or _____, twins
9. The tendency of heredity to restrict the development of some characteristics to just one or a few outcomes
10. In _____ societies, people think of themselves as separate entities and are largely concerned with their own personal needs.
15. Having two identical alleles at the same place on a pair of chromosomes
18. _____ studies compare the characteristics of family members in order to obtain heritability estimates.
19. _____ chromosomes: the 23rd pair of chromosomes; XX in females, XY in males
20. Directly observable characteristic

Down

1. Development resulting from ongoing, bidirectional exchanges between heredity and environment
3. _____ over: An exchange of genes between chromosomes next to each other during meiosis
4. Dominant-_____ inheritance: In heterozygous pairings, only one allele affects the child's characteristics
7. Rodlike structures in the cell nucleus that store and transmit genetic information
8. Cell formed by the union of the sperm and the ovum at conception
11. The 22 matching chromosome pairs in each human cell
12. _____ inheritance: Many genes determine a characteristic
13. _____ genes enhance or dilute the effects other genes
14. Human sperm and ova
16. The process of cell duplication
17. Long, double-stranded molecules that make up chromosomes (abbr.)

PUZZLE TERM REVIEW

Puzzle 2b

Across

2. Range of _____: a person's genetically determined response to a range of environmental conditions
6. Groups of people with beliefs and customs that differ from those of the larger culture
7. A pattern of inheritance in which both alleles influence the person's characteristics
8. _____ rate: the percentage of instances in which both members of a twin pair show a trait when it is present in one pair member
9. _____ twins have the same genetic makeup.
15. Genetic _____: alleles are chemically marked in such a way that one pair member is activated, regardless of its makeup
17. In _____ societies, people define themselves as part of a group and stress group over individual goals.
18. _____ Syndrome is a chromosomal disorder also referred to as Trisomy 21.
19. A segment of a DNA molecule that contains hereditary instructions
20. _____ policies: laws and government programs designed to improve the condition of children and families

Down

1. The process of cell division
3. In _____-family households, parent and child live with one or more adult relatives.
4. _____ estimates: Measure the extent to which individual differences in complex traits in a specific population are due to genetic factors
5. _____-environmental correlations: the notion that heredity influences the environments to which an individual is exposed
10. A sudden but permanent change in a segment of DNA
11. The genetic makeup of an individual
12. Genetic _____ is designed to help couples assess their chances of giving birth to a baby with a hereditary disorder.
13. _____ genetics: field devoted to uncovering the contributions of nature and nurture to individual differences in human traits and abilities
14. _____-picking: the tendency for individuals to actively choose environments that compliment their heredity
16. _____ diagnostic methods are medical procedures that permit the detection of problems before birth.

1. Directly observable physical and behavioral characteristics are called: (54)

    a. genotypes.
    b. phenotypes.
    c. alleles.
    d. chromosomes.

2. Rodlike structures in the nucleus of a cell that store and transmit genetic information are called: (54)

    a. gametes.
    b. genes.
    c. autosomes.
    d. chromosomes.

3. The process of cell duplication, in which the DNA ladder splits down the middle and each base pairs with a new mate, creating two identical DNA ladders, is called: (55)

    a. mitosis.
    b. meiosis.
    c. crossing over.
    d. genetic imprinting.

4. Sex cells are also referred to as: (55)

    a. autosomes.
    b. genotypes.
    c. gametes.
    d. sex chromosomes.

5. Monozygotic twins are: (57)

    a. genetically identical.
    b. genetically no more alike than ordinary siblings.
    c. conceived when two separate ova are fertilized.
    d. more common that other types of multiple births.

6. The pattern of genetic inheritance, seen in heterozygous pairings, in which only one allele affects the child's characteristics is called: (58)

    a. polygenic inheritance.
    b. X-linked inheritance.
    c. dominant–recessive inheritance.
    d. codominance.

7. Serious diseases are only rarely due to dominant alleles because: (59)

    a. dominance requires the same allele to be inherited from both parents.
    b. other genes usually alter the effects of dominant alleles.
    c. children inheriting the harmful dominant allele would always develop the disorder and seldom live long enough to pass on the trait.
    d. recessive genes usually overtake the harmful dominant allele.

46

8. In some heterozygous pairings, both alleles influence the person's characteristics. This pattern of inheritance is known as: (59)

    a. dominant–recessive inheritance.
    b. codominance.
    c. phenotypic inheritance.
    d   genotypic inheritance.

9. In which of the following patterns of inheritance are alleles chemically marked in such a way that only one pair member is activated, regardless of its makeup? (62)

    a. codominance
    b. homozygous inheritance
    c. polygenic inheritance
    d. genetic imprinting

10. Continuous traits, such as height or intelligence, are due to _____, in which many genes determine the characteristic. (63)

    a. polygenic inheritance
    b. monogenic inheritance
    c. heterozygous inheritance
    d. homozygous inheritance

11. The most common chromosomal abnormality is: (63)

    a. Klinefelter syndrome.
    b. PKU.
    c. cystic fibrosis.
    d. Down syndrome.

12. Techniques such as amniocentesis, chorionic villus sampling, and ultrasound are examples of: (67)

    a. fetal medicine.
    b. prenatal diagnostic methods.
    c. genetic engineering.
    d. neonatal medicine.

13. Which of the following is NOT true of adopted children? (71)

    a. Children adopted from foreign countries often struggle with identity development despite parental attempts to help them blend their birth and rearing backgrounds.
    b. Children adopted at older ages and children with disabilities are at the greatest risk for adoption failure.
    c. Adopted children exhibit more learning and emotional difficulties than do children in the general population.
    d. Most adopted children develop into well-adjusted adults.

14. Researchers view the family as: (74)

    a. a self-contained unit which is impervious to "third party" effects.
    b. a system of interdependent relationships.
    c. a stable system which is resistant to change.
    d. a network of unidirectional influences.

15. Which of the following is NOT true of lower-SES individuals? (76)
    a. They tend to have children at an earlier age than higher-SES individuals.
    b. Due to financial constraints, they tend to have fewer children than higher-SES individuals.
    c. They place a higher value on external characteristics of their children, such as obedience and cleanliness, than on psychological characteristics, such as happiness and autonomy.
    d. When interacting with their children, they use more criticisms and punishment than higher-SES parents.

16. Most homeless families consist of: (78)
    a. unemployed parents with young children.
    b. unemployed parents with school age children.
    c. single mothers with adolescent children.
    d. single mothers with young children.

17. _____ is more common in communities where residents feel socially isolated. (78)
    a. Child abuse and neglect
    b. Contact with relatives
    c. Church attendance
    d. Family cohesiveness

18. American values such as independence and self-reliance suggest that the United States can best be categorized as a(n) _____ society. (82)
    a. permissive
    b. autocratic
    c. collectivist
    d. individualistic

19. Which of the following has helped to protect African-American children from the harmful effects of poverty? (81)
    a. high-quality publicly-sponsored child care
    b. the vast resources available to families through public assistance programs
    c. the migration of African-Americans to small towns
    d. extended-family households

20. Laws and government programs designed to improve current conditions, such as those of children and families are called: (82)
    a. legal policies.
    b. domestic policies.
    c. public policies.
    d. democratic policies.

21. American public policies to safeguard children and youths: (82)
    a. are superior to those found in most other industrialized nations.
    b. lag behind those of other developed countries.
    c. are often ineffective due to inadequate knowledge and resources.
    d. are rapidly improving as the United States moves towards a more collectivist ideology.

22. A statistic that measures the extent to which continuous traits, such as intelligence, can be traced to heredity is called a: (85)

    a. heritability estimate.
    b. kinship estimate.
    c. concordance rate.
    d. canalization estimate.

23. Which of the following is NOT true about concordance rates? (86)

    a. A score of 100 means that if one twin has the trait, the other twin will always have the trait.
    b. If the concordance rate is higher for identical twins than for fraternal twins, heredity is believed to have an important effect on the trait.
    c. Concordance rates are used to study the role of heredity in traits that can be judged to be either present or absent.
    d. Since concordance rates are based on the study of twins, who always share the same genetic makeup, these estimates are unaffected by environmental variables.

24. Since all normal human babies roll over, sit up, crawl, and walk, one can conclude that infant motor behavior is a strongly _____ trait. (89)

    a. canalized
    b. imprinted
    c. instinctive
    d. encouraged

25. Identical twins reared apart, who nevertheless have many psychological traits and lifestyle characteristics in common, illustrate a form of genetic–environmental correlation called: (91)

    a. range of reaction.
    b. canalization.
    c. niche-picking.
    d. evocative.

50

CHAPTER 3

PRENATAL DEVELOPMENT

Chapter Summary

This chapter begins with a discussion of motivations for parenthood and current changes in birth patterns. Today, men and women are more likely to weigh the pros and cons of having children than they did in previous generations. The American family has declined in size over time, a trend that has child-rearing benefits. Births to women over thirty have increased, a change associated with both advantages and disadvantages for children.

At no other time is change as rapid as it is before birth. Prenatal development takes place in three phases: **(1)** the period of the zygote, during which the newly fertilized ovum travels down the fallopian tube and attaches itself to the uterine wall; **(2)** the period of the embryo, during which the groundwork for all body structures is laid down; and **(3)** the period of the fetus, the "growth and finishing" phase. The prenatal period is a vulnerable time. Teratogens such as drugs, smoking, alcohol, radiation, environmental pollution, maternal disease, inadequate nutrition, maternal stress, and Rh blood incompatibility can damage the developing organism. Prenatal health care is vitally important to ensure the health of mother and baby.

For most expectant parents, the prenatal period is not a time of medical hazard. Instead, it is a time of major life change in which mothers and fathers prepare for parenthood.

LEARNING OBJECTIVES

After reading this chapter, you should be able to:

3.1 Cite advantages and disadvantages of having children mentioned by modern American couples. (99)

3.2 Review current trends in family size and childbearing age, and discuss their impact on child development. (99-102)

3.3 List the phases of prenatal development, and describe the major milestones of each. (103-111)

3.4 Define the term teratogen, and summarize the factors which affect the impact of teratogens. (112)

3.5 List agents known to be or suspected of being teratogens, and discuss evidence supporting the harmful impact of each. (113-121)

3.6 Discuss maternal factors other than exposure to teratogens that can affect the developing embryo or fetus. (121-124)

3.7 Discuss the importance of prenatal health care and cite some of the barriers to seeking such care. (124-125)

3.8 Explain the factors that contribute to personal adjustment as expectant mothers and fathers prepare for parenthood. (126-128)

Motivations for Parenthood

1. List several of the advantages of parenthood mentioned by American couples. (99)

   _____

   _____

2. List several of the disadvantages of parenthood mentioned by American couples. (99)

   _____

   _____

3. List two major reasons that family size has declined in industrialized nations. (100)

   A. _____

   B. _____

4. Describe the benefits of growing up in a small family. (100)

   _____

   _____

   _____

5. True or False: Research supports the commonly held belief that only children are spoiled and selfish. (102)

6. Discuss some of the pros and cons of living in a one-child family, including perspectives of parents as well as children. (102)

   Pros (children): _____

   _____

   Cons (children): _____

   _____

   Pros (parents): _____

   _____

   Cons (parents): _____

   _____

7. True or False: Both males and females experience a decline in reproductive capacity with age. (102)

Social Issues: Education — A Global Perspective on Family Planning

1. Discuss some of the reasons why poverty is linked to higher birth rates. (100-101)

_____

_____

_____

_____

2. List two strategies which have been effective in breaking the cycle through which poverty and high birth rates perpetuate one another. (100-101)

A. _____

B. _____

Prenatal Development

1. Approximately once every 28 days, an ovum is released from one of a woman's two _____, and it travels through one of the two _____, which are long, thin structures that lead to the uterus. (103)

2. The period of the _____ lasts about two weeks, from fertilization until the tiny mass of cells drifts down and out of the fallopian tube and attaches itself to the uterus. (104)

3. Match each term with the appropriate definition. (104)

_____ will become the structures that provide protective covering and nourishment to the new organism

_____ hollow, fluid-filled ball that is formed by a tiny mass of cells four days after fertilization

_____ will become the new organism

1. blastocyst
2. embryonic disk
3. trophoblast

4. List two functions of the amniotic fluid. (105)

A. _____

B. _____

5. The _____ permits food and oxygen to reach the developing organism and waste products to be carried away. (106)

6. The period of the embryo lasts from _____ through the _____ week of pregnancy. (107)

7. True or False: The most rapid prenatal changes take place during the period of the embryo. (107)

8. List the organs and structures which will be formed from each of the three layers of the embryonic disk. (107)

Ectoderm: _____

Mesoderm: _____

Endoderm: _____

9. Summarize the events that take place during the second month of pregnancy. (108)

_____

_____

_____

_____

10. The period of the _____ is the longest prenatal period, lasting from the _____ month to the _____ month. Accordingly, this is sometimes referred to as the _____ and _____ phase. (108)

11. Prenatal development is divided into _____, or three equal periods of time. (108)

12. The white, cheeselike substance that protects the skin from chapping in the amniotic fluid is called _____, while the white, downy hair covering is called _____. (108)

13. What major milestone in brain development is reached at the end of the second trimester? (108)

_____

14. The age at which the baby can first survive if born early is called the age of _____. It occurs sometime between _____ and _____ weeks. (109)

15. True or False: Research shows that the fetus develops a preference for the tone and rhythm of the mother's voice during the last weeks of pregnancy. (109)

Biology and Environment: Temperament in the Womb

1. Describe the research findings on the relationship between fetal activity patterns during the last few weeks of pregnancy and infant temperament at 3 and 6 months after birth. (110)

_____

_____

_____

_____

Prenatal Environmental Influences

1. Define the term *teratogen* and describe four factors that affect the impact of teratogens. (112)

   Teratogen: _____

   _____

   A. _____

   B. _____

   C. _____

   D. _____

2. True or False: The fetal period is the time when teratogens are most likely to cause serious defects. (112)

3. When taken by mothers 4 to 6 weeks after conception, _____, a sedative widely available in some countries during the early 1960's, produced deformities of the embryo's developing arms and legs, and less frequently, caused damage to the ears, heart, kidneys, and genitals. (113)

4. True or False: Heavy caffeine intake during pregnancy is associated with prematurity, miscarriage, and newborn withdrawal symptoms. (114)

5. Describe the difficulties faced by babies who are prenatally exposed to heroine, methadone, or cocaine. (116)

_____

_____

_____

_____

6. True or False: Fathers who use cocaine may contribute to drug-related birth defects because cocaine can "hitchhike" its way to the zygote by attaching to the sperm. (116)

7. Summarize the effects of smoking during the prenatal period. (117)

_____

_____

_____

8. True or False: If a pregnant woman stops smoking at any time during the pregnancy, even during the last trimester, she reduces the chances that her baby will be negatively impacted. (117)

9. True or False: "Passive smoking" has not been determined to have a negative impact on the fetus. (117)

10. Infants whose mothers abused alcohol during pregnancy and who have a specific cluster of physical and behavioral abnormalities are said to have _____. Infants who show some, but not all, of the abnormalities associated with this disorder are said to suffer from _____. (117)

11. List some of the common impairments evidenced by children with fetal alcohol syndrome. (117)

_____

_____

_____

12. True or False: The physical and mental impairments seen in babies with fetal alcohol syndrome typically abate by the time the individual reaches adolescence or early adulthood. (118)

13. Describe two ways in which alcohol produces its devastating effects. (118)

A. _____

_____

B. _____

_____

14. True or False: There is no precise dividing line between safe and dangerous drinking levels during pregnancy. (118)

15. True or False: Low doses of radiation exposure, such as through medical x-rays, are believed to be safe for the developing fetus and have not been linked to any negative outcomes. (118)

16. Match each of the following environmental pollutants with its effect on development: (119)

_____ This teratogen, commonly found in paint chippings from old buildings and other industrial materials, is related to low birth weight, prematurity, brain damage, and physical defects.

1. Mercury
2. Lead
3. PCBs

_____ In the 1950s, children prenatally exposed to this teratogen in a Japanese community displayed physical deformities, mental retardation, abnormal speech, and uncoordinated movements.

_____ Women who ate fish contaminated with this substance gave birth to babies with slightly reduced birth weights, smaller heads, and later memory and intellectual deficits.

17. Describe the outcomes associated with embryonic and fetal exposure to maternal rubella. (119)

Embryonic: _____

_____

_____

Fetal: _____

_____

_____

18. When women carrying the AIDS virus become pregnant, they pass on the disease to their baby approximately _____ percent of the time. (120)

19. True or False: The AIDS disease progresses much more rapidly in infants than in older children and adults. (120)

20. Describe the benefits of regular, moderate exercise during pregnancy. (121)

_____

_____

21. Summarize the behavioral and health problems of prenatally malnourished babies. (122)

_____

_____

22. List the vitamin and mineral supplements which have been found to reduce prenatal complications and birth defects. (122)

A. _____ B. _____

C. _____ D. _____

E. _____

23. True or False: Prenatal malnutrition is currently limited to developing countries, and it has been entirely eradicated in the United States through government programs for low-income pregnant women. (123)

24. Summarize the developmental outcomes associated with severe emotional stress during pregnancy. (123)

_____

_____

_____

25. Describe three ways in which maternal emotional stress can affect the prenatal organism. (123)

A. _____

_____

B. _____

_____

C. _____

_____

26. True or False: When a pregnant woman is under severe emotional stress, the availability of social support networks greatly reduces the risks to the developing organism. (123)

27. Under what conditions can the Rh factor cause problems for the developing fetus? (123)

_____

_____

_____

28. True or False: Problems resulting from the Rh factor are more likely to affect later-born children. (123)

29. True or False: Research has shown that physical maturity among women in their forties, and physical immaturity among adolescents, can lead to increased prenatal difficulties and pregnancy complications. (124)

30. Describe some of the benefits of prenatal health care. (124)

_____

_____

_____

_____

31. List three common demographic characteristics of women who do not seek prenatal care until late in their pregnancies. (124-125)

A. _____ B. _____

C. _____

32. Discuss some of the barriers to obtaining prenatal health care mentioned by expectant mothers who delay or never seek such care. (124-125)

_____

_____

_____

_____

Social Issues: Health — The Prenatal Environment and Health in Later Life

1. True or False: Across numerous cross-cultural studies, low birth weight has been consistently linked to serious health problems later in life, including heart disease, stroke, and diabetes. (114)

2. High birth weight females show an increased risk of _____ _____ in adulthood. (114)

Preparing for Parenthood

1. Over _____ percent of pregnancies in industrialized nations result in healthy newborn babies. (126)

2. Pregnant mothers regard _____ as an extremely valuable source of information, second in importance only to their doctors. (126)

3. What changes and experiences help expectant parents come to view the baby as a reality? (127)

_____

_____

_____

4. True or False: Men and women who have had good relationships with their own parents are more likely to develop positive images of themselves as parents during the pregnancy. (127)

5. Describe the ways in which American culture and Japanese culture differ in their views of pregnancy. (127-128)

_____

_____

_____

_____

6. True or False: Having a baby typically improves a troubled marital relationship. (128)

7. Describe some of the ways in which pregnancy changes a marital relationship. (128)

_____

_____

_____

ASK YOURSELF . . .

REVIEW: Why are poverty and limited education linked to large family size? What are the consequences of a high birthrate for children's development and a nation's future?

_____

_____

_____

_____

APPLY: Rhonda and Mark are career-oriented, 35-year-old parents of an only child. They are thinking about having a second baby. What factors should they keep in mind as they decide whether to add to their family at this time in their lives?

_____

_____

_____

_____

REFLECT: Return to Table 3.1 on page 99, which lists advantages and disadvantages of parenthood. Which are more important and which are least important to you? What is your ideal family size? Explain.

_____

_____

_____

_____

REVIEW: Why is the period of the embryo regarded as the most dramatic prenatal phase? Why is the period of the fetus called the growth and finishing phase?

_____

_____

_____

_____

62

APPLY: Amy, who is 2 months pregnant, wonders how the developing organism is being fed and what parts of the body have formed. "I don't look pregnant yet. Does that mean not much development has taken place?" she asks. How would you respond to Amy?

_____

_____

_____

_____

CONNECT: How does the brain development relate to fetal behavior? What implications do individual differences in fetal behavior have for the baby's temperament after birth?

_____

_____

_____

_____

REVIEW: Why is it difficult to determine the effects of many environmental agents, such as drugs and pollution, on the embryo and fetus?

_____

_____

_____

_____

APPLY: Trixie has just learned she is pregnant. Since she has always been healthy and feels good right now, she cannot understand why the doctor wants her to come in for checkups so often. Why is early and regular prenatal care important for Trixie?

_____

_____

_____

_____

CONNECT: List teratogens and other maternal factors that affect brain development during the prenatal period. Why is the central nervous system often affected when the prenatal environment is compromised?

_____

_____

_____

_____

REFLECT: A recent survey reported that only 7 percent of American women of childbearing age are aware that taking a daily folic acid supplement around the time of conception reduces neural tube defects (U.S. Department of Health and Human Services, 1999). Were you aware of this finding? If you could publicize five environmental influences in a campaign aimed at safeguarding prenatal development, which ones would you choose, and why?

_____

_____

_____

_____

APPLY: Muriel, who is expecting her first child, recalls her own mother as cold and distant. Muriel is worried about whether she will be effective at caring for her new baby. What factors during pregnancy are related to maternal behavior?

_____

_____

_____

_____

REFLECT: Find out how your mother and your grandmothers managed regular activities, such as work and travel, during pregnancy. How were their daily lives different from those of contemporary pregnant women?

_____

_____

_____

_____

SUGGESTED STUDENT READINGS

Kleinfeld, J., Morse, B., Wescott, S. (Eds.) (2000). *Fantastic Antone grows up: Adolescents and adults with fetal alcohol syndrome*. Fairbanks, AK: University of Alaska Press. Primarily written as a guide for parents and caregivers, presents real-life accounts of the unique experiences of adolescents and young adults living with fetal alcohol syndrome.

Russell, A., Sobo, E. J., & Thompson, M.S. (Eds.) (2000). *Contraception across cultures: Technologies, choices, constraints*. New York: Berg. A collection of chapters highlighting the social, economic, political, and cultural contexts of contraception use, family planning, and reproductive health.

Susser, E. S., Brown, A. S., & Gorman, J. M. (Eds.) (1999). *Prenatal exposure in schizophrenia*. Washington, DC: American Psychiatric Press, Inc. Explores the genetic and environmental causes of schizophrenia. The authors focus on prenatal infection, prenatal malnutrition, and obstetric complications which may contribute to mental disorders.

Zeanah, C. H. Jr., et al. (Eds.) (2000). *Handbook of infant mental health (2nd ed.)*. New York: The Guilford Press. Describes the psychological experience of pregnancy, with particular emphasis on the origin of the infant-parent relationship.

PUZZLE TERM REVIEW

Puzzle 3

Across

2. Outer membrane that forms a protective covering and sends out villi from which the placenta emerges
3. Fetal Alcohol _____: condition of children who display some, but not all, of the defects of fetal alcohol syndrome
6. Age of _____: age at which the fetus can first survive if born early
12. Fetal Alcohol _____: mental retardation, slow growth, and facial abnormalities resulting from alcohol consumption during pregnancy
15. Viral infection that destroys the immune system (abbr.)
16. White, downy hair that covers the fetus
18. Parasitic disease caused by eating raw or undercooked meat or by contacting the feces of infected cats
19. Period of the _____: lasts from implantation through the 8th week of pregnancy
20. Period of the _____: growth and finishing phase
21. _____ tube: primitive spinal cord
23. _____ fluid: keeps the temperature in the womb constant and provides a cushion against jolts
24. Separates the mother's bloodstream from the fetus's but permits the exchange of nutrients and waste products

Down

1. Illness marked by increased maternal blood pressure and swelling in her face, hands, and feet
4. Three equal periods of time in prenatal development
5. Sedative available in the early 1960's that caused deformities of the arms and legs when taken between the 4th and 6th week after conception
7. German measles; causes a variety of prenatal abnormalities
8. White, cheeselike substance that covers the fetus and prevents chapping
9. Period of the _____: lasts from fertilization until the tiny mass of cells attaches to the uterine wall
10. Environmental agents that cause damage during the prenatal period
11. Zygote four days after fertilization, when it forms a hollow, fluid-filled ball
13. When present in the fetus's blood but not in the mother's, the _____ factor may cause the mother to build up antibodies that destroy the fetus's red blood cells.
14. The _____ cord connects the prenatal organism to the placenta
17. Ring of cells which will become the structures that provide protective covering and nourishment to the new organism
22. Embryonic _____: cluster of cells inside the blastocyst which will become the new organism

SELF-TEST

1. Which of the following is NOT mentioned by American couples as an advantage of parenthood? (99)
   a. giving and receiving warmth and affection
   b. having offspring to provide emotional and financial support for the parents as they age
   c. experiencing new growth and learning opportunities
   d. being accepted as a mature, responsible member of the community

2. The unfavorable outcomes associated with large family size are eliminated when: (101)
   a. parents are economically advantaged and provide a stimulating environment for their children.
   b. parents are more punitive in disciplining their children.
   c. siblings are spaced close together in age.
   d. parents have their children at a young age so that they are more energetic and better able to keep up with the demands of a large family.

3. Only children: (102)
   a. tend to grow up spoiled and selfish.
   b. tend to have difficulties relating to peers.
   c. are just as well adjusted as children with siblings.
   d. do not differ from children with siblings.

4. By the fourth day after conception, 60 to 70 cells form a hollow, fluid-filled ball called a(n): (104)
   a. blastocyst.
   b. embryonic disc.
   c. trophoblast.
   d. zygote.

5. The amniotic fluid: (105)
   a. produces blood cells until the developing liver, spleen, and bone marrow are mature enough to take over this function.
   b. permits oxygen and food to reach the developing organism.
   c. protects the fetus's skin from chapping.
   d. maintains a constant temperature in the womb and provides a cushion against jolts caused by the mother's movement.

6. The organ that separates the mother's bloodstream from the embryonic or fetal bloodstream, but permits exchange of nutrients and waste, is called the: (106)
   a. amnion.
   b. chorion.
   c. placenta.
   d. umbilical cord.

7. During the period of the _____, the most rapid prenatal changes take place, as the groundwork for all body structures and internal organs is laid down. (107)

    a. zygote
    b. fetus
    c. neonate
    d. embyro

8. The _____ is a primitive spinal cord, the top of which swells to form the brain. (107)

    a. umbilical cord
    b. neural tube
    c. ectoderm
    d. embryonic disk

9. _____ covers the baby's skin and prevents it from chapping in the amniotic fluid. (108)

    a. Lanugo
    b. The amnion
    c. Vernix
    d. The placenta

10. Which of the following is true about the relationship between temperament in the womb and temperament in early infancy? (110)

    a. Research has shown that there is no association between prenatal temperament and temperament in early infancy.
    b. Research has shown that fetal activity during the last few weeks of pregnancy is a modest predictor of infant temperament.
    c. Research has shown that fetal activity during the last few weeks of pregnancy is perfectly correlated with infant temperament.
    d. Researchers have yet to study this relationship.

11. Which of the following is NOT true about the effects of teratogens? (112)

    a. Larger doses over longer periods of time are usually associated with increased negative effects.
    b. The effects of teratogens vary with the age of the organism at the time of exposure.
    c. The consequences of prenatal exposure to teratogens may not be apparent for several decades.
    d. Teratogenic effects are limited to immediate physical damage.

12. Exposure to teratogens during the _____ period is associated with the most serious defects. (112)

    a. embryonic
    b. zygotic
    c. fetal
    d. neonatal

13. Infants who are prenatally exposed to cocaine: (116)

    a. show few ill effects beyond the dangerous withdrawal period.
    b. tend to be overly sensitive to environmental stimuli.
    c. typically have lasting difficulties.
    d. exhibit an easy temperament and are very receptive to cuddling.

14. The most well-known effect of smoking during pregnancy is: (117)

    a. low birth weight.
    b. infant death.
    c. childhood behavioral problems.
    d. long-term respiratory difficulties.

15. Mental retardation, slow physical growth, and facial abnormalities are among the dose-related effects of which of the following teratogens? (117)

    a. caffeine
    b. cocaine
    c. alcohol
    d. marijuana

16. What amount of alcohol is required to produce fetal alcohol effects? (118)

    a. extreme maternal alcoholism
    b. more than two drinks a day
    c. as little as one ounce a day
    d. the precise amount has not yet been determined

17. Following the bombings of Hiroshima and Nagasaki during World War II and the power plant accident in Chernobyl, Ukraine in 1986, there were dramatic increases in the incidents of miscarriages and birth defects due to prenatal _____ exposure. (118)

    a. mercury
    b. radiation
    c. lead
    d. thalidomide

18. Which of the following is NOT true of HIV/AIDS? (120)

    a. When women carrying the virus become pregnant, they pass the disease on to the developing organism 20 to 30 percent of the time.
    b. AIDS symptoms progress more rapidly in infants than in older children and adults.
    c. Most prenatal AIDS babies survive 4-6 years after the appearance of symptoms.
    d. The drug ZDV reduces prenatal AIDS transmission by as much as 95 percent, even in women with advanced cases of the disease.

19. Pregnant women should not eat undercooked meat or clean a cat's litter box due to the danger of: (120-121)

    a. toxoplasmosis.
    b. rubella.
    c. cytomegalovirus.
    d. tuberculosis.

20. Prenatal malnutrition is known to cause: (122)

    a. damage to the central nervous system.
    b. severe mental retardation.
    c. delayed motor development.
    d. serious cognitive impairments, including deficits in attention, memory, planning, and spatial abilities.

21. In cases where the mother is negative and the baby is positive, _____ can cause oxygen deprivation and result in miscarriage, mental retardation, heart damage, and death at birth. (123)

    a. eclampsia
    b. the androgen factor
    c. antibody incompatibility
    d. the Rh factor

22. All of the following are mentioned as barriers to early prenatal care in the United States EXCEPT: (124)

    a. inadequate health insurance for low-income families
    b. psychological stress
    c. difficulty finding a doctor
    d. absence of government-sponsored health services

23. Expectant parents: (127)

    a. need to have had a warm, secure relationship with their own parents in order to develop optimistic views of themselves as parents.
    b. frequently adapt to psychological challenges of pregnancy by seeking information from books.
    c. should not plan to modify their relationship just because their family is growing.
    d. are well-advised to reduce the physical activity of the expectant mother as much as possible.

24. Which of the following best reflects American and Japanese cultural values regarding activity during pregnancy? (127-128)

    a. Women in both American and Japanese cultures are typically very active until the end of pregnancy.
    b. Women in Japan commonly work and travel until the end of their pregnancies, but such activity during pregnancy is discouraged in the American culture.
    c. Women in America commonly work and travel until the end of their pregnancies, but such activity during pregnancy is discouraged in the Japanese culture.
    d. Women in both American and Japanese cultures typically cease work and strenuous leisure activities upon becoming pregnant out of a belief that this is necessary in order to protect the health of their babies.

25. When a couple has an unhappy relationship, the birth of a baby usually: (128)

    a. decreases family conflict.
    b. increases family conflict.
    c. has no effect on the relationship.
    d. increases family conflict initially, but results in decreased conflict as the couple adjusts to parenting.

CHAPTER 4

BIRTH AND THE NEWBORN BABY

Chapter Summary

Childbirth takes place in three stages: **(1)** dilation and effacement of the cervix; **(2)** delivery of the baby; and **(3)** birth of the placenta. Production of stress hormones helps the infant withstand the trauma of childbirth. The Apgar Scale permits assessment of the baby's physical condition immediately after birth. Natural or prepared childbirth and delivery in a birth center or at home are increasingly popular alternatives to traditional hospital delivery. Social support during labor and delivery can lead to more successful childbirth experiences. Nevertheless, childbirth in the United States is often accompanied by a variety of medical interventions. Although they help save the lives of many babies, these procedures can cause problems of their own when used routinely.

Although most births proceed normally, serious complications sometimes occur. Among the most common are oxygen deprivation and prematurity. Fortunately, many babies who experience severe birth trauma recover with the help of favorable child-rearing environments.

Infants begin life with a remarkable set of skills for relating to the surrounding world. Newborns display a wide variety of reflexes. In the early weeks, babies frequently move in and out of different states of arousal, although they spend the most time asleep, including important REM sleep, which stimulates the brain. Crying is the first way that babies communicate.

With experience, parents become better at interpreting the meaning of the infant's cries. Newborns' senses of touch, taste, smell, and sound are well developed. Vision is the least mature sensory capacity. The baby's many capacities have been put together into tests that permit behavioral assessment of the newborn.

The baby's arrival is exciting, but it brings with it profound changes. Special interventions exist to ease the transition to parenthood. Husbands and wives who support each other in their new roles typically adjust well.

LEARNING OBJECTIVES

After reading this chapter, you should be able to:

4.1   Describe the events leading up to childbirth and the three stages of labor. (134-137)

4.2   Discuss the baby's adaptation to labor and delivery, and describe the appearance of the newborn. (137-138)

4.3   Explain the purpose and main features of the Apgar Scale. (138-139)

4.4   Discuss the concept of natural childbirth, noting the typical features of a natural childbirth program, the benefits of the natural childbirth experience, and the role of social support in the natural childbirth process. (140)

4.5 Discuss the benefits and concerns associated with home delivery. (141)

4.6 Explain several medical techniques commonly used by doctors during labor and delivery, including fetal monitoring, labor and delivery medication, instrument delivery, induced labor, and cesarean delivery. Additionally, describe the circumstances that justify the use of each technique, and discuss the risks that each procedure may pose for mothers and babies. (141-144)

4.7 Discuss the risks associated with oxygen deprivation, preterm, small-for-date, low birth weight, and postterm births, and review the developmental outlook for infants born under such circumstances. (144-150)

4.8 Describe several interventions for preterm infants, including infant stimulation and parent training. (147-149)

4.9 Summarize findings of the Kauai Study relating to the long-term consequences of birth complications. (150)

4.10 Discuss parents' feelings of involvement with their newborn babies, including the findings on bonding. (151-152)

4.11 Name and describe major newborn reflexes, noting the functions served by each, and discuss the importance of assessing newborn reflexes. (152-154)

4.12 Describe the five infant states of arousal, with particular attention to sleep and crying. (154-157)

4.13 Describe the newborn baby's responsiveness to touch, taste, smell, sound, and visual stimulation. (157-160)

4.14 Describe Brazelton's Neonatal Behavioral Assessment Scale (NBAS), and explain its usefulness. (160)

4.15 Describe some common changes in the family system associated with the birth of a child, and discuss the impact of intervention programs on the transition to parenthood. (161-164)

STUDY QUESTIONS

The Stages of Childbirth

1. Describe three signs which indicate that labor is near. (134)

   A. _____

   B. _____

   C. _____

2. List the three stages of labor and note the major occurrences of each stage. (134-137)

   A. _____

   _____

   _____

B. _____

_____

_____

C. _____

_____

_____

3. The climax of Stage 1 is called _____, in which the frequency and strength of contractions are at their peak and the cervix opens completely. (135)

4. True or False: The production of stress hormones is adaptive for infants during childbirth. (138)

5. The average newborn baby is _____ inches long and weighs _____ pounds. (138)

6. The _____ is used to quickly assess the infant's physical condition at birth in terms of the following five characteristics: (138)

A. _____ B. _____ C. _____

D. _____ E. _____

7. With regard to the aforementioned assessment scale (see question 6), a score of ____ or better indicates a healthy infant, a score between ____ and ____ indicates that special assistance is required, and a score of ____ or below indicates a dire emergency. (138-139)

Biology and Environment: What Controls the Timing of Birth?

1. Name the placental hormone believed to initiate the complex hormonal system that controls the timing of birth. (136)

_____

2. How does this hormonal system ensure that labor will occur only when the fetus is ready to survive outside of the womb? (136-137)

_____

_____

Approaches to Childbirth

1. _____ childbirth techniques try to overcome the idea that childbirth is a painful ordeal that requires extensive medical intervention. (140)

2. List three components of a typical natural childbirth program. (140)

   A. _____

   B. _____

   C. _____

3. True or False: Empirical findings suggest that mothers who experience natural childbirth have more favorable attitudes toward the childbirth experience than mothers who do not. (140)

4. _____ is important to the success of natural childbirth, as it has been linked with the occurrence of fewer birth complications, as well as shorter labors. (140)

5. Name the position for delivery which is favored by the research findings, and discuss the benefits of this position. (140-141)

   _____

   _____

   _____

6. Discuss some of the reasons why increasing numbers of American women are opting for home delivery. (141)

   _____

   _____

   _____

   _____

7. Home births are typically handled by certified _____. (141)

8. Discuss the safety concerns surrounding home birth, and note the circumstances under which it is safe to give birth at home. (141)

_____

_____

_____

Medical Interventions

1. _____ are electronic instruments that track the baby's heart rate during labor. (141)

2. Cite four reasons why fetal monitoring is a controversial procedure. (142)

   A. _____

   B. _____

   C. _____

   D. _____

3. _____ are drugs used in mild doses to relieve pain, whereas _____ are stronger painkillers which block sensation. (142)

4. Discuss two ways in which the routine use of labor and delivery medications can cause problems during the childbirth process. (142)

   A. _____

   _____

   B. _____

   _____

5. True or False: Research findings definitively show that the use of labor and delivery medication has no lasting impact on the child's physical and mental development. (142)

6. In what circumstance is delivery with forceps or a vacuum extractor appropriate? (142)

   _____

   _____

7. True or False: Instrument delivery is used more than twice as often in the United States as it is in Europe. (142)

8. Induced labor is one that is started artificially by breaking the _____ and giving the mother a _____ that stimulates contractions. (143)

9. Induced labor is justified when _____ _____. (143)

10. In what ways does an induced labor proceed differently than a naturally occurring one? (143)

   _____

   _____

   _____

11. The rate of _____ is more than twice as great in induced labors as in spontaneous labors. (143)

12. True or False: The United States has one of the lowest rates of cesarean delivery in the world. (143)

13. Cesareans are often justified when the baby is in a _____ position, meaning that the buttocks or feet would be delivered first. (143)

14. How can cesarean delivery affect the adjustment of the newborn baby, and consequently, the early infant–mother relationship? (143-144)

   _____

   _____

   _____

Birth Complications

1. _____ is a general term for a variety of problems that result from brain damage before, during, or just after birth. A common cause of this condition is _____, or inadequate oxygen supply, during labor and delivery. (144)

2. Placenta _____ refers to a premature separation of the placenta, whereas placenta _____ refers to a detachment of the placenta resulting from implantation of the blastocyst low in the uterus so that the placenta covers the cervical opening. (144)

3. Describe the typical developmental outcomes of children who experience anoxia during labor and delivery. (145)

_____

_____

_____

4. Babies are considered premature if they are born _____ weeks or more before the end of a full 38-week pregnancy or if they weigh less than _____ pounds. (145)

5. True or False: Birth weight is the best available predictor of infant survival and healthy development. (145)

6. List the problems associated with low birth weight. (145-146)

_____

_____

_____

_____

7. Distinguish between preterm and small-for-date babies. (146)

Preterm: _____

_____

Small-for-date:_____

_____

8. Of the two types of babies, (preterm/small-for-date) infants usually have more serious problems. (Circle one) (146)

9. Discuss several methods of stimulation used to foster the successful development of preterm infants. (147)

_____

_____

_____

_____

10. True or False: Research suggests that all preterm children, regardless of family characteristics, require continuous, high-quality interventions well into the school years in order to maintain developmental gains. (147-148)

11. Infants born 42 weeks or more into the pregnancy are considered
_____. (149)

12. Discuss three factors related to the increased risk of oxygen deprivation and head injuries among postterm infants. (149-150)

A. _____

B. _____

C. _____

13. Findings from the Kauai study suggest that as long as birth injuries are not overwhelming, _____ can restore children's growth. (150)

Social Issues: Health — A Cross-National Perspective on Health Care and Other Policies for Parents and Newborn Babies

1. _____ refers to the number of deaths in the first year of life per 1,000 live births. (148)

2. In the United States, what group is at greatest risk for infant death during the first year of life? (148)

_____

3. _____ mortality, the rate of death in the first month of life, accounts for 67 percent of the infant death rate in the United States. (148)

4. List the two leading causes of neonatal mortality. (148)

A. _____

B. _____

5. Discuss the factors that are largely responsible for the high rates of infant mortality in the United States, and cite several factors which may lead to a reduction of the current infant mortality rates. (148)

_____

_____

_____

_____

Precious Moments After Birth

1. True or False: Fathers provide their infants with as much stimulation and affection as mothers do. (151)

2. True or False: The parent–infant relationship is highly dependent on close physical contact in the hours after birth in order for bonding to develop. (151)

3. _____ is an arrangement in which the infant stays in the mother's hospital room all or most of the time. (152)

The Newborn Baby's Capacities

1. A _____ is an inborn, automatic response to a particular form of stimulation. (152)

2. Match each reflex with the appropriate response or function descriptor. (153)

_____ Spontaneous grasp of adult's finger	1. Eye blink
_____ When the sole of foot is stroked, the toes fan out and curl	2. Tonic neck
_____ Helps infant find the nipple	3. Palmar grasp
_____ Prepares infant for voluntary walking	4. Babinski
_____ Permits feeding	5. Rooting
_____ Infant lies in a "fencing position"	6. Sucking
_____ Protects infant from strong stimulation	7. Swimming
_____ In our evolutionary past, may have helped infant cling to mother	8. Stepping
_____ Helps infants survive if dropped in water	9. Moro

3. When do most newborn reflexes disappear? (154)

_____

4. Explain the importance of assessing newborn reflexes. (154)

_____

_____

_____

5. Newborn infants move in and out of five _____, or degrees of sleep and wakefulness. (154)

6. Describe the characteristics of REM and NREM sleep. (155)

REM: _____

_____

NREM: _____

_____

7. Why do infants spend so much time in REM sleep? (155)

_____

_____

8. What is the most effective way to soothe a crying baby when feeding and diaper changing do not work? (156)

_____

9. How do the cries of preterm and ill infants differ from those of healthy infants, and how does this difference affect the response of parents? (156-157)

_____

_____

_____

10. True or False: Infants are born with a well-developed sense of touch, and consequently, they are quite sensitive to pain. (157-158)

11. True or False: Infants not only have taste preferences, but they are also capable of communicating these preferences to adults through facial expressions. (158)

12. Newborn infants respond to the smell of certain foods in a manner similar to that of adults, suggesting that some odor preferences are _____. (158)

13. True or False: Newborn infants are attracted to the scent of a lactating woman, but they are unable to discriminate the smell of their own mother's breast from that of an unfamiliar lactating woman. (158)

14. Infants prefer _____ sounds, such as noises and voices, to pure tones. (159)

15. True or False: Infants can discriminate almost all of the speech sounds of any human language. (159)

16. _____ is the least mature of the newborn baby's senses. (159)

17. Describe the newborn baby's visual acuity. (159)

_____

_____

18. True or False: Infants have well-developed color vision at birth, and they are immediately capable of discriminating colors. (159-160)

19. The most widely used instrument for assessing the behavior of infants during the newborn period is the _____
_____. (160)

20. Which areas of behavior does the NBAS evaluate? (160)

_____

_____

21. Since the NBAS is given to infants all around the world, researchers have been able to learn a great deal about individual and _____ differences in newborn behavior and the ways in which various childbearing practices affect infant behavior. Briefly discuss these findings. (160)

_____

_____

_____

_____

22. Why is a single NBAS score not a good predictor of later development, and what should be used in place of a single score? (160)

_____

_____

23. How are NBAS interventions beneficial for the early parent–infant relationship? (160)

_____

_____

The Transition to Parenthood

1. Discuss several changes in the family system following the birth of a new baby. (161-163)

   _____

   _____

   _____

   _____

2. True or False: Men experience a more difficult transition to parenthood than do women. (162)

3. In what ways does postponing childbearing until the late twenties or thirties ease the transition to parenthood? (162-163)

   _____

   _____

   _____

4. How does paternal involvement in infant care responsibilities affect the marital relationship? (163)

   _____

   _____

5. Discuss the ways in which interventions for parents who are not at risk differ from those for high-risk parents. (163-164)

   _____

   _____

   _____

Biology and Environment: Postpartum Depression and the Parent-Child Relationship

1. Approximately _____ to _____ percent of first-time mothers experience temporary postpartum blues, and as many as _____ percent develop postpartum depression. (162)

2. Discuss how the experience of postpartum depression affects the mother's interactions with her infant. (162)

_____

_____

_____

3. Explain the ways in which persistent maternal depression may impact the development of the child. (162)

_____

_____

_____

4. To prevent maternal depression from harming children, _____
_____ is vital. (162)

REVIEW: Name and briefly describe the three stages of labor.

_____

_____

_____

_____

APPLY: On seeing her newborn baby for the first time, Caroline exclaimed, "Why is she so out of proportion?" What observations prompted Caroline to ask this question? Explain why her baby's appearance is adaptive.

_____

_____

_____

_____

CONNECT: How do findings on the timing of birth illustrate bidirectional influences between mother and fetus? How do they illustrate the roles of both nature and nurture?

_____

_____

_____

_____

REVIEW: Describe the ingredients and benefits of natural childbirth. What aspect contributes greatly to favorable outcomes, and why?

_____

_____

_____

_____

APPLY: Sharon, a heavy smoker, has just arrived at the hospital in labor. Which one of the medical interventions discussed in the preceding sections is her doctor justified in using? (For help in answering this question, return to the discussion of prenatal effects of tobacco in Chapter 3, page 117.)

_____

_____

_____

84

CONNECT: Use of any one medical intervention during labor increases the chances that others will also be used. Provide as many examples as you can to illustrate this idea.

_____

_____

_____

_____

REFLECT: If you were an expectant parent, would you choose home birth? Why or why not?

_____

_____

_____

_____

REVIEW: Sensitive care can help preterm infants recover, but unfortunately they are less likely to receive such care than are full-term newborns. Explain why.

_____

_____

_____

_____

APPLY: Cecilia and Adena each gave birth to a baby 7 weeks preterm and weighing only 3 pounds. Cecilia did not finish high school and is single and on welfare. Adena and her husband graduated from college and earn a good income. Plan an intervention program appropriate for helping each baby develop favorably.

_____

_____

_____

_____

CONNECT: List factors discussed in this chapter and in Chapter 3 that increase the chances that an infant will be born underweight. How many of these factors could be prevented by better health care for mothers and babies?

_____

_____

_____

_____

REFLECT: Many people question the advisability of extraordinary medical measures to save extremely low-birth-weight babies (under 1½ pounds or 1,000 grams), since most who survive develop serious physical, cognitive, and emotional problems. Do you agree or disagree? Explain.

_____

_____

_____

_____

REVIEW: What functions does REM sleep serve in young infants? When newborn babies are awake, about how much time do they spend crying? Can sleep and crying tell us anything about the health of the newborn's nervous system? Explain.

_____

_____

_____

_____

APPLY: Jackie, who has had a difficult birth, observes her 2-day-old daughter, Kelly, being given the NBAS. Kelly scores poorly on many items. Jackie wonders if this means Kelly will not develop normally. How would you respond to Jackie's concern?

_____

_____

_____

_____

CONNECT: How do the diverse capacities of newborn babies contribute to their first social relationships? Provide as many examples as you can.

_____

_____

_____

_____

REVIEW: Explain how persisting postpartum depression seriously impairs children's development.

_____

_____

_____

_____

CONNECT: Louise has just given birth to her first child. Because her husband works long hours and is seldom available to help, she feels overwhelmed by the pressure of caring for a new baby. Why does Louise's 4-week maternity leave pose a risk to her mental health? (*Hint:* Consult the Social Issues: Health box on page 148.)

_____

_____

_____

_____

REFLECT: If you are a parent, what was the transition to parenthood like for you? What factors eased the stress of this major life change? What factors made it more difficult? If you are not a parent, pose these questions to someone you know who has recently become a parent.

_____

_____

_____

_____

SUGGESTED STUDENT READINGS

Barr, R. G., Hopkins, B., & Green, J. A. (Eds.). (2000). *Crying as a sign, symptom, and a signal: Clinical emotional, and developmental aspects of infant and toddler crying.* New York: Cambridge University Press. Takes a multidisciplinary look at this important infant behavior, describes normative developmental patterns of crying and discusses how they are manifested in various settings — emergency department, painful procedures, colic, temper tantrums, and nonverbal and mentally challenged infants.

Junn, E. N. & Boyatzis, C. J. (Eds.). (2000). *Annual editions: Child growth and development 2000/2001 (7th ed.).* Guilford, CT: Dushkin/McGraw-Hill. A compilation of selected articles taken from journals, magazines, and newspapers, this book presents current perspectives on child growth and development. Appropriate for students, researchers, and anyone interested in the field of child development.

Kotch, J. B., (1997). *Maternal and child health-programs, problems, and policy in public health.* Gaithersburg, MD: Aspen. Provides an overview of the health care needs of pregnant women, mothers and children of all ages. Particular attention is focused on services, policies, and institutional forces that directly influence maternal and child health. Weaknesses and strengths of current federal and state policies and health reform issues are discussed.

Tracey, N. (Ed.). (2000). *Parents of premature infants: Their emotional world.* London, England: Whurr Publishers, Ltd. A series of in-depth interviews which focuses on the emotions, thoughts, and fantasies of parents of premature infants.

PUZZLE TERM REVIEW

Puzzle 4a

Across

5. Climax of the first stage of labor in which the frequency and strength of contractions peak and the cervix opens completely
6. A mild pain-relieving drug
7. Respiratory _____ syndrome: A disorder of preterm infants in which the lungs are so immature that the air sacs collapse, causing breathing difficulties
8. _____ and effacement of the cervix: widening and thinning of the cervix during the first stage of labor
12. An "irregular" sleep state in which brain wave activity is similar to that of the waking state (abbr.)
13. Parents' feelings of affection and concern for the newborn baby
15. An inborn, automatic response to a particular form of stimulation

Down

1. Positioning of the baby in the uterus such that the buttocks or feet would be delivered first
2. States of _____: different degrees of sleep and wakefulness
3. _____ mortality: the number of deaths in the first year of life per 1,000 live births
4. A strong pain-killing drug that blocks sensation
9. _____ labor: a labor started artificially by breaking the amnion and giving the mother a hormone that stimulates contractions
10. The _____ Scale is used to assess the newborn immediately after birth.
11. _____ mortality: the number of deaths in the first month of life per 1,000 live births
14. A "regular" sleep state in which the heart rate, breathing, and brain wave activity are slow and regular (abbr.)

PUZZLE TERM REVIEW

Puzzle 4b

Across

2. An arrangement in which the baby stays in the mother's hospital room all or most of the time (2 words)
3. Infants who spend more than 42 weeks in the uterus
4. Metal clamps placed around the baby's head; used to pull the baby from the birth canal
6. Infants born several weeks or months before their due date
9. Infants whose birth weight is below normal when length of pregnancy is taken into account (3 words)
11. _____ extractor: a plastic cup attached to a suction tube; used to deliver the baby
12. Inadequate oxygen supply
13. _____ childbirth: an approach designed to overcome the idea that birth is a painful ordeal requiring extensive medical intervention
14. A small incision made during childbirth to increase the size of the vaginal opening

Down

1. _____ depression: feelings of sadness and withdrawal that appear shortly after childbirth and continue for weeks or months
4. _____ monitors: electronic instruments that track the baby's heart rate during labor
5. _____ delivery: a surgical delivery in which the doctor makes an incision in the mother's abdomen and lifts the baby out of the uterus
7. A test developed to assess the behavior of the infant during the newborn period (abbr.)
8. A general term for a variety of problems, all of which involve muscle coordination, that result from brain damage before, during, or just after birth (2 words)
10. Visual _____: fineness of visual discrimination

SELF-TEST

1. All of the following are signs that labor is near EXCEPT: (134)

   a. separation of the placenta.
   b. false labor.
   c. lightening.
   d. the bloody show.

2. Which of the following takes place during Stage 1 of the childbirth process? (134)

   a. delivery of the baby
   b. prelabor
   c. dialation and effacement of the cervix
   d. birth of the placenta

3. The _____ is used to assess the physical condition of the newborn at 1 and 5 minutes after birth. (138)

   a. Brazelton Neonatal Behavioral Assessment Scale
   b. Apgar Scale
   c. Bayley Scales of Infant Development
   d. Neonatal Reflex Inventory

4. Natural, or prepared, childbirth: (140)

   a. tries to overcome the idea that birth is a painful ordeal that requires extensive medical intervention.
   b. is typically handled by a certified midwife rather than a doctor.
   c. is reported by mothers to be extremely painful, and consequently, leads to less favorable maternal attitudes toward the childbirth experience.
   d. is associated with increased risk of birth complications.

5. Home delivery: (141)

   a. is recommended for women who are at risk for birth complications.
   b. commonly leads to serious birth complications, and therefore, should not be considered a safe option under any circumstances.
   c. accounts for approximately 15 percent of all births.
   d. is a safe option for healthy, well-assisted women.

6. Fetal monitors are electronic instruments that: (141)

   a. track the baby's heart rate during labor.
   b. track the baby's progress through the birth canal.
   c. monitor the mother's vital signs during labor and delivery.
   d. monitor fetal brain wave activity for signs of distress during labor and delivery.

7. Which of the following is NOT true of instrument delivery? (142)

   a. Instrument delivery is used when the mother's pushing does not move the baby through the birth canal in a reasonable period of time.
   b. Instrument delivery is associated with a higher risk of infant head injury.
   c. Instrument delivery is a surgical birth.
   d. Instrument delivery is used more than twice as often in the United States as in Europe.

8. An induced labor: (143)

   a. proceeds the same way as a naturally occurring labor.
   b. allows the mother more control over the delivery.
   c. leads to contractions that are longer, harder, and more closely spaced together.
   d. typically requires lesser amounts of labor and delivery medication.

9. Cesarean delivery: (143)

   a. emphasizes relaxation and breathing techniques.
   b. is rarely used in the United States except in extreme medical emergencies.
   c. may cause the baby to be sleepy and unresponsive.
   d. makes future vaginal births impossible.

10. Which of the following is NOT true of the breech position? (143)

   a. The baby is turned so that the buttocks or feet would be delivered first.
   b. Doctors can sometimes turn the baby into a head-down position.
   c. Breech births always require a cesarean delivery.
   d. The breech position increases the baby's chances of experiencing oxygen deprivation during labor and delivery.

11. Anoxia, or oxygen deprivation, during labor and delivery may lead to: (144)

   a. cerebral palsy.
   b. placenta abruptio.
   c. respiratory distress syndrome.
   d. Down syndrome.

12. An infant born two months early but weighing an appropriate amount for the time spent in the uterus is called: (146)

   a. small-for-date.
   b. preterm.
   c. postterm.
   d. low birth weight.

13. Which of the following is true regarding the use of stimulation with preterm infants? (147)

   a. Doctors recommend that all preterm infants are placed in a highly stimulating environment in order to foster development.
   b. Research suggests that stimulation is harmful for fragile preterm infants.
   c. Preterm infants differ in their responses to stimulation, and therefore, the amount and kind of stimulation should be adjusted to fit the individual child.
   d. Studies suggest that stimulation is unrelated to developmental outcomes among preterm infants.

14. Which of the following is NOT true of postterm pregnancies? (149-150)

   a. Infants born after the 42nd week of pregnancy are considered postterm.
   b. Postterm infants are at increased risk of anoxia and head injuries.
   c. Postterm infants are at high risk for long-term developmental delays.
   d. Doctors usually have to induce labor in cases of postterm pregnancies.

15. Findings from the Kauai study revealed that: (150)

    a. postterm births are strongly associated with exposure to environmental pollution.
    b. newborn reflexes typically disappear in the first six months of life.
    c. the impact of early biological risk factors far outweigh personal characteristics and social experiences in contributing to developmental functioning throughout childhood.
    d. in a supportive home environment, even children with serious birth problems can develop successfully.

16. The _____ reflex helps a breast-fed baby to find the mother's nipple. (153)

    a. rooting
    b. sucking
    c. tonic neck
    d. Moro

17. A careful assessment of an infant's reflexes provides the pediatrician with important information about the infant's: (154)

    a. muscle tone.
    b. sensory capacities.
    c. responsiveness to physical stimulation.
    d. nervous system.

18. REM sleep: (155)

    a. accounts for a lesser percentage of sleep time in infants than in children and adults.
    b. seems to fulfill young infants' need for stimulation since they spend such little time in an alert state.
    c. is a "regular" sleep state in which the body is almost motionless, and the heart rate, breathing, and brain wave activity are slow and regular.
    d. is less frequent in the fetus and in preterm infants than in full-term infants.

19. The most effective way to sooth a crying baby is to: (156)

    a. lift the baby to the shoulder.
    b. swaddle the baby.
    c. offer a pacifier.
    d. play rhythmic sounds.

20. The cries of brain-damaged infants and those who have experienced prenatal and birth complications are often: (156)

    a. more difficult for adults to interpret.
    b. weak and sporadic.
    c. shrill and piercing.
    d. easier to sooth than the cries of other infants.

21. Research on the sense of smell indicates that: (158)
    a. infants do not have a well-developed sense of smell until several months after birth.
    b. newborn infants recognize the smell of their own mother's breast and amniotic fluid.
    c. odor preferences are gradually developed through environmental exposure to a variety of scents.
    d. infants can distinguish pleasant and unpleasant odors but cannot identify the location of an odor, and therefore, cannot defend themselves from unpleasant odors by turning their heads in the other direction.

22. Newborn infants: (159)
    a. prefer pure tones to complex sounds.
    b. are most attentive to low-pitched, monotonous patterns of sound.
    c. can discriminate all but a few sounds of any human language.
    d. can only discriminate the speech sounds of their native language.

23. Because the visual system is not yet well-developed, _____, or fineness of discrimination, is limited in newborn infants. (159)
    a. depth perception
    b. tunnel vision
    c. binocular vision
    d. visual acuity

24. Which of the following is NOT true of the Neonatal Behavioral Assessment Scale (NBAS)? (160)
    a. The NBAS evaluates the baby's reflexes, state changes, and responsiveness to physical and social stimuli.
    b. A single NBAS score is an excellent predictor of later development.
    c. The NBAS can be used to examine cultural differences in newborn behavior.
    d. The NBAS can be used to facilitate a healthy parent–child relationship.

25. Which of the following is NOT true of the transition to parenthood? (161-163)
    a. The roles of the husband and wife typically become less traditional.
    b. Women typically experience a more difficult transition to parenthood than do men.
    c. The demands of new parenthood often lead to a decline in marital satisfaction.
    d. Postponing childbearing until the late twenties or thirties eases the transition to parenthood.

CHAPTER 5

PHYSICAL DEVELOPMENT IN INFANCY AND TODDLERHOOD

Chapter Summary

Body size increases dramatically during the first 2 years of life, following organized patterns of growth. Fat increases faster than muscle, and the skull expands rapidly to accommodate the rapidly growing brain. Neurons form intricate connections and their fibers myelinate, causing a rapid increase in brain weight. Already, the two hemispheres of the cortex have begun to specialize, although the brain retains considerable plasticity during the first few years. In addition, specific sensitive periods in brain development are now recognized, when the brain must receive appropriate stimulation for it to reach its full potential.

A variety of factors affect early physical growth. Heredity contributes to height, weight, and rate of physical maturation. Nutrition is essential for rapidly growing babies, and breast milk is especially suited to meet their needs. Malnutrition during the early years can result in permanent stunting of physical growth and of brain development. Affection and stimulation are also essential for healthy physical growth.

Infants are marvelously equipped to learn immediately after birth. Classical conditioning, operant conditioning, habituation–dishabituation, and imitation are important early learning capacities that assist infants in finding out about their physical and social worlds.

Although motor development follows the same organized sequences as physical growth, it does not follow a fixed maturational timetable. According to dynamic systems theory, previously learned skills are combined in increasingly complex ways to result in new abilities. Central nervous system development, movement possibilities of the body, the task the child has in mind, and environmental supports combine to influence the development of motor skills.

Hearing and vision undergo major advances during the first 2 years as infants organize stimuli into complex patterns, improve their perception of depth and objects, and combine information across sensory modalities. The Gibsons' differentiation theory helps us understand the course of perceptual development.

LEARNING OBJECTIVES

After reading this chapter, you should be able to:

5.1 Describe changes in body size, body proportions, and muscle-fat makeup during the first 2 years of life. (170-172)

5.2 Discuss skeletal growth during the first 2 years of life, including the growth of the skull and the appearance of teeth. (172-173)

5.3 Describe brain development during infancy and toddlerhood at the level of individual brain cells and at the level of the cerebral cortex. (173-177)

5.4 Explain the concepts of brain lateralization and brain plasticity. (175-177)

5.5 Describe research findings related to the existence of sensitive periods in brain development, and note the evidence of brain growth spurts and need for appropriate stimulation. (177-178)

5.6 Discuss the changes in the organization of sleep and wakefulness between birth and 2 years of age. (178-180)

5.7 Discuss the impact of heredity on early physical growth. (180)

5.8 Discuss the nutritional needs of infants and toddlers, the advantages of breast-feeding, and the extent to which chubby babies are at risk for later overweight and obesity. (181-183)

5.9 Discuss the impact of severe malnutrition on the development of infants and toddlers, and cite two dietary diseases associated with this condition. (183-184)

5.10 Describe the growth disorder known as nonorganic failure to thrive, noting common symptoms and family circumstances surrounding the disorder. (184)

5.11 Describe how infants learn through classical conditioning, operant conditioning, habituation, and imitation. (185-188)

5.12 Describe the sequence of motor development in first two years of life. (189-190)

5.13 Explain the dynamic systems theory of motor development, and discuss the support for this approach stemming from microgenetic and cross-cultural research. (190-193)

5.14 Describe the development of reaching and grasping, and explain how early experiences affect these skills. (193-195)

5.15 Summarize the development of hearing in infancy, giving special attention to speech perception. (196)

5.16 Summarize the development of vision in infancy, with particular attention to depth perception and pattern perception. (197-202)

5.17 Discuss the development of object perception during the first year of life. (202-204)

5.18 Explain the concept of intermodal perception. (204-205)

5.19 Explain the differentiation theory of perceptual development. (205-206)

STUDY QUESTIONS

Body Growth

1. By the end of the first year, the infant's height is _____ percent greater than it was at birth, and by 2 years it is _____ greater. By 5 months, birth weight has _____, at 1 year it has tripled, and at 2 years it has _____. (170)

2. True or False: Infants and toddlers grow in spurts, wherein they may experience relatively long stretches without any growth and then add as much as half-an-inch in a 24-hour period. (170)

3. True or False: Trends in body growth tend to be consistent cross-culturally. (170-171)

4. The cephalocaudal growth trend refers to growth from _____ to _____, whereas the proximodistal growth trend refers to growth from _____ to _____. (171)

5. Why do infants experience an increase in body fat during the first year of life? (172)

_____

_____

6. True or False: Boys and girls have an equal muscle-to-fat ratio during infancy. (172)

7. The best way of estimating a child's physical maturity is to use _____, a measure of the development of the bones in the body. Explain how this estimate is obtained. (172)

_____

_____

_____

8. At birth, the bones of the skull are separated by six gaps, or soft spots, called _____. Explain their function. (173)

_____

_____

9. On the average, a Caucasian baby's first tooth appears at about _____ months of age, whereas an African-American baby's first tooth appears at around _____ months of age. (173)

10. True or False: 65 percent of teething infants show symptoms such as increased irritability, sleepiness, ear rubbing, facial rash, and mild fever. (173)

Brain Development

1. The human brain has 100 to 200 billion _____, or nerve cells, that store and transmit information. Between them are tiny gaps, or _____, across which messages pass. (173-174)

2. True or False: Few neurons are produced after the prenatal period. (174)

3. As neurons form connections, _____ becomes vital for their survival. (174)

4. Explain the process of synaptic pruning. (174)

_____

_____

_____

5. About one-half the brain's volume is made up of _____, which do not carry messages, but instead are responsible for _____, the coating of neural fibers with an insulating fatty sheath that improves the efficiency of message transfer. (174)

6. How are the glial cells and the myelinization process related to brain development in the first two years of life? (174)

_____

_____

_____

7. The _____ is the largest, most complex brain structure, accounting for 85 percent of the brain's weight and containing the greatest number of neurons and synapses. (174)

8. For most people, the left hemisphere of the cortex is responsible for _____ abilities and _____ emotion while the right hemisphere is responsible for _____ abilities and _____ emotion. (175)

9. Explain the concepts of lateralization and brain plasticity, noting how the two are related. (175)

_____

_____

_____

_____

10. True or False: Overstimulation of infants and toddlers threatens their interest in learning and may create conditions similar to those of stimulus deprivation. (178)

11. Describe the major changes in the organization of sleep and wakefulness during the first two years of life, and discuss how the social environment impacts these changing arousal patterns. (178,180)

_____

_____

_____

_____

_____

Social Issues: Health — The Mysterious Tragedy of Sudden Infant Death Syndrome

1. The unexpected death of an infant under 1 year of age that remains unexplained after thorough investigation is labeled _____ (176)

2. True or False: SIDS is the leading cause of infant mortality between one week and twelve months of age. (176)

3. True or False: Researchers have recently determined the precise cause of SIDS. (176)

4. Describe some early physical problems that are common among SIDS victims. (176)

_____

_____

_____

5. Discuss the environmental factors associated with SIDS. (176)

_____

_____

_____

Cultural Influences: Cultural Variations in Sleeping Arrangements

1. True or False: Although rare in the United States, parent–infant cosleeping is common in many other countries around the world. (179)

2. Explain the role of collectivist versus individualistic cultural values in determining infant sleeping arrangements. (179)

_____

_____

_____

_____

Factors Affecting Early Physical Growth

1. True or False: When diet and health are adequate, height and rate of physical growth are largely determined by heredity. (180)

2. Describe the phenomenon of *catch-up growth.* (180)

_____

_____

3. Describe several nutritional and health advantages of breast-feeding. (181-182)

_____

_____

_____

_____

4. Discuss the benefits of breast-feeding as they relate to mothers and infants in poverty-stricken regions of the world. (181)

_____

_____

_____

5. True or False: The breast milk produced for a preterm baby differs from that produced for a full-term baby. (182)

6. True or False: Fatness in infancy typically leads to obesity at older ages. (182-183)

7. Describe the causes of marasmus and kwashiorkor, two dietary diseases associated with severe malnutrition, and review the developmental outcomes associated with these extreme forms of malnutrition. (183)

_____

_____

_____

_____

_____

_____

8. Interventions for malnourished children must improve the _____ situation as well as the child's nutrition. (183)

9. True or False: Malnutrition is largely confined to developing countries and recent surveys indicate that it is almost nonexistent in the United States. (184)

10. What is *nonorganic failure to thrive*, and what are some common symptoms? (184)

_____

_____

_____

_____

11. Discuss the family circumstances surrounding nonorganic failure to thrive. (184)

_____

_____

_____

Learning Capacities

1. Define *learning*. (185)

_____

2. _____ conditioning is a form of learning in which a neutral stimulus is paired with a stimulus that leads to a reflexive response. (185)

3. Match the following terms to the appropriate definitions. (185)

_____ A neutral stimulus that leads   1. Unconditioned Stimulus (UCS)
        to a reflexive response, if   2. Conditioned Stimulus (CS)
        learning occurs   3. Unconditioned Response (UCR)
_____ A learned response exhibited toward 4. Conditioned Response (CR)
        a previously neutral stimulus
_____ A reflexive response
_____ A stimulus that automatically
        leads to a reflexive response

4. Using the above definitions as a guide (see question 3), outline the three steps
    involved in classical conditioning. (185-186)

A. _____

    _____

B. _____

    _____

C. _____

    _____

5. In classical conditioning, if the CS is presented alone enough times, without
    being paired with the UCS, the CR will no longer occur. This is referred to as
    _____. (185)

6. Young infants can be classically conditioned most easily when the association
    between the two stimuli has _____ value. (185)

7. _____ conditioning is a form of learning in which a spontaneous
    behavior is followed by a stimulus that changes the probability that the behavior
    will occur again. (186)

8. Define the terms *reinforcer* and *punishment* as they relate to operant conditioning.
    (186)

Reinforcer: _____

    _____

Punishment: _____

    _____

102

9. _____ refers to a gradual reduction in the strength of a response due to repetitive stimulation. The recovery seen when a new stimulus is introduced and responsiveness returns to a high level is referred to as _____. (187)

10. True or False: Habituation is evident as early as the third trimester of pregnancy. (187)

11. As infants get older, they habituate to stimuli more quickly, indicating that _____. (187-188)

12. True or False: The imitation observed in newborns appears to represent active attempts to match what they "see" with what they "feel," much as it does in adults. (188)

13. Describe some of the things that infants are able to learn through the imitation process. (188)

_____

_____

_____

Motor Development

1. Distinguish between gross and fine motor development, and provide examples of each. (189-190)

   Gross: _____

   _____

   Fine: _____

   _____

2. Whereas the _____ of motor development is fairly uniform across all children, large individual differences exist in the _____ of motor progress. (189)

3. Discuss the organization and direction of motor development in relation to the cephalocaudal and proximodistal trends. (190)

   _____

   _____

   _____

4. According to the dynamic systems theory of motor development, mastery of motor skills involves acquisition of increasingly complex systems of action. Explain what this term means. (190-191)

_____

_____

_____

_____

5. List four factors that contribute to the development of each new motor skill. (191)

A. _____

B. _____

C. _____

D. _____

6. True or False: Dynamic systems theory regards motor development as a genetically determined process. (191)

7. What did Esther Thelen's microgenetic studies reveal about infant motor development? (191)

_____

_____

_____

8. Give at least one example of how cultural variations in infant-rearing practices affect motor development. (191-192)

_____

_____

_____

9. True or False: Voluntary reaching requires visual guidance of the arms and hands. (193)

10. The grasp reflex of the newborn period is replaced by the _____ grasp, a clumsy motion in which the fingers close against the palm. By the end of the first year, infants use the thumb and index finger opposably in a well-coordinated _____ grasp. (194)

11. Toilet training is best delayed until what age? _____ Why is this the case? (195)_____

_____

Perceptual Development

1. Distinguish between sensation and perception. (196)

   Sensation: _____

   Perception: _____

2. What is the greatest change that takes place in hearing over the first year of life? (196)

   _____

3. Describe the changes in auditory perception over the first year of life which prepare infants for language acquisition. (196)

   By 6 months: _____

   _____

   _____

   6-12 months: _____

   _____

   _____

4. What is depth perception, and why is it important in infant development? (197)

   _____

   _____

   _____

5. Describe the visual cliff, and cite the limitations of this approach for the study of infant depth perception. (197)

   _____

   _____

   _____

6. _____ provides a great deal of information about depth, and it is the first depth cue to which infants are sensitive. (197)

7. _____ depth cues arise because our eyes have slightly different views of the visual field. (198)

8. _____ depth cues are the ones that artists use to make a painting look three-dimensional (e.g., changes in texture, overlapping objects). (198)

9. True or False: There is a close correspondence between depth perception and motor development. (198)

10. List two changes in depth perception that are associated with independent movement. (198)

    A. _____

    B. _____

11. The principle of _____, which accounts for early pattern preferences, states that if infants can detect a difference in contrast between two or more patterns, they will prefer the one with more contrast. (199)

12. Summarize the development of face perception across the first year of life. (202-203)

    Birth-1 month: _____

    _____

    2-4 months: _____

    _____

    5-12 months: _____

    _____

13. True or False: Size and shape constancy appear to emerge gradually over time as infants acquire more advanced knowledge of objects in the environment. (203-204)

14. True or False: When two objects are touching and either move in unison or stand still, infants younger than 4 months of age do not perceive the boundary between the two objects, and therefore, cannot distinguish them. (204)

15. _____ perception combines stimulation from more than one sensory system. (204)

16. True or False: From birth, infants are capable of combining information from multiple sensory systems. (204)

17. Explain the differentiation theory of perceptual development. (205-206)

_____

_____

_____

Biology and Environment: Development of Infants with Severe Visual Impairments

1. True or False: Children with severe visual impairments show delays in motor, cognitive, language, and social development. (200)

2. Discuss how severe visual impairments impact motor exploration and spatial understanding. (200)

_____

_____

_____

_____

3. How do severe visual impairments affect the caregiver–infant relationship? (200-201)

_____

_____

_____

4. List several techniques that can help infants with severe visual impairments become aware of their physical and social surroundings. (201)

A. _____

_____

B. _____

_____

C. _____

_____

ASK YOURSELF . . .

REVIEW: How does stimulation affect early brain development? Cite evidence at the level of neurons and at the level of the cerebral cortex.

_____

_____

_____

_____

APPLY: When Joey was born, the doctor found that his anterior fontanel had started to close prematurely. Joey had surgery to open the fontanel when he was 3 months old. From what you know about the function of the fontanels, why was early surgery necessary?

_____

_____

_____

_____

CONNECT: Suppose you were offered two cognitive enrichment programs for your 1-year-old. The first emphasizes gentle talking and touching, exposure to a wide variety of interesting sights and sounds, pleasurable social games, such as pat-a-cake and peekaboo. The second program teaches words and numbers and includes French and classical-music lessons. On the basis of findings on brain development, which program would you choose, and why?

_____

_____

_____

_____

REFLECT: What is your attitude towards parent–infant cosleeping? Is it influenced by your cultural background? Explain.

_____

_____

_____

_____

REVIEW: Explain why breast-feeding offers babies protection against disease and early death in poverty-stricken regions of the world.

_____

_____

_____

_____

APPLY: Ten-month-old Shaun is below average in height and painfully thin. He has one of two serious growth disorders. Name them, and indicate what clues you would look for to tell which one Shaun has.

_____

_____

_____

_____

CONNECT: How are bidirectional influences between parent and child involved in the impact of malnutrition on psychological development? After her adoption, how did those influences change for Grace, leading to rapid gains in intellectual development?

_____

_____

_____

_____

REVIEW: Using examples, describe the differences between classical and operant conditioning. Why is each type of learning useful to infants?

_____

_____

_____

_____

APPLY: Nine-month-old Byron has a toy with large, colored push buttons on it. Each time he pushes a button, he hears a nursery tune. Which learning capacity is the manufacturer of this toy taking advantage of?

_____

_____

_____

_____

APPLY: Recall that infants with nonorganic failure to thrive are unlikely to smile at a friendly adult. Also, they keep track of nearby adults in an anxious, fearful way. Explain these reactions using the learning capacities discussed in the preceding sections.

_____

_____

_____

_____

CONNECT: Return to the section on intervening with preterm infants on page 147 of Chapter 4. Why might a preterm baby seek contact with a soft, "breathing" teddy bear, as reported in our discussion of operant conditioning on pages 186-187?

_____

_____

_____

_____

REVIEW: Cite evidence indicating that motor development is not hardwired into the brain but rather a joint product of biological, psychological, and social factors.

_____

_____

_____

_____

APPLY: Rosanne read in a magazine that infant motor development could be accelerated through visual stimulation, so she hung mobiles and pictures above her newborn baby's crib and surrounded it with a brightly colored, patterned crib bumper. Is Rosanne doing the right thing? Why or why not?

_____

_____

_____

_____

CONNECT: Cite several examples of how motor development influences infants and toddlers social experiences. How might social experiences, in turn, influence motor development?

_____

_____

_____

_____

REFLECT: Do you favor early training of infants in motor skills, such as crawling, walking, running, hopping, and stairclimbing? Why or why not?

_____

_____

_____

_____

REVIEW: Cite evidence indicating that infants' expanding knowledge of objects and people influences their pattern perception.

_____

_____

_____

APPLY: Not until age 2 months did Jana show keen interest in the bright wallpaper with detailed pictures on the wall of her room. What new visual abilities probably account for this change?

_____

_____

_____

_____

APPLY: After several weeks of crawling, Benjie learned to avoid going head-first down a steep incline. Now he has started to walk. Can his mother trust him not to try walking down the steep surface? Explain, using the concept of affordances.

_____

_____

_____

_____

CONNECT: Motor development and perceptual development are closely linked. Provide as many examples as you can to support this statement.

_____

_____

_____

_____

SUGGESTED STUDENT READINGS

Bruer, J. T. (1999). *The myth of the first three years.* New York: Free Press. Challenges the widely accepted belief that the first 3 years of life determine whether or not a child will develop into a successful, thinking person. Drawing on research on brain development, shows that learning and cognitive development occur not just in infancy and toddlerhood, but also throughout childhood and adulthood. Stresses the dangers of a view that overemphasizes early learning to the detriment of long-term parental and educational responsibilities.

Gopnik, A., Meltzoff, A. N., & Kuhl, P. K. (1999). *The scientist in the crib: Minds, brains, and how children learn.* New York: William Morrow. Brings together a wealth of research on infant and toddler learning to show how, and how much, very young children know and parents naturally teach them. Includes chapters on the young child's knowledge about people, objects, and language and scientists' discoveries about the young brain and mind.

Nelson, C. A. (Ed.) (2000). The Minnesota symposia on child psychology, Vol.31: *The effects of early adversity on neurobehavioral development.* Mahwah, NJ: Lawrence Erlbaum Associates. A collection of chapters that examines the effects of early biological and/or psychological adversity on child development. Also illustrates the importance of a dynamic systems approach to the study of early development.

Pruitt, D. B. (Ed.) (1998). *Your child: What every parent needs to know about childhood development from birth to preadolescence.* New York, NY: Harpercollins Publishers. Written primarily for parents and caregivers, this book examines the develop-mental milestones of childhood. Includes questions and answers to commonly asked questions about day-to-day growth and development.

PUZZLE TERM REVIEW

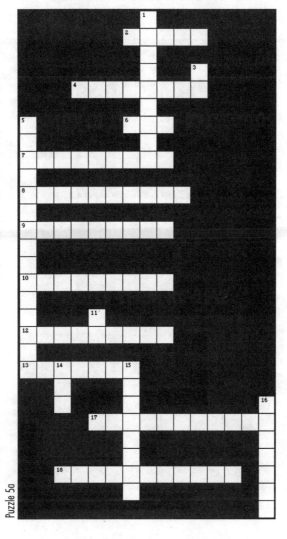

Puzzle 5a

Across

2. Cells that serve the function of myelinization are called _____ cells.
4. A disease usually appearing in the first year of life that is caused by a diet low in all essential nutrients
6. In classical conditioning, a stimulus that leads to a reflexive response (abbr.)
7. Six soft spots that separate the bones of the skull at birth
8. In classical conditioning, decline of the CR as a result of presenting the CS enough times without the UCS
9. Growth centers in the bones
10. Learning by copying another person; also called modeling or observational learning
12. In the differentiation theory of perceptual development, _____ features are those that remain stable in a constantly changing perceptual world.
13. Nerve cells that store and transmit information
17. A disease usually appearing between 1 and 3 years of age that is caused by a diet low in protein
18. An estimate of physical maturity based on development of the bones of the body (2 words)

Down

1. _____ conditioning: a form of learning that involves associating a neutral stimulus with a stimulus that leads to a reflexive response
3. In classical conditioning, a neutral stimulus that through pairing with an UCS leads to a new response (abbr.)
5. _____ theory: view that perceptual development involves detection of increasingly fine-grained, invariant features of the environment
11. In classical conditioning, an originally reflexive response that is produced by a CS after learning has occurred (abbr.)
14. In classical conditioning, a reflexive response that is produced by an UCS (abbr.)
15. The gaps between neurons, across which chemical messages are sent
16. Synaptic _____: loss of connective fibers by seldom-stimulated neurons

PUZZLE TERM REVIEW

Puzzle 5b

Across

3. _____ perception combines information from more than one sensory system.
4. In operant conditioning, a stimulus that decreases the occurrence of a response
5. The largest, most complex brain structure is the _____ cortex.
6. _____ failure to thrive: a growth disorder caused by a lack of affection and stimulation
7. Size _____: perception of an object's size as the same, despite changes in the size of its retinal image
10. Well-coordinated grasp involving thumb and forefinger opposition
11. Increase in responsiveness after stimulation changes
13. _____ systems theory of motor development: views new motor skills as a reorganization of previously mastered skills that lead to more effective ways of exploring and controlling the environment
14. The unexpected death of an infant under 1 year of age that remains unexplained after thorough investigation (abbr.)
15. Clumsy grasp in which the fingers close against the palm
16. _____ sensitivity: if babies can detect a difference in contrast between two or more patterns, they will prefer the one with more contrast

Down

1. The poorly coordinated, primitive reaching movements of newborn babies
2. A process in which neural fibers are coated with an insulating fatty sheath that improves the efficiency of message transfer
4. _____ trend: a pattern of physical growth that proceeds from the center of the body outward
8. _____ trend: a pattern of physical growth that proceeds from head to tail
9. A gradual reduction in the strength of a response as a result of repeated stimulation
12. In operant conditioning, a stimulus that increases the occurrence of a response
17. _____ conditioning: a form of learning in which a spontaneous behavior is followed by a stimulus that changes the probability that the behavior will occur again

SELF-TEST

1. The _____ trend refers to a pattern of physical growth which proceeds from the center of the body outward. (171)

    a. intermodal
    b. cephalocaudal
    c. proximodistal
    d. inverse

2. Skeletal age is estimated by: (172)

    a. using the child's weight to estimate bone density.
    b. x-raying the child's bones and examining the epiphyses.
    c. determining bone density through the use ultrasound.
    d. examining the fontanels.

3. _____ are nerve cells in the brain that store and transmit information. (173)

    a. Glial cells
    b. Neurons
    c. Synapses
    d. Epiphyses

4. The process in which neural fibers are coated with an insulating fatty sheath that improves the efficiency of message transfer is called: (174)

    a. myelinization.
    b. synaptic pruning.
    c. neural sheathing.
    d. brain plasticity.

5. Which is the largest, most complex brain structure, containing the greatest number of neurons and synapses? (174)

    a. frontal lobe
    b. cerebellum
    c. corpus callosum
    d. cerebral cortex

6. Brain plasticity refers to: (175)

    a. the level of specialization of the two hemispheres of the brain.
    b. the degree to which the areas of the brain are committed to specific functions.
    c. the extent of neural development at a particular period of development.
    d. the loss of neural connections resulting from inadequate stimulation.

7. The greatest change in the organization of sleep and wakefulness during the first two years of life is that: (178)

    a. with age, infants require more naps.
    b. short periods of sleep and wakefulness are put together.
    c. there is a drastic decline in total sleep time.
    d. by the end of the first year, infants no longer have night wakings.

8. Which of the following is NOT a nutritional or health benefit of breast-feeding? (181-182)

    a. high protein, low fat content facilitates lateralization of the brain
    b. smoother transition to solid foods
    c. protection against disease
    d. nutritional completeness

9. Marasmus is caused by: (183)

    a. overeating during the first year of life.
    b. a severe iron deficiency.
    c. a diet low in protein.
    d. a diet low in all essential nutrients.

10. Nonorganic failure to thrive: (184)

    a. is associated with a known biological cause.
    b. is caused by a lack of stimulation and affection.
    c. results from an inadequate diet in early infancy.
    d. is associated with long-term deficits, even when treated early.

11. In classical conditioning, the _____ must consistently produce a reflexive reaction before learning can take place. (185)

    a. unconditioned stimulus (UCS)
    b. conditioned stimulus (CS)
    c. unconditioned response (UCR)
    d. conditioned response (CR)

12. In classical conditioning, if the conditioned stimulus (CS) is presented alone enough times, without being paired with the unconditioned stimulus (UCS), the conditioned response (CR) will no longer occur. This is known as: (185)

    a. dishabituation.
    b. termination.
    c. extinction.
    d. disassociation.

13. Which of the following is true with regard to classical conditioning? (185)

    a. Infants are easily conditioned by pairing any two stimuli.
    b. Infants are conditioned most easily to fear responses.
    c. Classical conditioning is most effective when the neutral stimulus is presented several minutes after the unconditioned stimulus (UCS).
    d. Classical conditioning is valuable to infants because it makes the environment more orderly and predictable.

14. Which of the following best reflects the views of infant behavior suggested by classical conditioning and operant conditioning perspectives? (186)

    a. In classical conditioning, infants are viewed as passive learners, whereas in operant conditioning, infants are viewed as active learners.
    b. In operant conditioning, infants are viewed as passive learners, whereas in classical conditioning, infants are viewed as active learners.
    c. Both classical conditioning and operant conditioning view infants as active learners.
    d. Both classical conditioning and operant conditioning view infants as passive learners.

15. In operant conditioning, a stimulus that increases the likelihood of a response is a: (186)

   a. punishment.
   b. reward.
   c. reinforcer.
   d. conditioned stimulus.

16. After repeatedly listening to a particular tone for a period of time, an infant shows a gradual reduction in responding to this tone. When a new tone is introduced, the infant returns to a high level of responding. This recovery of responsiveness is known as: (187)

   a. habituation.
   b. dishabituation.
   c. differentiation.
   d. extinction.

17. Crawling, standing, and walking are examples of: (189)

   a. fine motor development.
   b. gross motor development.
   c. coordinated motor development.
   d. dynamic motor development.

117

18. According to the dynamic systems theory of motor development: (190-191)

   a. new skills are acquired by revising and combining earlier accomplishments.
   b. new skills are acquired independently of previously learned skills.
   c. motor development is a genetically determined process.
   d. the pathways to motor skill acquisition are universal.

19. In which sequence do infants develop voluntary reaching and grasping behaviors? (193-194)

   a. pincer grasp, ulnar grasp, prereaching
   b. ulnar grasp, pincer grasp, prereaching
   c. prereaching, ulnar grasp, pincer grasp
   d. prereaching, pincer grasp, ulnar grasp

20. Which of the following is NOT true of auditory development over the first year of life? (196)

   a. Infants maintain the ability to distinguish almost all of the sounds of any human language.
   b. Infants start to organize sounds into complex patterns.
   c. Infants begin to detect clauses and phrases in sentences.
   d. Infants begin to analyze the internal structure of words and sentences.

21. Which of the following is NOT a depth cue used by infants in the development of depth perception? (197-198)

   a. motion
   b. binocular depth cues
   c. pictorial depth cues
   d. monocular depth cues

22. According to the principle of contrast sensitivity, infants 2 months of age and older would prefer to look at: (198-199)

    a. a large, bold checkerboard.
    b. a small, complex checkerboard.
    c. a simple pattern with a lot of color.
    d. an image representing a familiar object.

23. The development of object perception is dependent upon the presence of: (203-204)

    a. contrast sensitivity.
    b. well-developed color vision.
    c. pictorial cues.
    d. size and shape constancy.

24. From the start, infants expect sight, sound, and touch to go together, a capacity called: (204)

    a. intermodal perception.
    b. sensory perception.
    c. systematic perception.
    d. integrative perception.

25. According to the differentiation theory of perceptual development: (205)

    a. infants seek out variant, or ever-changing, features of the environment.
    b. infants seek out invariant, or stable, features of the environment.
    c. infants have an innate capacity to give order to their environment.
    d. infants impose meaning on their perceptions, thereby constructing categories of objects and events in the environment.

CHAPTER 6

COGNITIVE DEVELOPMENT IN INFANCY AND TODDLERHOOD

Chapter Summary

According to Piaget, from earliest infancy children actively build psychological structures, or schemes, as they manipulate and explore their world. The vast changes that take place in Piaget's sensorimotor stage are divided into six substages. By acting on the world, infants make strides in intentional behavior, mastery of object permanence, and physical reasoning. In the final substage, they transfer their action-based schemes to a mental level, and representation appears. Research indicates that a variety of sensorimotor milestones emerge earlier than Piaget believed and that cognitive development in infancy and toddlerhood does not follow distinct, even stages. Debate continues concerning the degree to which cognitive development depends on motor, perceptual, or innate capacities.

Information processing, an alternative to Piaget's theory, focuses on the development of mental strategies for storing and interpreting information. With age, infants' attention becomes more effective and flexible, and memory improves and is supported by mental representation. Findings on infant categorization support the view that young babies structure experience in adultlike ways. Vygotsky's sociocultural theory stresses that cognitive development is socially mediated as adults help infants and toddlers master challenging tasks.

A variety of infant intelligence tests have been devised to measure individual differences in early mental development. Although most predict later performance poorly, those that emphasize speed of habituation and dishabituation to visual stimuli and object permanence show better predictability. Home, child care, and early intervention for at-risk infants and toddlers are powerful influences on intellectual progress.

Behaviorist and nativist theories provide contrasting accounts of language development. The interactionist view emphasizes that innate abilities and environmental influences combine to produce children's extraordinary language achievements. During the first year, infants prepare for language in many ways. First words appear around 12 months, 2-word utterances between 18 months and 2 years. At the same time, substantial individual differences exist in rate and style of early language progress. Conversational give-and-take and child-directed speech (a simplified form of parental language) support infants' and toddlers' efforts to become competent speakers.

LEARNING OBJECTIVES

After reading this chapter, you should be able to:

6.1 Describe Piaget's view of development, noting key concepts of his theory. (212-213)

6.2 Describe the major cognitive achievements of Piaget's six sensorimotor substages. (213-216)

6.3 Discuss recent research on sensorimotor development and its implications for the accuracy of Piaget's sensorimotor stage. (216-220)

6.4 Describe the prominent views of cognitive development, including the perceptual view, the nativist view, and the compromise position. (221-223)

6.5 Describe the structure of the information-processing system, as elaborated in information-processing theory, discuss how this approach differs from Piaget's perspective, and review the strengths and limitations of the information-processing theory of cognitive development. (224-229)

6.6 Discuss the advancements in attention, memory, and categorization taking place during infancy and toddlerhood. (225-228)

6.7 Explain how Vygotsky's concept of the zone of proximal development expands our understanding of early cognitive development. (229-230)

6.8 Describe the mental testing approach, the meaning of intelligence test scores, and the extent to which infant tests predict later performance. (232-233)

6.9 Discuss environmental influences on early mental development, including home, child care, and early intervention for at-risk infants and toddlers. (233-238)

6.10 Describe three major theories of language development, indicating the emphasis each places on biological and environmental influences. (239-241)

6.11 Describe how infants prepare for language, and explain how adults support their emerging capacities. (241-242)

6.12 Describe the characteristics of infants' first words and two-word phrases, and explain why language comprehension develops ahead of language production. (243-245)

6.13 Describe individual and cultural differences in early language development and the factors that influence these differences. (245-246)

6.14 Explain how child-directed speech and conversational give-and-take support early language development. (246-247)

STUDY QUESTIONS

Piaget's Cognitive-Developmental Theory

1. During Piaget's _____ stage, which spans the first two years of life, infants and toddlers "think" with their eyes, ears, and hands. (212)

2. In Piaget's theory, what is a *schema*? (212)

_____

_____

3. True or False: Piaget believed that psychological structures, or children's organized ways of making sense of experience, are stable across childhood. (212)

4. List and define the two processes that account for changes in schemes. (212-213)

   A. _____

   _____

   B. _____

   _____

5. During _____, we use our current schemes to interpret the external world. In _____, we create new schemes or adjust old ones to produce a better fit with the environment. (213)

6. The _____ (2 words) occurs when infants stumble onto a new experience caused by their own motor activity and then try to repeat the event again and again, thereby strengthening the response into a new schema. (213)

7. Match each of the following sensorimotor substages with its appropriate description (214-216)

   _____ Infants' primary means of adapting   1. Substage 1
   to the environment is through
   reflexes   2. Substage 2

   _____ Infants engage in goal-directed   3. Substage 3
   behavior and begin to attain object   4. Substage 4
   permanence
                                                   5. Substage 5
   _____ Toddlers repeat behaviors with
   variation, producing new effects   6. Substage 6

   _____ Infants' adaptations are oriented
   toward their own bodies

   _____ Infants' attention begins to turn
   outward toward the environment

   _____ Toddlers gain the ability to create
   mental representations

8. Explain the differences between primary, secondary, and tertiary circular reactions. (214-215)

   Primary: _____

   _____

Secondary: _____

_____

Tertiary: _____

_____

9. Eight- to 12-month-old infants gain an understanding that objects exist even when they are out of sight, a principle known as _____. They typically make the _____ error, however, searching only in the first hiding place when an object has been moved from one hiding place to another. (215)

10. _____ imitation is the ability to remember and copy the behavior of models who are not immediately present. (216)

11. True or False: More recent studies suggest that Piaget overestimated infant capabilities. (216)

12. Explain the violation-of-expectation method, which is often used by researchers to identify infants' grasp of object permanence and other aspects of physical reasoning. (217)

_____

_____

_____

_____

13. List the two ways that infants first understand object permanence, according to recent research. (217-218)

A. _____

_____

B. _____

_____

14. True or False: Infants demonstrate the A-not-B search error because of memory deficits; that is, they cannot remember an object's new location after it has been hidden in more than one place. (218)

15. Briefly summarize the evidence that refutes memory-based explanations of A-not-B search error. (218)

_____

_____

_____

_____

16. List several aspects of physical reasoning displayed by infants in the first year of life. (218-219)

_____

_____

_____

17. True or False: Although Piaget's theory suggests that infants are incapable of mental representation until about 18 months of age, new studies show that infants exhibit deferred imitation, a form of representation, as early as six weeks of age. (219)

18. By 10 to 12 months of age, infants can solve problems by _____, meaning that they take a strategy from one problem and apply it to other relevant problems. (220)

19. True or False: New studies reveal that while Piaget underestimated the age at which cognitive capacities emerge, these cognitive attainments do, in fact, develop in the neat, stepwise fashion that Piaget predicted. (221)

20. Contrast the perceptual and nativist views of cognitive development. (221-222)

_____

_____

_____

_____

21. The _____ is a nativist view that assumes that each type of knowledge has its own module, or genetically prewired neural system in the brain, and timetable of maturation. (222)

22. Identify three criticisms of the modular view of the mind. (222)

A. _____

B. _____

C. _____

23. List two important contributions of Piaget. (223)

A. _____

_____

B. _____

_____

Information Processing

1. In what way is information-processing theory similar to Piaget's theory, and in what way is it different? (224)

Similar: _____

_____

Different: _____

_____

2. Most models of human information processing divide the mind into three basic parts. Name and describe each of these parts. (224)

A. _____

_____

B. _____

_____

C. _____

_____

3. As information flows through the information-processing system, it can be operated on and transformed using _____, thereby increasing the efficiency of thinking and the chances that we will retain the information for later use. (224)

4. True or False: Long-term memory has a limitless capacity. (224)

5. Discuss several key changes in attention from infancy to toddlerhood. (225-226)

_____

_____

_____

_____

6. True or False: Habituation-dishabituation research in the laboratory setting underestimates infants' ability to remember real-world events. (226)

7. At first, memory is highly _____ dependent. For example, if 2- to 6-month-old infants are not tested in the same situation in which they were trained, their memory is poor. (226)

8. _____, the simplest form of memory, involves a simple indication as to whether a new experience is identical or similar to a previous one. _____, on the other hand, is much more challenging because it involves remembering something in the absence of perceptual support. (226)

9. True or False: Infants are unable to categorize stimuli based upon multiple properties, and, therefore, they store information in a highly disorganized fashion. (228)

10. The earliest categories used by infants are _____, based on similar overall appearance or prominent object part. By the end of the first year, categories become _____, based on common functions and behavior. (228)

11. Information-processing research underscores the _____ of human thinking from infancy into adult life. (228)

12. True or False: Research on infant memory and categorization supports Piaget's view that early cognitive development takes place in discrete stages. (229)

13. What is the greatest drawback of the information-processing approach to cognitive development? (229)

_____

_____

_____

Biology and Environment: Infantile Amnesia

1. What is *infantile amnesia*? (227)

   _____

   _____

2. _____ memory refers to representations of special, one-time events that are long-lasting because they are imbued with personal meaning. (227)

3. Discuss the two developments that are necessary for memories to become autobiographical. (227)

   A. _____

   _____

   B. _____

   _____

4. True or False: Many researchers believe that the offset of infantile amnesia requires the emergence of autobiographical memory. (227)

The Social Context of Early Cognitive Development

1. Explain Vygotsky's concept of the *zone of proximal development*. (229)

   _____

   _____

   _____

2. Compared to Piagetian and information-processing views, what important feature of cognitive development does Vygotsky's theory emphasize? (230)

   _____

   _____

Cultural Influences: Social Origins of Make-Believe Play

1. Vygotsky believed that society provides children with opportunities to represent _____ meaningful activities in play. (231)

2. True or False: When adults participate, toddlers' make-believe play is more elaborate and advanced. (231)

Individual Differences in Early Mental Development

1. How does the testing approach differ from the cognitive theories discussed earlier in this chapter? (232)

   _____

   _____

   _____

2. Most infant intelligence tests measure _____ and _____ responses. (232)

3. One commonly used infant test is the _____ _____ of Infant Development, designed for children between 1 month and 3-and-one-half years. (232)

4. Describe how intelligence scores are computed. (232)

   _____

   _____

   _____

5. The _____ quotient is a score that permits an individual's perform-ance on an intelligence test to be compared to the performance of other individuals of the same age. (232)

6. True or False: Scores on infant intelligence tests are excellent predictors of later intelligence. Why or why not? (232-233)

   _____

   _____

   _____

7. Because infant test scores do not tap the same dimensions of intelligence measured at older ages, they are conservatively labeled _____, or DQs, rather than IQs. (233)

8. For what purpose are infant intelligence tests largely used? (233)

   _____

   _____

9. True or False: Findings show that habituation and dishabituation to visual stimuli are the best available infant predictors of intelligence from early childhood into adolescence. (233)

10. Describe the *Home Observation for Measurement of the Environment* (HOME), and discuss how HOME scores are related to early mental development. (233-234)

_____

_____

_____

_____

11. Discuss the impact of low versus high quality child care on mental development. (234-235)

_____

_____

_____

_____

12. Describe the overall condition of child care for infants and toddlers in the United States. (235-236)

_____

_____

_____

13. List and describe at least four signs of developmentally appropriate infant and toddler child care. (236)

A. _____

B. _____

C. _____

D. _____

14. Describe the nature of center-based and home-based interventions for infants and toddlers, and discuss the effectiveness of these programs with relation to infant and toddler mental development. (236-237)

Center-based interventions: _____

_____

_____

Home-based interventions: _____

_____

_____

Language Development

1. On average, children say their first word at _____ months of age. (238)

2. The behaviorist perspective suggests that language, like any other behavior, is acquired through _____. (239)

3. Discuss Chomsky's nativist perspective of language acquisition, noting how this approach differs from the behaviorist perspective. Be sure to explain the language acquisition device in your response. (239)

_____

_____

_____

_____

4. Name the two language-specific areas of the brain, and cite the function of each. (240)

A. _____

_____

B. _____

_____

5. True or False: Research supports the idea that there is a sensitive period for language development. (240)

6. List two challenges to Chomsky's theory. (240-241)

   A. _____

   B. _____

7. The interactionist perspective of language development emphasizes interactions between _____ and _____. (241)

8. Although several interactionist theories exist, all stress the _____ context of language learning. (241)

9. _____ refers to vowel-like noises made by infants, whereas _____ refers to the repetition of consonant-vowel combinations in long strings. (241)

10. True or False: The timing of early babbling seems to be due to maturation, since babies everywhere start babbling at about the same age and produce a similar range of early sounds. (241)

11. How do cooing and babbling help to prepare infants for language? (242)

   _____

   _____

   _____

12. Describe the notion of joint attention, and discuss its impact on early language development. (242)

   _____

   _____

   _____

13. True or False: Turn-taking games such as pat-a-cake and peekaboo contribute to the infant's acquisition of language skills. (242)

14. Briefly describe the nature of toddlers' first words (for example, to which subjects do these words commonly refer?) (243)

   _____

   _____

   _____

15. _____ is an early vocabulary error in which a word is applied too narrowly, to a smaller number of objects and events than is appropriate. Conversely, _____ is an early vocabulary error in which a word is applied too broadly, to a wider collection of objects and events than is appropriate. (243)

16. Provide an example of underextension and an example of overextension. (243)

    Underextension: _____

    Overextension: _____

17. True or False: Toddlers' overextensions are typically random, showing little sensitivity to categorical relations. (243)

18. Explain the nature of *telegraphic speech*. (244)

    _____

    _____

    _____

19. In language development, _____ refers to the words and word combinations that children *use*, whereas _____ refers to the words and word combinations that children *understand*. (244)

20. Why does language comprehension develop ahead of language production? (244-245)

    _____

    _____

    _____

21. True or False: Girls are slightly ahead of boys in early vocabulary growth. (245)

22. Distinguish between referential and expressive styles of early language learning. Which style is associated with faster vocabulary development? (245)

    Referential: _____

    _____

    Expressive: _____

    _____

23. Describe the characteristics of *child-directed speech*. (246)

_____

_____

_____

24. True or False: From birth, infants prefer to listen to child-directed speech more than other kinds of adult talk. (247)

25. Conversational _____ between parent and toddler is one of the best predictors of early language development and academic competence during the school years. (247)

Biology and Environment: Parent-Child Interaction and Cognitive Development of Deaf Children

1. True or False: Deaf children with hearing parents experience fewer delays in language and complex make-believe play than do deaf children with deaf parents. (248)

2. How do the parent-child communication patterns of hearing parents and deaf children differ from those of deaf parents and deaf children? (248)

_____

_____

_____

_____

3. Hearing parents lack experience with _____ communication, which enables deaf parents to respond readily to a deaf child's needs. (248)

ASK YOURSELF . . .

REVIEW: Construct your own table providing an overview of infant and toddler cognitive development. Which entries in the table are consistent with Piaget's theory? Which ones develop earlier than Piaget anticipated?

_____

_____

_____

_____

APPLY: Seven-month-old Mimi banged her rattle on the tray of her high-chair. Then she dropped the rattle, which fell out of sight on her lap. She did not try to retrieve it. Does Mimi know that the rattle still exists? Why doesn't she search for it? Use research findings to explain your answer.

_____

_____

_____

_____

CONNECT: Recall from Chapter 5 (page 204) that around the middle of the first year, infants depend less on motion and more on features (shape, color, and texture) to perceive object unity. How might this change help infants understand physical causality, which also emerges around this time?

_____

_____

_____

_____

REFLECT: Which explanation of infants' cognitive competencies do you prefer, and why?

_____

_____

_____

_____

133

REVIEW: Cite evidence that categorization becomes less perceptual and more conceptual with age. What factors support this shift? How can adults facilitate the development of categorization?

_____

_____

_____

_____

APPLY: Caitlin played with toys in a far more intentional, goal-directed way as a toddler than as an infant. What impact is Caitlin's more advanced toy play likely to have on the development of attention? How is her cultural background likely to affect her attentional strategies?

_____

_____

_____

_____

CONNECT: Review the research on page 220, indicating that by age 10 to 12 months, infants solve problems by analogy. How might that capacity relate to a context-free memory, which develops about the same time?

_____

_____

_____

_____

REFLECT: Describe your earliest autobiographical memory. How old were you when the event occurred? Do your responses fit with research on infantile amnesia?

_____

_____

_____

_____

REVIEW: What probably accounts for the finding that speed of habituation and dishabituation to visual stimuli predicts later IQ better than does an infant mental test score?

_____

_____

_____

_____

APPLY: Fifteen-month-old Joey's developmental quotient (DQ) is 115. His mother wants to know exactly what this means and what she should do at home to support his mental development. How would you respond to her questions?

_____

_____

_____

_____

CONNECT: Using what you learned about brain development in Chapter 5, explain why intensive intervention for poverty-stricken children beginning in the first 2 years has a greater impact on IQ than an intervention at a later age.

_____

_____

_____

_____

REFLECT: Suppose you were seeking a child-care program for your baby. What would you want it to be like, and why?

_____

_____

_____

_____

REVIEW: Why is the interactionist perspective attractive to many investigators of language development? How does it differ from the behaviorist and nativist perspectives? Cite evidence that supports it.

_____

_____

_____

_____

APPLY: Prepare a list of research-based recommendations for how to support language development during the first 2 years.

_____

_____

_____

_____

CONNECT: Cognition and language are interrelated. List examples of how cognition fosters language development. Next, list examples of how language fosters cognitive development.

_____

_____

_____

_____

SUGGESTED STUDENT READINGS

Bruer, J. T. (1999). *The myth of the first three years*. New York: Free Press. Challenges the widely accepted belief that the first 3 years of life determine whether or not a child will develop into a successful, thinking person. Drawing on research on brain development, the author shows that learning and cognitive development occur not just in infancy and toddlerhood, but also throughout childhood and adulthood. Stresses the dangers of a view that overemphasizes early learning to the detriment of long-term parental and educational responsibilities.

Cowan, N. (Ed.). (1997). *The development of memory in childhood*. Hove, England: Psychology Press/Erlbaum (UK) Taylor & Francis. Written primarily for students of psychology and allied disciplines, this book presents the neurobiological, cognitive, and social aspects of memory development in infants and children.

Gopnik, A., Meltzoff, A. N., & Kuhl, P. K. (1999). *The scientist in the crib: Minds, brains, and how children learn*. New York: William Morrow. Brings together a wealth of research on infant and toddler learning to show how, and how much, very young children know and parents naturally teach them. Includes chapters on the young child's knowledge about people, objects, and language and scientists' discoveries about the young brain and mind.

Reynolds, A. J. (2000). *Success in early intervention: The Chicago child-parent centers*. Lincoln, NE: University of Nebraska Press. Presents an overview of the Child-Parent Center (CPC) program in Chicago, the second oldest federally funded early childhood intervention program in the United States. The author emphasizes the unique features of this program, including mandatory parental involvement and a single, sustained educational system which extends from preschool to third grade. Also includes follow-up data from a study on the long-term outcomes of the CPC program.

PUZZLE TERM REVIEW

Puzzle 6a

Across

3. In language development, the words and word combinations that children use
7. Style of early language learning in which toddlers use language mainly to label objects
8. Mental _____: procedures that operate on and transform information, thereby increasing the efficiency of thinking and the chances that information will be retained
9. Style of early language learning in which toddlers use language mainly to talk about feelings and needs
10. Piaget's first stage, during which infants and toddlers "think" with their eyes, ears, and hands
12. In language development, the words and word combinations that children understand
13. Type of memory that involves noticing whether a new experience is identical or similar to a previous one
14. Physical _____: the causal action one object exerts on another through contact
16. Type of memory that involves remembering something in the absence of perceptual support
17. Repetition of consonant–vowel combinations in long strings
18. _____ search error: if an object is moved from hiding place A to hiding place B, 8- to 12-month old infants will search only in the first hiding place

Down

1. The ability to remember and copy the behavior of models who are not immediately present is know as _____ imitation.
2. Zone of _____ development: Range of tasks that the child cannot yet handle alone but can do with the help of more skilled partners
3. Object _____: understanding that objects still exist even when they are out of sight
4. _____-of-expectation method: researchers habituate infants to an event and then determine whether they dishabituate to a possible event or an impossible event.
5. Checklist for gathering information about the quality of children's home lives (abbr.)
6. Standards devised by NAEYC that specify program characteristics that meet the developmental and individual needs of young children are called _____ appropriate practice.
11. _____ representation: internal image of an absent object or past event
12. When infants stumble onto a new experience caused by their own motor activity and then try to repeat the event again and again, they are exhibiting a _____ reaction.
15. In Piaget's theory, a specific structure, or organized way of making sense of experience, which changes with age

PUZZLE TERM REVIEW

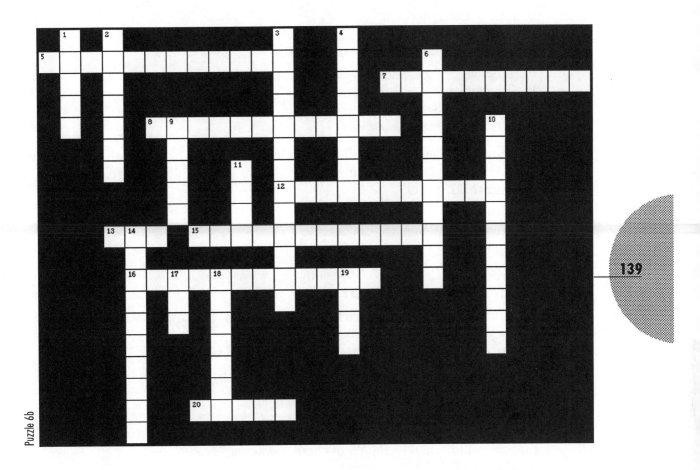

Puzzle 6b

Across

5. _____ quotient: a score that permits an individual's performance on an intelligence test to be compared to the performances of other individuals of the same age
7. Type of play involving pleasurable motor activity with or without objects
8. The external world is represented in terms of current schemas
12. Type of play in which children pretend, acting out everyday and imaginary images
13. Biologically-based, innate system that permits children to speak in a rule-oriented fashion as soon as they learn enough words (abbr.)
15. The internal arrangement and linking together of schemas so that they form a strongly interconnected cognitive system
16. New schemas are created and old ones adjusted to produce a better fit with the environment
20. _____'s area: area of the brain that controls language production

Down

1. _____extension: early vocabulary error in which a word is applied too narrowly, to a smaller number of objects and events than is appropriate
2. The _____ register is the part of the mental system in which sights and sounds are held until they decay or are transferred to short-term memory.
3. _____ quotient: a score on an infant intelligence test; based primarily on perceptual and motor responses
4. _____'s area: area of the brain responsible for interpreting language
6. _____, or goal-directed, behavior is a sequence of actions in which schemas are deliberately combined to solve a problem.
9. _____-term memory: conscious part of memory where we actively work on a limited amount of information
10. _____ speech: toddlers' two-word utterances that leave out smaller and less important words
11. _____-term memory: contains our permanent knowledge base
14. Process of building new schemas through direct contact with the environment
17. Form of speech marked by high-pitched, exaggerated expression, clear pronunciations, and distinct pauses between speech segments (abbr.)
18. _____ view of the mind: regards the mind as a collection of genetically prewired neural systems, each equipped to make sense of a certain type of knowledge
19. _____extension: early vocabulary error in which a word is applied too broadly, to a wider collection of objects and events than is appropriate

SELF-TEST

1. In Piaget's theory, a(n) _____ is an organized way of making sense of experience that changes with age. (212)
   a. schema
   b. adaptation
   c. sensory register
   d. *zone of proximal development*

2. According to Piaget, when children create new schemas or adjust old ones to produce a better fit with the environment, they are using which of the following processes? (213)
   a. assimilation
   b. accommodation
   c. equilibrium
   d. organization

3. Infants are exhibiting a circular reaction when they: (213)
   a. stumble onto a new experience caused by their own motor activity, and then they try to repeat the event again and again.
   b. use current schemas to interpret their external world.
   c. deliberately combine schemas in order to solve a problem.
   d. search for an object only in hiding place A after the object has been moved from place A to place B.

4. When toddlers repeat behaviors with variation in order to provoke new effects, they are exhibiting which type of circular reaction? (215)
   a. primary
   b. secondary
   c. tertiary
   d. fluid

5. The understanding that objects continue to exist when they are out of sight is referred to as: (215)
   a. physical causality.
   b. mental representation.
   c. object permanence.
   d. stimulus constancy.

6. During Substage 6 of the sensorimotor stages, infants develop the ability to create _____, or internal images of absent objects and past events. (216)
   a. schemas
   b. mental strategies
   c. symbolic images
   d. mental representations

7. The ability to remember and copy the behavior of a model who is not immediately present is known as: (216)
   a. functional imitation.
   b. delayed imitation.
   c. deferred imitation.
   d. social modeling.

8. Recent research on sensorimotor development suggests that Piaget: (216)

    a. overestimated infant capabilities.
    b. underestimated infant capabilities.
    c. overlooked many important areas of cognitive development.
    d. correctly predicted the neat, stepwise fashion in which cognitive attainments develop.

9. To study infants' grasp of physical reasoning, researchers often use a violation-of-expectation method in which: (217)

    a. infants are habituated to a physical event, and then researchers determine whether they dishabituate faster to a possible event or an impossible event.
    b. infants are asked to seek an object after it has been moved from one hiding place to another.
    c. infants are instructed to perform a response after seeing it modeled by an adult.
    d. infants are asked to retrieve an object that has been hidden from their view.

10. Which of the following views assumes that each type of knowledge has its own genetically prewired neural system in the brain? (222)

    a. the information-processing perspective
    b. the perceptual view
    c. the modular view of the mind
    d. the cognitive-developmental perspective

11. How does the information-processing approach differ from Piaget's theory? (224)

    a. Whereas Piaget used general concepts to describe how children think, the information-processing approach strives to be more explicit and precise, investigating exactly what individuals of different ages can do when faced with a task or problem.
    b. Whereas information processing uses general concepts to describe how children think, Piaget was more explicit and precise, investigating exactly what individuals of different ages can do when faced with a task or problem.
    c. Whereas Piaget regarded children as active, inquiring beings, the information-processing perspective regards children as passive beings who are acted upon by their environment.
    d. Whereas Piaget's theory focused on many different aspects of thinking, the information-processing approach provides a single, unified theory of cognitive development.

12. In information processing, procedures that operate on and transform information, increasing the efficiency of thinking and the chances that information will be retained, are called: (224)

    a. schemas.
    b. organizational processes.
    c. representational strategies.
    d. mental strategies.

13. Which of the following is the conscious part of our mental system, where we actively work on a limited amount of information? (224)

    a. perceptual register
    b. sensory register
    c. short-term memory
    d. long-term memory

14. Which type of memory involves noticing whether a new experience is identical or similar to a previous one? (226)

    a. recall
    b. recognition
    c. autobiographical
    d. retrospective

15. The greatest drawback of the information-processing perspective is that it: (229)

    a. fails to account for the continuity of human thinking from infancy into adulthood.
    b. regards infants and toddlers as passive beings who are acted on by their environment rather than acknowledging them as active, inquiring beings.
    c. explains cognitive development in terms of discrete stages.
    d. analyzes cognition in terms of its components, but has difficulty putting the components back together into a comprehensive theory.

16. Vygotsky's zone of proximal development refers to: (229)

    a. individual differences in the processes through which children acquire new skills and abilities.
    b. a range of tasks that the child can accomplish when working with a peer who is at the same developmental level.
    c. a range of tasks that the child cannot yet handle alone but can accomplish with the help of more skilled partners.
    d. a range of tasks over which the child has complete mastery and can perform independently.

17. The testing approach to mental development: (232)

    a. focuses on cognitive products and tries to predict future performance.
    b. explains the processes which account for changes in children's thinking over time.
    c. emphasizes separate components of cognitive development, such as attention, memory, and categorization.
    d. explores the early foundations of cognitive processing.

18. A(n) _____ quotient is a score on an infant intelligence test; based primarily on perceptual and motor responses. (233)

    a. intelligence
    b. developmental
    c. sensorimotor
    d. aptitude

19. Infant intelligence tests: (232-233)

    a. measure many of the same skill and ability areas that are measured by adult intelligence tests.
    b. measure only stable aspects of intelligence in order to increase predictive validity.
    c. are useful indicators of the true abilities of infants and toddlers at the time the test is administered.
    d. are poor predictors of later intelligence.

20. Which of the following is NOT true with regard to early environment and mental development? (235)

    a. A stimulating home environment marked by parental involvement and affection is associated with IQ gains in early childhood.
    b. An early home environment that is devoid of stimulation and parental involvement and affection is predictive of potentially significant declines in IQ.
    c. Family living conditions continue to predict children's IQ beyond the contribution of parental IQ.
    d. Although high quality child care sustains the benefits of growing up in an economically advantaged family, it is ineffective for reducing the negative impact of a stressed, poverty-stricken home life.

21. In Chomsky's theory, the _____ is a biologically-based system that permits children, no matter what language they hear, to speak in a rule-oriented fashion as soon as they have learned enough words. (239)

    a. language acquisition device
    b. bio-linguistic mechanism
    c. linguistic processing device
    d. zone of proximal development

22. Which area of the brain is responsible for interpreting language? (240)

    a. Chomsky's area
    b. Broca's area
    c. Wernicke's area
    d. parietal lobe

23. Children's knowledge of categorical relations would lead us to predict that they would be most likely to overextend the word *doggie* to: (243)

    a. other furry, four-legged animals.
    b. all other animals.
    c. any living thing.
    d. nearly anything; their errors are random.

24. A toddler whose early vocabulary consists mainly of words referring to objects is using a(n) _____ style. (245)

    a. expressive
    b. referential
    c. concrete
    d. attributional

25. Which of the following is NOT true of child-directed speech? (246)

    a. CDS is characterized by high-pitched, exaggerated expression.
    b. CDS contains many simplified words.
    c. Speakers of CDS commonly repeat phrases.
    d. CDS rarely contains questions or directions.

144

CHAPTER 7

EMOTIONAL AND SOCIAL DEVELOPMENT IN INFANCY AND TODDLERHOOD

Chapter Summary

Erikson's psychoanalytic theories provide an overview of the emotional and social tasks of infancy and toddlerhood. For Erikson, trust and autonomy grow out of warm, supportive parenting and reasonable expectations for impulse control during the second year.

Emotions play an important role in the organization of relationships with caregivers, exploration of the environment, and discovery of the self. Infants' ability to express basic emotions, such as happiness, anger, sadness, and fear, and respond to the emotions of others expands over the first year. As toddlers become more self-aware, self-conscious emotions, such as shame, embarrassment, and pride, begin to emerge. Emotional self-regulation improves with brain maturation, gains in cognition and language, and sensitive child rearing.

Children's unique temperamental styles are apparent in early infancy. Heredity influences early temperament, but child-rearing experiences determine whether a child's temperament is sustained or modified over time.

Ethological theory is the most widely accepted view of the development of the infant-caregiver relationship. According to this perspective, attachment evolved over the history of our species to promote survival. Research shows that responding promptly, consistently, and appropriately to infant signals supports secure attachment, whereas insensitive caregiving is linked to attachment insecurity. Because children and parents are embedded in larger contexts, family circumstances influence attachment quality. Cultural factors also affect attachment patterns. Infants form attachment bonds with a variety of familiar people, including mothers, fathers, and siblings. Although quite limited, peer sociability is present in the first 2 years, and it is fostered by the early caregiver-child bond. Continuity of caregiving seems to be involved in the relationship of attachment security to later development.

LEARNING OBJECTIVES

After reading this chapter, you should be able to:

7.1   Discuss the first two stages of Erikson's psychosocial theory, noting the psychological conflict at each stage, as well as how each of these conflicts can be positively resolved. (255)

7.2   Describe the development of basic emotions, including happiness, anger, sadness, and fear, throughout the first two years of life. (257-259)

7.3 Summarize the changes in infants' ability to understand and respond to the emotions of others, with particular attention to the emergence of social referencing. (259-260)

7.4 Explain the nature of self-conscious emotions, noting why they emerge during the second year and indicating their role in development. (260)

7.5 Trace the development of emotional self-regulation during the first two years. (260-261)

7.6 Discuss the four underlying components of temperament, and identify the three temperamental styles elaborated by Thomas and Chess. (262-264)

7.7 Compare and contrast Thomas and Chess's model of temperament with that of Rothbart. (263-264)

7.8 Explain how temperament is measured, and discuss the stability of temperament over time. (264-265)

7.9 Summarize the genetic and environmental influences on temperament, and describe the goodness-of-fit model. (265-269)

7.10 Describe and compare drive reduction, psychoanalytic, and ethological theories of attachment. (269-271)

7.11 Describe the Strange Situation procedure for measuring attachment, and discuss the four patterns of attachment that have been identified using this technique. (271-273)

7.12 Discuss the factors that affect attachment security. (274-279)

7.13 Discuss infants' attachment relationships with fathers and siblings, noting the factors that impact these relationships. (279-281)

7.14 Describe the link between infant-mother attachment and later cognitive, emotional, and social development, and explain how continuity of caregiving affects this link. (282)

7.15 Trace the emergence of self-awareness, and explain how it influences early emotional and social development, categorization of the self, and development of self-control. (283-286)

STUDY QUESTIONS

Erikson's Theory of Infant and Toddler Personality

1. How did Erikson expand upon Freud's view of development during the oral stage? (255)

_____

_____

2. According to Erikson, what is the psychological conflict of the first year, and how is it resolved on the positive side? (255)

_____

_____

_____

3. In what way did Erikson expand upon Freud's view of development during the anal stage? (255)

_____

_____

4. Erikson believed that the psychological conflict during the second year of life, autonomy versus _____ and _____, is resolved favorably when parents provide young children with _____ and _____. (255)

Emotional Development

1. _____ offer the most reliable cues as to which emotions infants are experiencing. (256)

2. True or False: Infants come into the world with the ability to express basic emotions such as happiness, anger, fear, sadness, and surprise. (257)

3. Trace the development of smiling behavior across early infancy, noting changes in the stimuli that trigger infant smiles. (257-258)

Newborn: _____

_____

By the end of 1st month: _____

_____

By 3 months: _____

_____

4. True or False: The frequency and intensity of infants' anger expressions increase with age. (258)

5. Explain how cognitive and motor development affect infants' angry reactions. (258)

_____

_____

_____

_____

6. Sadness is especially common in infants when parent-infant interaction is _____. (258)

7. The most frequent expression of fear in infants is _____ anxiety. (259)

8. Cite several factors that influence infants' and toddlers' reactions to strangers. (259)

_____

_____

_____

_____

9. True or False: In the first few months of life, infants are able to match the emotional tone of the caregiver during face-to-face interactions. (259)

10. Define *social referencing* and explain the functions it serves for infants and toddlers. (259-260)

Definition: _____

Functions: _____

_____

_____

11. _____ emotions are those that involve injury to or enhancement of our sense of self. List some examples of this type of emotion. (260)

_____

12. List two factors that support the emergence of self-conscious emotions during the second year. (260)

A. _____

B. _____

13. Self-conscious emotions play an important role in children's _____-related and _____ behaviors. (260)

14. True or False: The situations in which adults encourage children's expressions of self-conscious emotions vary from culture to culture. (260)

15. Emotional _____ refers to the strategies we use to adjust our emotional state to a comfortable level of intensity so that we can accomplish our goals. (260-261)

16. How does a caregiver's style of responding to an infant's emotional cues impact the infant's development of emotional self-regulation? (261)

_____

_____

_____

17. How does language development affect toddlers' emotional self-regulation? (261)

_____

_____

_____

Temperament and Development

1. Temperament refers to stable individual differences in _____, _____, _____, and _____. (262)

2. Cite two important findings from the New York longitudinal study on temperament. (262)

   A. _____

   B. _____

3. List and describe the three temperamental types that have emerged from the work of Thomas and Chess. (263)

   A. _____

   _____

   B. _____

   _____

   C. _____

   _____

4. True or False: All children fit into one of the three temperament categories described above. (264)

5. Rothbart's six dimensions represent which three underlying components of temperament? (264)

   A. _____ B. _____ C. _____

6. Discuss the advantages and disadvantages of using parent reports to assess children's temperament. (264)

   Advantages: _____

   _____

   Disadvantages: _____

   _____

7. True or False: Temperamental stability from one age period to the next is generally low to moderate. (265)

8. Describe the findings from twin studies relating to the biological basis of temperament. (265)

   _____

   _____

   _____

9. True or False: Lack of consistent ethnic and sex differences in early temperament have called into question the role of heredity. (265-266)

10. How do environmental influences affect temperament, generally speaking? (266-268)

    _____

    _____

    _____

11. Explain the goodness-of-fit model. (268-269)

    _____

    _____

    _____

Biology and Environment: Biological Basis of Shyness and Sociability

1. Kagan, a researcher who studies shyness and sociability in children, believes that individual differences in arousal of the _____, an inner brain structure that controls avoidance reactions, contributes to these contrasting temperamental styles. (266)

2. List four physiological responses that are correlated with shyness in children. (266-267)

   A. _____

   B. _____

   C. _____

   D. _____

Development of Attachment

1. Define *attachment*. (269)

   _____

   _____

2. True or False: Both psychoanalytic and behaviorist theories emphasize feeding as the central context in which infants and caregivers build a close emotional bond. (270)

3. List two problems with psychoanalytic and drive reduction theories of attachment. (270)

   A. _____

   B. _____

4. Explain the ethological theory of attachment. (270-271)

   _____

   _____

   _____

5. Match each phase of attachment with the appropriate description. (270-271)

_____ Attachment to the familiar caregiver is evident, and infants
display separation anxiety

_____ Infants are not yet attached and
do not mind being left with an
unfamiliar adult

_____ Separation anxiety declines as
children gain an understanding of
the parent's comings and goings
and can predict his/her return

_____ Infants start to respond differen-
tially to a familiar caregiver than
to a stranger

1. The preattachment phase
2. The attachment in the making phase
3. The phase of clear-cut attachment
4. Formation of a reciprocal relationship

6. According to Bowlby, children develop an *internal working model* based on their experiences during the four phases of attachment. Define and explain this term. (271)

_____

_____

_____

7. Describe the Strange Situation technique. (272)

_____

_____

_____

_____

8. Summarize the reasoning behind the use of the Strange Situation as a measure
of attachment security. (272)

_____

_____

_____

9. Match each of the following attachment classifications assessed by the Strange Situation with the appropriate description. (272-273)

_____ Before separation, these infants seek closeness to the parent and fail to explore. When she returns, they display angry, resistive behavior, may continue to cry after being picked up, and cannot be easily comforted.

_____ Before separation, these infants use the parent as a base from which to explore. They are upset by the parent's absence, and when she returns, they seek contact and are easily comforted.

_____ Before separation, these infants seem unresponsive to the parent. When she leaves, they react to the stranger in much the same way as to the parent. Upon her return, they are slow to greet her.

_____ When the parent returns, these infants show confused, contradictory behaviors, such a looking away while being held.

1. Secure
2. Avoidant
3. Resistant
4. Disorganized/Disoriented

10. The Attachment _____ is used as an alternative to the Strange Situation for measuring attachment. Briefly describe this method. (273)

_____

_____

_____

_____

11. True or False: In terms of attachment stability, securely attached infants maintain their attachment status more often than do insecurely attached infants. (273)

12. True or False: The secure pattern is the most common attachment classification in all societies studied to date. (274)

13. List four important influences that affect attachment security. (274-277)

   A. _____

   B. _____

   C. _____

   D. _____

14. True or False: Research on adopted children reveals that children can develop a first attachment bond as late as 4 to 6 years of age. (274)

15. Describe several adjustment problems evidenced by children and adolescents who lacked the opportunity to develop attachment bonds during infancy and childhood. (274-275)

   _____

   _____

   _____

16. A special form of communication known as *interactional* _____ appears to separate the experiences of securely from insecurely attached infants. Describe this pattern of communication. (275)

   _____

   _____

   _____

17. How does the parental care experienced by avoidant infants differ from that experienced by resistant infants? (275)

   _____

   _____

   _____

18. Among maltreated infants, _____ attachment is especially high. (275)

19. In _____ families, difficulties such as prematurity, birth complications, and newborn illness are linked to attachment insecurity. (276)

154

20. True or False: Researchers have concluded that infant temperament exerts an extremely powerful influence on attachment security, as evidenced by the fact that infants typically display an attachment quality that is consistent across familiar adult caregivers (such as, mother, father, or professional caregiver). (276)

21. True or False: Style of caregiving can override the impact of infant characteristics on attachment security. (276)

22. Explain how family circumstances, such as job loss, a failing marriage, or financial difficulties, affect infant attachment. (276-277)

_____

_____

_____

_____

23. True or False: The way parents view their childhood experiences is more influential than the actual experiences themselves in determining how parents rear their own children. (277)

24. Describe how mothers and fathers differ in the way they relate to and interact with babies, and discuss how these patterns are changing due to the revised work statusof women. (279)

_____

_____

_____

_____

_____

25. List two conditions associated with increased paternal involvement with caregiving. (279)

A. _____

B. _____

26. When a new baby arrives, how is a preschool-age sibling likely to respond? Include both negative and positive reactions in your answer. (279-280)

_____

_____

_____

_____

27. Discuss three ways in which mothers can promote positive relationships between infants and their preschool-age siblings. (280-281)

A. _____

_____

B. _____

_____

C. _____

_____

28. Peer sociability in the first two years is fostered by _____. (282)

29. True or False: Early attachment style consistently predicts psychological adjustment in later childhood. (282)

30. _____ determines whether attachment security is linked to later development. Briefly explain this relationship. (282)

_____

_____

_____

Social Issues: Health

Is Child Care in Infancy a Threat to Attachment Security?

1. True or False: American infants placed in full-time child care before 12 months of age are more likely than home-reared infants to display insecure attachment. (278)

2. Discuss several reasons why we must be cautious about concluding that child care is harmful to infants' attachment security. (278)

_____

_____

_____

_____

Cultural Influences: Father-Infant Relationships Among the Aka

1. Describe how the relationship between Aka husbands and wives encourages fathers' participation in child-rearing. (280)

_____

_____

_____

_____

Self-Development

1. The earliest aspect of the self to emerge is the _____-self, a sense of self as a subject, or agent, who is separate from objects and other people but attends to and acts on them. (283)

2. During the second year, toddlers start to construct a second aspect of self, the _____-self, a reflective observer who treats the self as an object of knowledge and evaluation. (284)

3. Discuss several ways in which self-awareness is associated with early emotional and social development. (284)

_____

_____

_____

_____

4. Describe categorizations of the self that appear in toddlerhood, and cite an example of how children use this knowledge to organize their behavior. (284-285)

_____

_____

_____

_____

5. _____ is the capacity to resist an impulse to engage in socially disapproved behavior. List three developmental milestones which are essential for the development of this capacity. (285)

A. _____

B. _____

C. _____

6. True or False: Among toddlers who experience warm, sensitive caregiving and reasonable expectations for mature behavior, compliance is more common than opposition. (285)

7. List several ways of helping toddlers develop compliance and self-control. (286)

_____

_____

_____

_____

ASK YOURSELF...

APPLY: Derek's mother fed him in a warm and loving manner during the first year. But when he became a toddler, she kept him in a playpen for many hours because he got into too much mischief while exploring freely. Use Erikson's theory to evaluate Derek's early experiences.

_____

_____

_____

_____

CONNECT: Do Erikson's recommendations for fostering autonomy in toddlerhood fit with Vygotsky's concept of the zone of proximal development, described on page 229 of Chapter 6? Explain.

_____

_____

_____

_____

REVIEW: Why do many infants show stranger anxiety in the second half of the first year? What factors can increase or decrease wariness of strangers?

_____

_____

_____

_____

APPLY: At 14 months, Timmy danced joyfully to the tune, Old MacDonald, as several adults and children watched. At 20 months, he stopped dancing after a few steps, hiding his face behind his hands. What explains this change in Timmy's behavior?

_____

_____

_____

_____

CONNECT: How do babies of depressed mothers fare in development of self-regulation? (See Chapter 4, page 162)

_____

_____

_____

_____

REFLECT: Do you believe it is important to teach infants and toddlers to control the expression of negative emotion? Explain.

_____

_____

_____

_____

REVIEW: Why is stability of temperament only low to moderate?

_____

_____

_____

_____

APPLY: At age 18 months, highly active Jake climbed out of his highchair long before his meal was finished. Exasperated, his father made him sit at the table until he had eaten all of his food. Soon Jake's behavior escalated into a full-blown tantrum. Using the concept of goodness of fit, suggest another way of handling Jake.

_____

_____

_____

_____

CONNECT: Do findings on ethnic and sex differences in temperament illustrate genetic-environmental correlation, discussed on page 89 of Chapter 2? Explain.

_____

_____

_____

_____

REFLECT: How would you describe your temperament as a young child? What type of parenting fits well with that temperament?

_____

_____

_____

_____

REVIEW: Which attachment patterns tend to be stable over infancy and toddlerhood? Which ones often change, and why?

_____

_____

_____

APPLY: What attachment pattern did Timmy display when Vanessa picked him up from child care, and what factors probably contributed to it? Will Timmy's insecurity necessarily compromise his development? Explain.

_____

_____

_____

_____

CONNECT: Review research on emotional self-regulation on pages 260-261. How do the caregiving experiences of securely attached infants promote development of emotional self-regulation?

_____

_____

_____

_____

REFLECT: How would you characterize your internal working model? What factors, in addition to your early relationship with your parents, might have influenced it?

_____

_____

_____

_____

APPLY: Nine-month-old Harry turned his cup upside down, spilling juice on the tray of his highchair. His mother directed, "Harry, put your cup back the right way!" Why can't Harry comply? When will he be able to do so?

_____

_____

_____

_____

CONNECT: What type of early parenting fosters the development of emotional self-regulation, attachment, and self-control? Why, in each instance, is it effective?

_____

_____

_____

_____

SUGGESTED STUDENT READINGS

Booth, A., & Crouter, A. C. (Eds.), (1998). *Men in families: When do they get involved? What difference does it make?* Mahwah, NJ: Lawrence Erlbaum Associates, Inc., Publishers. Presents contemporary research regarding the role of the father in child development. Topics include: controversial findings on the effects of paternal involvement, men's current family roles, and future roles for fathers and husbands.

Bronson, M. B. (2000). *Self-regulation in early childhood: Nature and nurture.* New York: The Guilford Press. A collection of chapters examining the development of self-regulation through the first 8 years of life. Also includes practical advice to parents and educators for enhancing self-regulatory skills throughout infancy and early childhood.

Campbell, A., & Muncer, S. (Eds.), (1997). *The social child.* Washington, DC: Psychology Press. An edited book that provides a survey of pressing issues in the field of social development. Chapters cover information on cross-cultural findings, behavioral genetics, social cognition, family influences, and effects of the media on children's behavior.

Meins, E. (1997). *Security of attachment and the social development of cognition.* Washington, DC: Psychology Press. Investigates how children's attachment styles are associated with various aspects of cognitive development throughout the preschool years. Accounts for individual differences using principles from both Bowlby's and Vygotsky's theories.

PUZZLE TERM REVIEW

Puzzle 7a

Across

2. A child who reacts negatively to and withdraws from novel stimuli
6. Voluntary obedience to adult requests and commands
9. _____ caregiving involves prompt, consistent, and appropriate responses to infant signals.
10. Temperament style characterized by inactivity, mild, low-key reactions to environmental stimuli, negative mood, and slow adjustment to new experiences
12. The capacity to understand another's emotional state and to *feel with* that person
13. Temperament style characterized by irregular daily routines, slow acceptance of new experiences, and negative, intense reactions
14. Positive outcome of Erikson's psychological conflict of infancy
15. Stable individual differences in quality and intensity of emotional reaction, activity level, attention, and emotional self-regulation

Down

1. A child who reacts positively to and approaches novel stimuli
2. _____ anxiety: an infant's expression of fear in response to unfamiliar adults
3. Sense of self as subject, or agent, who is separate from but attends to and acts on objects and other people
4. Model of attachment which states that an effective match between child-rearing practices and a child's temperament leads to favorable adjustment
5. Temperament style characterized by establishment of regular routines in infancy, general cheerfulness, and easy adaptation to new experiences
7. Reflective observer who treats the self as an object of knowledge and evaluation
8. The capacity to resist an impulse to engage in socially disapproved behavior (2 words)
10. Interactional _____: a sensitively-tuned emotional dance, in which the caregiver responds to infant signals in a well-timed, appropriate fashion, and both partners match emotional states
11. Positive outcome of Erikson's psychological conflict of toddlerhood

PUZZLE TERM REVIEW

Puzzle 7b

Across

4. _____ working model: a set of expectations derived from early caregiving experiences; guides all future close relationships
6. The _____ smile is evoked by the stimulus of the human face.
10. A procedure involving short separations from and reunions with the parent that assesses the quality of the attachment bond (2 words)
12. _____ emotions can be directly inferred from facial expressions; examples include happiness, sadness, anger, fear, and surprise
13. Infants use the caregiver as a secure _____ from which to explore, returning for emotional support.
14. Attachment _____: method for assessing the quality of the attachment bond in which a parent sorts a set of descriptors of attachment-related behaviors on the basis of how will they describe the child
15. Attachment style characterizing infants who are not distressed by parental separation and who avoid the parent when she returns

Down

1. The strong, affectional tie that humans feel toward special people in their lives
2. The _____ theory of attachment views the infant's emotional tie to the caregiver as an evolved response that promotes survival.
3. Social _____: relying on a trusted person's emotional reaction to decide how to respond in an uncertain situation
5. _____ anxiety: the infant's distressed reaction to the departure of a familiar caregiver
7. Self-_____ emotions involve injury or enhancement to the sense of self; examples include shame, embarrassment, guilt, pride
8. Attachment style characterizing infants who remain close to the parent prior to separation and display angry behavior upon reunion
9. Attachment style characterizing infants who respond in a confused, contradictory fashion when reunited with the parent (a.k.a. disoriented attachment)
10. Attachment style characterizing infants who are distressed at parental separation and are easily comforted upon parental return
11. Emotional self-_____: strategies for adjusting one's emotional state to a comfortable level of intensity

SELF-TEST

1. Erikson's stage of basic trust versus mistrust builds on Freud's _____ stage. (255)

    a. oral
    b. anal
    c. phallic
    d. ego

2. According to Erikson, the great conflict of the autonomy versus shame and doubt stage is resolved favorably when: (255)

    a. parents are very controlling and set rigid limits.
    b. parents adopt a permissive attitude, allowing the child complete freedom to explore.
    c. parents provide children with suitable guidance and reasonable choices.
    d. the child is successfully toilet trained by the age of two.

3. Emotions that can be directly inferred from facial expressions are known as: (257)

    a. basic emotions.
    b. social emotions.
    c. self-conscious emotions.
    d. referential emotions.

4. Research on happiness indicates that: (257-258)

    a. infants do not begin to smile until around 3 months of age.
    b. by 3 months of age, infants smile more often when they see a dynamic eye-catching object than when they interact with people.
    c. smiling reflects faster processing of information than does laughter.
    d. infants smile and laugh when they conquer new skills, expressing their delight in motor and cognitive mastery.

5. Which of the following is NOT true of angry reactions of infants? (258)

    a. As infants get older, their angry expressions decrease in frequency and intensity.
    b. Older infants react with anger to a wider range of situations than do younger infants.
    c. Anger is adaptive because it permits infants to defend themselves or to overcome obstacles.
    d. Infants' angry reactions change with age due to advancements in cognitive and motor development.

6. Stranger anxiety: (259)

    a. is a universal phenomenon, demonstrated by children in all cultures.
    b. is lessened if the parent remains nearby.
    c. is diminished if the unfamiliar adult immediately picks up the infant.
    d. is relatively uncommon among most children.

7. When an unfamiliar adult offers Heather a toy, she hesitates and looks at her mother, who smiles and nods. Heather then reaches out and takes the toy. This is an example of: (259-260)
    a. self-control.
    b. social referencing.
    c. emotional contagion.
    d. compliance.

8. Which of the following are characterized as self-conscious emotions? (260)
    a. happiness and sadness
    b. fear and anger
    c. interest and surprise
    d. shame and embarrassment

9. The capacity to adjust one's emotional state to a comfortable level of intensity is known as: (260-261)
    a. emotive self-referencing.
    b. affective monitoring.
    c. emotional self-regulation.
    d. emotional self-control.

10. Which of the following is NOT one of the three underlying components of temperament? (262)
    a. sociability
    b. attention
    c. activity level
    d. emotion

11. A child who is inactive, shows mild, low-key reactions to environmental stimuli, and is negative in mood would best fit into which of the following categories of temperament? (263)
    a. easy
    b. difficult
    c. slow-to-warm-up
    d. apathetic

12. Which of the following is true with regard to the stability of temperament? (265)
    a. Temperament is highly stable from infancy to adulthood.
    b. Temperament is moderately stable from one age period to the next.
    c. Temperament is not at all stable from one age period to the next.
    d. Temperament stabilizes in late childhood and is consistent after that time.

13. The notion that an effective match between child-rearing practices and a child's temperament will lead to favorable outcomes is known as: (268)
    a. secure base.
    b. goodness-of-fit.
    c. interactional synchrony.
    d. sensitive caregiving.

14. The _____ theory of attachment views the infant's emotional tie to the caregiver as an evolved response that promotes survival. (270)
    a. psychoanalytic
    b. drive reduction
    c. ethological
    d. ecological

15. According to Bowlby, during which phase of attachment development do infants display separation anxiety, becoming upset when the caregiver leaves? (271)
    a. the preattachment phase
    b. the attachment in the making phase
    c. the phase of clear-cut attachment
    d. the formation of a reciprocal relationship phase

16. Based on their experiences during Bowlby's four phases of attachment development, children construct a(n) _____, or a set of expectations about the availability of attachment figures, their likelihood of providing support during times of stress, and the self's interaction with those figures. (271)
    a. attachment schema
    b. secure attachment
    c. secure base
    d. internal working model

17. When placed in the Strange Situation, infants who seek closeness to their mother before separation but display angry behavior when she returns are classified as having which pattern of attachment? (272)
    a. secure
    b. avoidant
    c. resistant
    d. disorganized/disoriented

18. Which of the following is a measure of attachment quality in which parents are asked to sort a set of descriptors of attachment-related behaviors on the basis of how well they describe the child? (273)
    a. Child Attachment Inventory
    b. Attachment Q-Sort
    c. Strange Situation
    d. Individual Attachment Quality Checklist

19. Which is the most stable pattern of attachment, with nearly 70 percent of children retaining this classification over the second year? (273)
    a. secure
    b. avoidant
    c. resistant
    d. disorganized/disoriented

20. Which of the following is NOT true of the relationship between caregiving and attachment style? (275)

a. Secure attachment is associated with almost 100 percent interactional synchrony between mother and infant.
b. Avoidant infants tend to receive overstimulating and intrusive care.
c. Resistant babies typically experience inconsistent care.
d. Among maltreated infants, disorganized/disoriented attachment is especially high.

21. Fathers: (279)

a. are less involved in caregiving, and, therefore, often have an insecure attachment with their infants.
b. experience less anxiety than do mothers about daily separations from their child.
c. tend to engage in more exciting, physical play with infants than do mothers.
d. are more likely than mothers to provide toys, talk to infants, and initiate conventional games such as pat-a-cake and peekaboo.

22. _____ determines whether attachment security is linked to later development. (282)

a. Continuity of caregiving
b. Individual temperament
c. Quality of caregiving during infancy
d. Strength of the child's internal working model

23. Which term refers to one's sense of self as a subject, or agent, who is separate from objects and other people but attends to and acts on them? (283)

a. me-self
b. I-self
c. objective-self
d. agentic-self

24. As soon as children develop the ability to categorize themselves, they exhibit a sharp increase in: (285)

a. their capacity to resist an impulse to engage in socially disapproved behavior.
b. their ability to understand another's emotional state.
c. sociable play with peers.
d. gender-stereotyped play.

25. Which of the following is NOT one of the ways of helping toddlers develop compliance and self-control? (286)

a. respond to the toddler warmly and sensitively
b. set rigid expectations for behavior
c. offer many prompts and reminders
d. support language development

170

CHAPTER 8

PHYSICAL DEVELOPMENT IN EARLY CHILDHOOD

Chapter Summary

Compared to infancy, body size increases more slowly during early childhood, and the child's shape becomes more streamlined. The brain continues to grow faster than other parts of the body. The cortex, especially, shows gains in myelinization and formation of synapses, followed by synaptic pruning. Hand preference strengthens, a sign of greater brain lateralization. In addition, connections between different parts of the brain increase. These changes support improvements in a wide variety of physical and cognitive skills.

Factors affecting physical growth and health in infancy and toddlerhood continue to be influential in early childhood. Heredity affects physical growth by regulating the production of hormones. Extreme emotional deprivation can interfere with the production of growth hormone, thereby stunting children's growth. Sleep difficulties, in the form of night waking and nightmares, are common during the preschool years. Appetite declines due to a slower rate of physical growth. Since caloric intake is reduced, preschoolers need a high-quality diet. Disease can lead to malnutrition, seriously undermining children's growth, an effect that is especially common in developing countries. Unintentional injuries are the leading cause of childhood death. Efforts at several levels, including laws that promote safety, improvement of community environments, and efforts to change parents' and children's behavior, are necessary.

An explosion of new motor skills takes place in early childhood. Gross motor skills such as running, jumping, throwing, and catching appear and become better coordinated. Gains in fine motor development can be seen in preschoolers' ability to dress themselves, draw representational pictures, and print letters of the alphabet. As in other areas, heredity and environment combine to influence early childhood motor development.

Gains in perception continue during the preschool years. They are especially apparent in children's detection of the fine-grained structure of written symbols.

LEARNING OBJECTIVES

After reading this chapter, you should be able to:

8.1 Describe changes in body size, body proportions, and skeletal maturity during early childhood, and discuss asynchronies in physical growth. (294-297)

8.2 Discuss brain development in early childhood, including synaptic growth and pruning, lateralization and handedness, and other advances in brain development that help to establish links between parts of the brain. (297-299)

8.3 Describe the factors affecting physical growth and health during early childhood, noting the impact of heredity and hormones, emotional well-being, sleep habits and problems, nutrition, infectious disease, and childhood injury. (300-308)

8.4 Summarize individual, familial, community, and societal factors related to childhood injuries, and describe ways to prevent them. (308-309)

8.5 Cite major milestones of gross and fine motor development in early childhood. (310-316)

8.6 Discuss individual differences in early childhood motor skills, and cite ways to enhance early motor development. (316-317)

8.7 Summarize perceptual development in early childhood, paying special attention to the discrimination of written symbols. (318)

STUDY QUESTIONS

Body Growth

1. True or False: In contrast to the rapid increases in body size seen during infancy, early childhood is marked by a slow pattern of growth. (294)

2. On average, children add ____ to ____ inches in height and about ____ pounds in weight each year. (294)

3. Describe changes in body proportions during early childhood. (294)

_____

_____

_____

4. True or False: Growth norms and trends in body size are cross-culturally consistent. (294-295)

5. Changes in the _____, or growth centers in which cartilage hardens into bone, provide doctors with an estimate of _____, the best available measure of progress toward physical maturity. (295)

6. During early and middle childhood, information about skeletal age is helpful in diagnosing _____. (295)

7. True or False: The age at which children start to lose their primary teeth varies by sex and cultural ancestry. (296)

8. Describe the *general growth curve*, which represents changes in body size from infancy to adolescence. (296)

_____

_____

_____

9. List two exceptions to the trend depicted by the general growth curve. (296-297)

A. _____

B. _____

Brain Development

1. True or False: By four years of age, the child's brain has produced an overabundance of synaptic connections, contributing to the plasticity of the young brain. (297)

2. Describe the process of *synaptic pruning*. (297)

_____

_____

_____

3. For most children, the _____ hemisphere is especially active between 3 and 6 years of age and then levels off. In contrast, activity in the _____ hemisphere increases steadily throughout early and middle childhood, with a slight spurt between 8 to 10 years. (297)

4. Explain how findings on hemispheric lateralization fit with what we know about cognitive development. (297-298)

_____

_____

_____

_____

5. The _____ cerebral hemisphere is the hemisphere responsible for skilled motor action. (298)

6. True or False: The brains of left-handers tend to be less strongly lateralized than those of right-handers. (298)

7. List three theories regarding the origins of handedness. (298-299)

A. _____

_____

B. _____

_____

C. _____

_____

8. For each of the following brain structures, describe developmental changes in early childhood, and indicate their impact on children's physical and cognitive skills: (299)

Cerebellum

Changes: _____

_____

Impact: _____

Reticular Formation

Changes: _____

_____

Impact: _____

Corpus Callosum

Changes: _____

_____

Impact: _____

Factors Affecting Growth and Health

1. The _____ gland, located near the base of the brain, releases hormones affecting physical growth. (300)

2. Describe the impact of growth hormone (GH) and thyroid stimulating hormone (TSH) on body growth and indicate what happens when there are deficiencies of these hormones. (300)

GH: _____

_____

_____

TSH: _____

_____

_____

3. Describe the cause and characteristics of deprivation dwarfism. (300)

Cause: _____

Characteristics: _____

_____

4. How can deprivation dwarfism be distinguished from biologically-based GH deficiency and from normal shortness? (300)

_____

5. In what way does sleep contribute to body growth? (302)

_____

6. True or False: It is normal for children's appetite to decline in early childhood. (302)

7. Cite three factors that influence young children's food preferences and eating habits. (303)

A. _____

B. _____

C. _____

8. List at least four ways to encourage good nutrition in early childhood. (303)

A. _____

B. _____

C. _____

D. _____

175

9. Explain how malnutrition and disease interact to undermine physical growth. (304)

_____

_____

_____

10. True or False: In developing countries, widespread diarrhea increases children's risk of growth retardation and death. (304)

11. True or False: Among industrialized nations, the United States has the highest rates of immunization. (304-305)

12. Cite two factors that contribute to inadequate immunization in the United States. (306)

A. _____

B. _____

13. True or False: Childhood illness increases with child care attendance. (306)

14. Discuss several strategies for controlling the spread of infectious disease in child care. (306)

_____

_____

_____

_____

15. True or False: Unintentional injuries are the leading cause of childhood mortality in industrialized countries. (307)

16. List the three most common causes of injury during the early childhood years. (308)

A. _____

B. _____

C. _____

17. Cite two child characteristics that increase the risk of injury. (308)

A. _____ B. _____

18. Describe family characteristics related to injury. (308)

_____

_____

_____

19. List three factors that likely contribute to the high childhood injury death rate in the United States. (308)

A. _____

B. _____

C. _____

20. A variety of programs based on _____
(modeling and reinforcement) have been effective in improving child safety practices. (309)

21. List at least four ways to reduce unintentional injuries in early childhood. (309)

A. _____

B. _____

C. _____

D. _____

Biology and Environments: Treating Short Children with Growth Hormone

1. True or False: Research consistently shows that short stature is associated with adjustment problems, including poor social skills, social isolation, low self-esteem, and poor academic achievement. (301)

2. Discuss the effectiveness of growth hormone (GH) treatment in achieving height gains for both GH deficient and short, normal-GH children. (301)

_____

3. List the drawbacks of GH treatment. (301)

_____

_____

_____

Cultural Influences:

Child Health Care in the United States and Other Western Nations

1. List two factors that have prevented government-sponsored health services from being offered to all children in the United States. (305)

    A. _____

    B. _____

2. How does child health care in the United States differ from that of many European nations? (305)

    _____

    _____

    _____

    _____

3. Under the new health initiative, CHIP, or _____ _____ _____ _____, states receive $4 billion a year in federal matching funds for upgrading children's health insurance. (305)

Social Issues: Health

Otitis Media and Development

1. Discuss the impact of otitis media on language development and academic functioning. (307)

    _____

    _____

    _____

    _____

2. List several ways of preventing early otitis media. (307)

    _____

    _____

    _____

Motor Development

1. Which principle that governed motor development in the first 2 years continues to operate in early childhood? (310)

   _____

2. As children's bodies become more streamlined and their center of gravity shifts downward, _____ improves greatly, paving the way for new motor skills involving large muscles of the body. (310)

3. List four gross motor skills that develop throughout early childhood. (310-311)

   A. _____

   B. _____

   C. _____

   D. _____

4. To parents, fine motor development is most evident in which two areas? (312)

   A. _____ B. _____

5. Cite the self-help skills that emerge at the following ages: (312)

   2 years: _____

   3 years: _____

   4 to 5 years: _____

   5 to 6 years: _____

6. List the three-stage sequence through which drawing skills typically progress and the approximate age at which each is reached. (313-314)

   A. _____ Age: _____

   B. _____ Age: _____

   C. _____ Age: _____

7. Describe evidence indicating that culture has a significant impact on the development of drawing skills. (315)

_____

_____

_____

8. Discuss sex differences in motor development during early childhood. (316-317)

_____

_____

_____

9. True or False: Sex differences in motor development during early childhood are influenced more by social norms than by actual physical differences between boys and girls. (317)

10. True or False: Research suggests that preschoolers who are exposed to formal lessons, such as gymnastics, are far ahead of peers in motor development. (317)

11. List three ways to foster motor development. (317)

    A. _____

    B. _____

    C. _____

Perceptual Development

1. True or False: By age 3 or 4, children can tell writing from scribbling and pictures, even though they cannot yet identify the letters of the alphabet. (318)

2. Letters that are _____ are especially hard for young children to tell apart. Explain why this is the case. (318)

_____

_____

_____

ASK YOURSELF . . .

REVIEW: Explain why brain growth in early childhood involves not only an increase in neural connections but loss of synapses and cell death.

_____

_____

_____

_____

APPLY: Both Crystal and Shana are shorter and lighter than 97 percent of other North American 4-year-olds girls. What are the possible causes of their very short stature?

_____

_____

_____

_____

CONNECT: What stance on the nature-nurture issue does evidence on development of handedness support? Document your answer with research findings.

_____

_____

_____

_____

REVIEW: What sleep problems can Western parents anticipate during the preschool years, and what factors contribute to those problems?

_____

_____

_____

_____

APPLY: One day, Leslie prepared a new snack to serve at preschool: celery stuffed with ricotta cheese and pineapple. The first time she served it, few children touched it. What can Leslie do to encourage her pupils to accept the snack? What tactics should she avoid?

_____

_____

_____

_____

CONNECT: Using ecological systems theory, suggest ways to reduce childhood injuries by intervening in the microsystem, mesosystem, and macrosystem. Why are interventions at each of these levels necessary?

_____

_____

_____

_____

REFLECT: As a preschooler, did you insist on bedtime rituals? Were you a picky eater? Did you sustain any serious injuries? If possible, find out from a parent or other family member. What factors might be responsible for your early childhood behaviors?

_____

_____

_____

_____

REVIEW: Describe typical changes in children's drawings of people and objects during early childhood.

_____

_____

_____

_____

APPLY: Mabel and Chad want to do everything they can to support their 3-year-old daughter's athletic development. What advice would you give them?

_____

_____

_____

_____

CONNECT: Does preschoolers' developing skill at gripping a pencil fit with dynamic systems theory of motor development? Explain, returning to Chapter 5, page 190, if you need to review.

_____

_____

_____

_____

SUGGESTED STUDENT READINGS

Bracken, B. A. (Ed.) (1999). *The psychoeducational assessment of preschool children (3rd Ed.).* Boston: Allyn & Bacon. Written primarily for early childhood educators and child psychologists, this book highlights current theories, guidelines, practices, and procedures for assessing preschool children.

Rookes, P., & Willson, J. (2000). *Perception: Theory, development, and organization.* London: Routledge. Explores the basic biological and psychological processes involved in the development of perception. Also discusses the role of culture in early childhood perceptual development.

Slaby, R. G., Roedell, W. C., Arezzo, D., & Hendrix, K. (1995). *Early violence prevention: Tools for teachers of young children.* A practical guide for teachers and caregivers dealing with preschool children's aggressive behavior. Also includes effective teaching strategies for early violence prevention.

Puzzle 8

Across

3. A brain structure that aids in balance and control of body movements
5. Oral _____ therapy: a treatment for diarrhea in which sick children are given a glucose, salt, and water solution to replace lost body fluids
8. The _____ gland, located near the base of the brain, releases hormones affecting physical growth.
9. The _____ growth curve represents overall changes in body size: rapid growth during infancy, slower gains in early and middle childhood, and rapid growth once again during adolescence
10. Corpus _____: a large bundle of fibers that connects the two hemispheres of the brain

Down

1. _____ formation: a brain structure that maintains alertness and consciousness
2. _____ dwarfism is a growth disorder caused by emotional deprivation.
4. The _____ cerebral hemisphere of the brain is responsible for skilled motor action.
6. A pituitary hormone that stimulates the thyroid gland to release thyroxine, which is necessary for normal brain development and body growth (abbr.)
7. _____ hormone: a pituitary hormone that affects the development of all body tissues except the central nervous system and the genitals
11. Otitis _____: middle ear infection

SELF-TEST

1. Which of the following best reflects the pattern of growth during early childhood? (294)

   a. Girls tend to be slightly larger than boys.
   b. Individual differences in body size become less apparent than in infancy and toddlerhood.
   c. Body fat increases compared to infancy and toddlerhood.
   d. Growth occurs more slowly than in infancy and toddlerhood.

2. During early and middle childhood, information about skeletal age is helpful for: (295)

   a. examining sex differences in patterns of growth.
   b. establishing universal growth norms.
   c. diagnosing growth disorders.
   d. tracking children's motor development and capacity to perform various motor skills.

3. Which of the following is NOT true of dental development? (296)

   a. The age at which children lose their primary teeth is heavily influenced by genetic factors.
   b. Cultural ancestry plays little role in children's dental development.
   c. Decay in primary teeth is a strong predictor of decay in permanent teeth.
   d. Tooth decay is especially prevalent among low-SES children.

4. The _____ depict(s) rapid growth during infancy, slower gains in early and middle childhood, and rapid growth again during adolescence. (296)

   a. universal growth norms
   b. synchronous growth trend
   c. general growth curve
   d. holistic growth pattern

5. Synaptic pruning: (297)

   a. reduces the number of synapses.
   b. produces an overabundance of synaptic connections.
   c. supports the plasticity of the brain.
   d. enables many synapses to serve identical functions, thus helping to ensure that children will acquire certain abilities.

6. Language skills increase rapidly in early childhood, whereas spatial skills develop very gradually over childhood and adolescence. These trends in cognitive development are consistent with findings that: (297-298)

   a. the two hemispheres of the brain develop at different rates.
   b. the hemispheres of the brain are no longer lateralized after early childhood.
   c. synaptic pruning supports plasticity of the brain.
   d. skill acquisition is independent of brain development.

7. Which of the following is NOT true with regard to handedness? (298-299)
   a. For right-handed people, language is housed in the left hemisphere of the brain, whereas for left-handed people, language is typically shared between the two hemispheres.
   b. The brains of left-handers tend to be more strongly lateralized than those of right-handers.
   c. Hand preference among twins is thought to be related to body position during the prenatal period.
   d. There are wide cultural differences in the percentage of left-handers within the population.

8. The _____, a bundle of fibers that connects the two hemispheres of the brain, is instrumental in the integration of thought processes, including perception, memory, attention, language, and problem solving. (299)
   a. cerebellum
   b. reticular formation
   c. corpus callosum
   d. cerebral cortex

9. A gland located near the base of the brain that releases hormones affecting physical growth is the: (300)
   a. adrenal gland.
   b. growth gland.
   c. thyroid gland.
   d. pituitary gland.

10. Deprivation dwarfism results from: (300)
    a. extreme malnutrition in early childhood.
    b. a deficiency in thyroxine.
    c. diminished production of growth hormone associated with emotional deprivation.
    d. limited exposure to perceptual stimulation.

11. Which of the following is NOT true of sleep habits and problems in early childhood? (302)
    a. Rigid bedtime rituals often cause sleep problems in children.
    b. Intense bedtime struggles may result from inconsistent discipline.
    c. On average, total sleep declines during early childhood.
    d. Difficulty falling asleep is typically due to lingering separation anxiety.

12. Mario only eats carrots and turkey, and his parents are concerned that he may not be eating enough other foods. What should they do to increase Mario's acceptance of new foods? (303)
    a. serve only one new food at each meal, and put a large amount on his plate
    b. continue to expose him to a variety of new foods without insisting that he eat them
    c. continually offer the new food throughout the course of the meal and prompt Mario to eat it
    d. tell Mario that he can have carrots and turkey only after he tries the new food

13. Which of the following statements is true? (304)

    a. Ordinary childhood illnesses have consequences for physical growth among all children.
    b. In industrialized nations, childhood diseases have continued to increase dramatically over the past 50 years.
    c. The United States has the highest immunization rate of all industrialized nations, with nearly 100% of all children receiving a full program of immunizations in the first two years.
    d. While childhood illnesses typically have no adverse consequences on physical growth among well-nourished children, the consequences for growth among malnourished children may be severe.

14. The leading cause of death among children over 1 year of age is: (308)

    a. motor vehicle collisions.
    b. infectious diseases.
    c. drowning.
    d. choking.

15. With regard to childhood injury, the United States: (308)

    a. ranks lowest among industrialized nations in childhood injury mortality.
    b. ranks among the highest in childhood injury mortality among industrialized nations.
    c. has experienced a rapid decline in injury deaths over the past 30 years.
    d. has a high rate of injury for low-SES children, but fares much better than other countries when comparing injury rates for children from economically advantaged families.

16. Programs based on _____ have been successful in improving child safety. (309)

    a. classical conditioning
    b. shaping
    c. applied behavior analysis
    d. radical behaviorism

17. In early childhood, _____ improves greatly, paving the way for new motor skills involving large muscles of the body. (310)

    a. visual acuity
    b. muscle tone
    c. balance
    d. hand-eye coordination

18. Gross motor development involves improvement in children's ability to: (312)

    a. put puzzles together.
    b. build with small blocks.
    c. cut and paste.
    d. throw and catch a ball.

19. Gains in fine motor development are due to increased control of the: (312)

    a. arms and legs.
    b. hands and fingers.
    c. legs and feet.
    d. torso.

20. Children's drawing skills: (315)

   a. develop in varying sequences, depending on cultural practices.
   b. follow the same sequence of development, regardless of culture.
   c. vary considerably from culture to culture in the early stages, but arrive at the same endpoint in the sequence (i.e., realistic drawings).
   d. develop independently of cultural conventions.

21. Letter reversals, such as writing the letter "D" backwards, are: (316)

   a. common well into the second grade.
   b. common during the preschool years but indicative of a learning disability after the age of 5 or 6.
   c. common in many children well into early adolescence.
   d. cause for concern, regardless of the age of the child.

22. Which if the following statements is NOT true of sex differences in motor development during early childhood? (316-317)

   a. Boys are ahead of girls in skills that emphasize force and power.
   b. Girls have better development of fine motor skills than do boys.
   c. Girls perform better than boys on tasks requiring balance and precision of movement, such as hopping and skipping.
   d. Sex differences in early motor development are largely due to genetic differences in physical capacity.

23. Parents can enhance children's mastery of motor skills through all of the following EXCEPT: (317)

   a. providing play spaces and age-appropriate equipment for running, climbing, jumping, and throwing.
   b. encouraging children's use of self-help skills and artistic expression through daily routines.
   c. providing a supportive environment which emphasizes fun rather than perfection of correct technique.
   d. exposing children to formal lessons, such as gymnastics or tumbling.

24. Which letter pair should a child first be able to differentiate? (318)

   a. B versus V
   b. C versus G
   c. M versus W
   d. E versus F

25. Which of the following activities helps children learn to differentiate between mirror image forms? (318)

   a. reading
   b. drawing
   c. writing
   d. working puzzles

CHAPTER 9

COGNITIVE DEVELOPMENT IN EARLY CHILDHOOD

Chapter Summary

Early childhood brings dramatic advances in mental representation. Aside from the development of language and make-believe play, Piaget's description of the preoperational stage emphasizes young children's cognitive limitations. Newer research reveals that preschoolers show the beginnings of logical, reflective thought when tasks are simplified and made relevant to their everyday experiences. Piaget's theory has had a powerful influence on education, promoting child-oriented approaches to teaching and learning.

Whereas Piaget believed that language is of little importance in cognitive development, Vygotsky regarded it as the foundation for all higher cognitive processes. As adults and more skilled peers provide children with verbal guidance on challenging tasks, children incorporate these dialogues into their self-directed speech and use them to regulate their own behavior. A Vygotskian classroom emphasizes assisted discovery, including verbal support from teachers and peer collaboration.

A variety of information-processing skills improve during early childhood. With age, preschoolers sustain attention for longer periods of time, and their recognition memory becomes highly accurate. Recall develops more slowly because preschoolers are not yet effective users of memory strategies. Like adults, young children remember everyday events in a logical, well-organized fashion, and their memory for special, one-time events improves. Preschoolers also make great strides in problem solving skills, generating a variety of strategies for finding solutions. Around the same time, children begin to construct a set of beliefs about mental activities. Through informal experiences, preschoolers also develop a basic understanding of written symbols and mathematical concepts.

A stimulating home environment, warm parenting, and reasonable demands for mature behavior continue to predict mental development in early childhood. Formal academic training in early childhood undermines motivation and other aspects of emotional well-being. Although test score gains resulting from early intervention such as Head Start eventually decline, at-risk children show long-term benefits in school adjustment. High-quality child care can serve as effective intervention, whereas poor-quality child care undermines children's development regardless of SES background.

Language development proceeds at a rapid pace during early childhood. By the end of the preschool years, children have an extensive vocabulary, use most of the grammatical constructions of their language competently, and are effective conversationalists. Opportunities for conversational give-and-take with adults enhance these skills.

Learning Objectives

After reading this chapter, you should be able to:

9.1 Describe advances in mental representation during the preschool years, including changes in make-believe play. (324-326)

9.2 Describe what Piaget believed to be the deficiencies of preoperational thought. (327-329)

9.3 Discuss recent research on preoperational thought and note the implications of such findings for the accuracy of Piaget's preoperational stage. (329-335)

9.4 Describe three educational principles derived from Piaget's theory. (335-336)

9.5 Contrast Piaget's view of children's private speech with that of Vygotsky. (337)

9.6 Describe features of social interaction that foster cognitive development. (337-339)

9.7 Discuss how Vygotsky's ideas have been applied in educational settings. (339)

9.8 Summarize recent challenges to Vygotsky's theory. (339)

9.9 Describe the development of attention, memory, and problem solving during early childhood. (341-344)

9.10 Discuss preschoolers' understanding of mental activities, noting factors that contribute to early metacognition, as well as limitations of the young child's theory of mind. (344-346)

9.11 Describe early literacy and mathematical development during the preschool years, and discuss appropriate ways to enhance children's development in these areas. (346-349)

9.12 Describe the nature of early childhood intelligence tests, and explain the impact of home environment, preschool and child care, and educational television on mental development. (350-355)

9.13 Trace the development of vocabulary, grammar, and conversational skills in preschool children, and cite factors that support language development in early childhood. (356-360)

STUDY QUESTIONS

Piaget's Theory: The Preoperational Stage

1. As children move from the sensorimotor to the preoperational stage, the most obvious change is an extraordinary increase in _____ mental activity. (324)

2. How does language increase the efficiency of cognition? (324)

    _____

    _____

3. According to Piaget, (language/sensorimotor activity) gives rise to representational thought. (324)

4. List three important changes in make-believe play during early childhood, and give an example of each. (325)

A. _____

_____

Example: _____

B. _____

_____

Example: _____

C. _____

_____

Example: _____

5. _____ play is make-believe play with others. (325)

6. List several advantages of make-believe play. (326)

A. _____

B. _____

C. _____

7. True or False: Recent research indicates that the creation of imaginary companions is a sign of maladjustment. (326)

8. _____ refers to the ability to view a symbolic object as both an object in its own right and a symbol. Provide an example. (326)

_____

_____

9. According to Piaget, young children are not capable of *operations*. Define this term. (327)

_____

_____

10. Piaget believed that _____, the inability to distinguish the symbolic viewpoints of others from one's own, is the most serious deficiency of preoperational thought. (327-328)

11. The preoperational belief that inanimate objects have lifelike qualities is called _____. (328)

12. _____ refers to the idea that certain physical characteristics of objects remain the same even when their outward appearance changes. (328)

13. Match each term to the appropriate definition. (328)

_____ The tendency to focus on one aspect of a situation and neglect other important features

_____ The inability to mentally go through a series of steps in a problem and then reverse direction, returning to the starting point

_____ The tendency to treat the initial and final stages of a problem as completely unrelated

_____ Being easily distracted by a concrete, perceptual appearance of objects

1. Centration
2. Perception Bound
3. States rather than Transformations
4. Irreversibility

14. Preschoolers have difficulty with _____; that is, they cannot yet organize objects into classes and subclasses on the basis of similarities and differences. (329)

15. True or False: Recent research using adjusted, developmentally appropriate tasks provides support for Piaget's notion of egocentrism. (329-330)

16. Piaget overestimated preschoolers' animistic beliefs because he asked children about _____ (330)

17. Under what conditions do children show better performance than Piaget suggested on tasks examining conservation and causal reasoning? (330-331)

_____

_____

_____

18. By the second half of the first year, children have formed a variety of _____ categories, such as furniture, animals, and vehicles. Over the early preschool years, children's general categories differentiate as they form many _____-_____ categories, such as chairs, tables, dressers, and beds. Soon after, they break down these intermediate level categories into _____, such as rocking chairs and desk chairs. (332-333)

19. Preschoolers' rapidly growing _____ and expanding _____ support their skill at categorizing. (333)

20. What experience helps children learn to distinguish between appearance and reality? (334)

   _____

   _____

21. Does recent research support or refute Piaget's theory? Explain your answer. (334-335)

   _____

   _____

   _____

   _____

22. Findings indicate that children attain logical operations (gradually/suddenly). (334)

23. List and describe three educational principles derived from Piaget's theory. (335-336)

   A. _____

   _____

   B. _____

   _____

   C. _____

   _____

Social Issues: Education: Young Children's Understanding of Death

1. Name and describe the three components of the death concept, listing them in the order in which they develop. (332)

   A. _____

   _____

   B. _____

   _____

   C. _____

   _____

2. Most children grasp the three components of the death concept by age _____. (332)

3. How can adults help children develop an accurate understanding of death? (333)

   _____

   _____

   _____

Vygotsky's Sociocultural Theory

1. True or False: Vygotsky placed a greater emphasis than did Piaget on the role of language in cognitive development. (336)

2. Contrast Piaget's view of children's private speech with that of Vygotsky. (337)

   _____

   _____

   _____

   _____

3. Most research findings have supported (Piaget's/Vygotsky's) view of children's private speech. (337)

4. Under what circumstances are children likely to use private speech? (337)

   _____

   _____

5. According to Vygotsky, where does private speech come from? (337-338)

_____

_____

6. Identify and describe two features of social interaction that facilitate children's cognitive development. (338)

A. _____

_____

B. _____

_____

7. Vygotskian classrooms promote _____, in which teachers guide children's learning with explanations, demonstrations, and verbal prompts. This process is helped along by _____, in which children with varying abilities work in groups, teaching and helping one another. (339)

8. Vygotsky saw _____ as the ideal social context for fostering cognitive development in early childhood. (339)

9. Discuss several limitations of Vygotsky's theory. (339)

_____

_____

_____

_____

Cultural Influences: Young Children's Daily Life in a Yucatec Mayan Village

1. Describe the daily experiences of children living in the Mayan village of the Yucatan, Mexico, and discuss how such experiences affect Mayan preschoolers' skills and behavior (relative to their Western agemates). (340)

_____

_____

_____

_____

_____

Information Processing

1. During early childhood, attention becomes more _____, which involves thinking out a sequence of acts ahead of time and allocating attention accordingly in order to reach a goal. (341)

2. Explain the difference between recognition and recall. (341-342)

   _____

   _____

   _____

3. Preschoolers' recall memory is much (better/poorer) than their recognition memory. Why is this the case? (342)

   _____

   _____

   _____

4. What is *episodic memory*? (342)

   _____

   _____

5. Preschoolers remember familiar experiences in terms of _____, general descriptions of what occurs in a particular situation. Discuss the utility of this strategy. (342)

   _____

   _____

6. _____ memory refers to representations of one-time events that are particularly meaningful in terms of the life story that each of us creates about ourselves. (343)

7. Explain the two styles, elaborative and repetitive, which are used by adults to elicit children's autobiographical narratives, and note which style leads to better memory of events over time. (343)

Elaborative: _____

_____

Repetitive: _____

_____

8. Describe Siegler's *overlapping-waves theory* of problem solving. (343)

_____

_____

_____

9. List several factors that facilitate children's movement from less efficient to more efficient problem-solving strategies. (343-344)

A. _____

B. _____

C. _____

10. A theory of mind, also called _____, is a set of ideas about mental activities. (344)

11. Between ages 3 and 4, children figure out that both _____ and _____ determine behavior. (344)

12. An illustration of preschoolers' developing theory of mind comes from games that test whether they know that _____ beliefs, ones that do not accurately represent reality, can guide people's actions. (344)

13. Discuss four factors that contribute to the development of children's theory of mind. (345-346)

A. _____

_____

B. _____

_____

C. _____

_____

D. _____

_____

14. Cite two general ways in which preschoolers' awareness of inner cognitive activities is incomplete. What can we conclude about the difference between the young child's theory of mind and that of the older child? (346)

A. _____

B. _____

Conclusion: _____

_____

15. True or False: Preschoolers have an understanding of written language long before they learn to read and write. (346)

16. How do preschoolers' ideas about written language differ from those of adults? (346, 348)

_____

_____

_____

_____

17. List several ways in which adults can foster literacy development in young children. (348)

_____

_____

_____

18. In the second year, children begin to grasp the concept of _____, or order relationships between quantities (for example, three is more than two, and two is more than one). (349)

19. Between ages 4 and 5, children grasp the principle of _____, the understanding that the last number in a counting sequence indicates the quantity of items in the set. (349)

20. True or False: Cross-cultural research suggests that basic arithmetic knowledge emerges universally around the world. (349)

Biology and Environment: Mindblindness and Infantile Autism

1. Describe the characteristics associated with infantile autism. (347)

_____

_____

_____

2. Researchers agree that infantile autism stems from _____, usually due to genetic or prenatal environmental causes. (347)

3. Describe three hypotheses regarding the specific causes of autism. (347)

A. _____

_____

B. _____

_____

C. _____

_____

Individual Differences in Mental Development

1. How does the content of early childhood intelligence tests differ from that of infant and toddler intelligence tests? (350)

_____

_____

2. True or False: By age 5 to 6, children's intelligence test scores become good predictors of later intelligence and academic achievement. (350)

3. Describe the content of early childhood intelligence tests. (350)

_____

_____

4. List two ways in which low-SES and ethnic minority preschoolers are likely to respond differently than middle-SES children to a testing situation. (350)

A. _____

_____

B. _____

_____

5. True or False: Performance on intelligence tests is rarely affected by cultural and situational factors. (350-351)

6. Summarize the aspects of young children's home environments that the HOME has found to support intellectual growth. (351)

_____

_____

_____

_____

7. Currently, _____ percent of American preschool children have mothers who are employed. (352)

8. Describe the difference between child-centered preschools and academic preschools. (352)

Child-centered: _____

_____

Academic: _____

_____

9. True or False: Children in academic preschools demonstrate higher levels of achievement than those in child-centered preschools, including greater mastery of motor, academic, language, and social skills. (352)

10. List the main components of a typical Head Start program. (352)

_____

_____

_____

11. Describe the long-term impact of preschool intervention on low-SES children's development, comparing outcomes of university-based programs with those of Head Start programs. (352-353)

_____

_____

_____

_____

12. True or False: After children graduate from Head Start, they demonstrate a rapid decline in intelligence test scores. (352)

13. Explain the *two-generation approach* to early intervention. (353)

_____

_____

_____

14. True or False: Preschoolers exposed to poor-quality child care, regardless of family SES level, score lower on measures of cognitive and social skills. (354)

15. List four characteristics of high quality child care. (355)

A. _____

B. _____

C. _____

D. _____

16. True or False: The more often children watch *Sesame Street*, the higher they score on tests designed to measure the program's learning goals. (355)

17. Discuss the impact of television viewing on children's cognitive development. (355)

_____

_____

_____

_____

Language Development

1. True or False: Preschoolers learn an average of 5 new words each day, increasing their vocabulary from 200 words at age 2 to 10,000 words at age 6. (356)

2. Explain how children build their vocabularies so quickly over the preschool years. (356)

_____

_____

_____

3. Children learn to fast map _____ especially rapidly because these words refer to concrete items that they already know much about. _____ and _____ words, however, take somewhat longer to learn. (356)

4. The principle of _____ refers to an assumption made by children in the early stages of vocabulary growth that words refer to entirely separate (nonoverlapping) categories. (357)

5. When children figure out the meaning of a word by observing how it is used in the structure of a sentence, they are using _____ bootstrapping. (357)

6. True or False: Children are able to effectively use social cues to identify word meanings. (357)

7. What is grammar? (Provide a brief definition.) (357)

_____

_____

8. When children overextend grammatical rules to words that are exceptions- for example, saying "I runned fast" instead of "I ran fast"-they are making an error called _____. (358)

9. True or False: By the end of the preschool years, children have mastered most of the grammatical constructions of their language. (358)

10. Define semantic bootstrapping. (358)

_____

_____

11. True or False: The idea of a built-in language acquisition device has been universally accepted by researchers. (358-359)

12. The practical, social side of language that is concerned with how to engage in effective and appropriate communication with others is known as _____. (359)

13. Preschoolers (are/are not) capable of effective communication, such as initiating conversation, responding appropriately to another's comments, and conversational turn-taking. (359)

14. True or False: Having an older sibling facilitates the acquisition of pragmatic language. (359)

15. True or False: Preschoolers adjust their speech to fit the age, sex, and social status of their listeners. (359)

16. Explain the conditions under which preschoolers are likely to experience a break down of conversational skills. (359-360)

_____

_____

_____

17. Describe several techniques that adults can use to promote preschoolers' language skills. (360)

_____

_____

_____

ASK YOURSELF . . .

REVIEW: Select two of the following characteristics of the preoperational stage: egocentrism, perception-bound thought, illogical reasoning, lack of hierarchical classification. Cite findings that led Piaget to conclude preschoolers are deficient in those ways. Then present evidence indicating that preschoolers are more capable thinkers than Piaget assumed.

_____

_____

_____

_____

APPLY: At home, 4-year-old Will understands that his tricycle isn't alive and can't move by itself. Yet when Will went fishing with his family and his father asked, "Why do you think the river is flowing along?" Will responded, "Because it's alive and it wants to." What explains this contradiction in Will's reasoning?

_____

_____

_____

_____

REFLECT: Did you have an imaginary companion as a young child? If so, what was your companion like, and why did you create it? Were your parents aware of your companion? What was their attitude toward it?

_____

_____

_____

_____

REVIEW: Describe characteristics of social interaction that support children's cognitive development. How does such interaction create a zone of proximal development?

_____

_____

_____

_____

APPLY: Tanisha sees her 5-year-old son, Toby, talking out loud to himself while he plays. She wonders whether she should discourage this behavior. Use Vygotsky's theory to explain why Toby talks to himself. How would you advise Tanisha?

_____

_____

_____

_____

CONNECT: Are intersubjectivity and scaffolding involved in *child-directed speech*, discussed on page 246 of Chapter 6? Explain.

_____

_____

_____

_____

REVIEW: What factors influence children's problem-solving strategies, and why do they follow an overlapping-waves pattern of development?

_____

_____

_____

_____

APPLY: Lena notices that her 4-year-old son Gregor recognizes his name in print and counts to twenty. She wonders why Gregor's preschool teacher permits him to spend so much time playing instead of teaching him academic skills. Gregor's teacher responds, "I am teaching him academics through play." Explain why play is the best way for preschoolers to develop academically.

_____

_____

_____

_____

CONNECT: Cite evidence on the development of memory, theory of mind, and literacy and mathematical understanding that is consistent with Vygotsky's sociocultural theory.

_____

_____

_____

_____

REVIEW: Describe differences between child-centered and academic preschools. What findings indicate that parents who want to foster their preschooler's academic development should choose a child-centered preschool?

_____

_____

_____

_____

APPLY: Senator Smith heard that IQ and achievement gains resulting from Head Start do not last, so he plans to vote against funding for the program. Write a letter to Senator Smith explaining why he should support Head Start.

_____

_____

_____

_____

REFLECT: What TV programs did you watch as a child? How do you think they affected your play and learning?

_____

_____

_____

_____

REVIEW: What can adults do to support language development in early childhood? Provide a list of recommendations, noting research that supports each.

_____

_____

_____

_____

APPLY: One day, Jason's mother explained to him that the family would take a vacation in Miami. The next morning, Jason emerged from his room with belongings spilling out of a suitcase and remarked, "I gotted my bag packed. When are we going to Your-ami?" What do Jason's errors reveal about his approach to mastering language?

_____

_____

_____

_____

CONNECT: Explain how children's strategies for word learning support the inter-actionist perspective on language development, described on page 241 of Chapter 6.

_____

_____

_____

_____

SUGGESTED STUDENT READINGS

Barnett, D. W., Bell, S. H., & Carey, K. T. (1999). *Designing preschool interventions: A practitioner's guide.* New York: The Guilford Press. Written primarily for school practitioners, special education teachers, and early childhood educators, this book examines a variety of preschool interventions available to children with learning and behavioral difficulties. Also includes guidelines for conducting assessments, practical approaches to evaluating intervention outcomes, and legal and ethical concerns.

Berk, L. E., & Winsler, A. (1995). *Scaffolding children's learning: Vygotsky and early childhood education.* Washington, DC: National Association for the Education of Young Children. Written in an easy-to-read style, this book presents the main principles of Vygotsky's theory. Focuses on educational applications of Vygotsky's theory.

Bloom, P. (2000). *How children learn the meanings of words.* Cambridge, MA: The MIT Press. Examines the dynamic cognitive processes involved in the acquisition of word meaning. The author argues that learning new words, even simple nouns, requires complex interactions between the child's conceptual, social, and linguistic capacities.

Kinder, M. (Ed.). (2000). *Kids' media culture.* Durham, NC: Duke University Press. Explores the effects of children's media on development. Also compares the books, cartoons, and television shows of the 1950s and 1960s with today's mass media. Finally, this book addresses concerns with television in schools and how various forms of mass media communicate messages about gender and socialization.

Saracho, O. N., & Spodek, B. (Eds.). (1998). *Multiple perspectives on play in early childhood education.* Albany, NY: State University of New York Press. A collection of chapters addressing theory and research on the role of play in learning and development. Also includes useful information about incorporating play into classroom activities.

PUZZLE TERM REVIEW

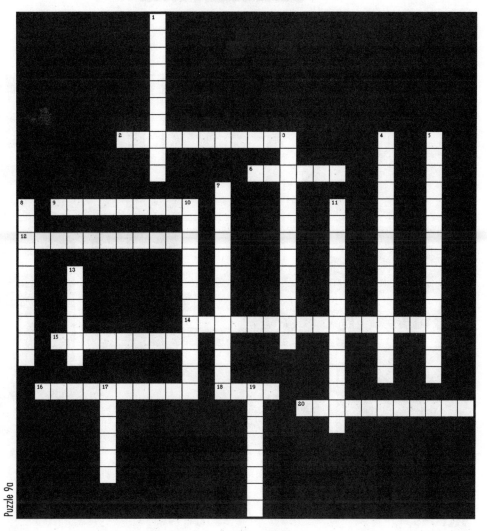

Puzzle 9a

Across

2. The inability to distinguish the symbolic viewpoints of others from one's own.
6. Infantile _____ is the most severe behavior disorder of childhood.
9. _____ thinking refers to the belief that inanimate objects have lifelike qualities.
12. The ability to tell whether a stimulus is the same as or similar to one you have seen before
14. _____ memory: representations of one-time events that are particularly meaningful in terms of the life story that each of us creates about ourselves.
15. Federal program that provides low-SES children with a year or two of preschool, along with nutritional and medical services
16. The tendency to focus on one aspect of a situation and neglect other important features
18. _____ representation: representation of a symbolic object as both an object in its own right and a symbol
20. A changing quality of support over the course of a teaching session in which the adult adjusts the assistance provided to fit the child's current level of performance.

Down

1. Mental representations of actions that obey logical rules
3. Thinking about thought
4. States rather than _____: the tendency to treat the initial and final states in a problem as completely unrelated
5. The inability to mentally go through a series of steps and then reverse direction, returning to the starting point
7. Preschools in which the teacher provides a variety of activities from which children select; most of the day is devoted to free play
8. _____ bound: being easily distracted by the concrete, perceptual appearance of objects
10. The understanding that certain physical features of an object remain the same, even when their outward appearance changes
11. Piaget's second stage; marked by rapid growth in representation
13. _____ participation calls attention to adult and child contributions to cooperative dialogue.
17. Requires that the child generate a mental image of an absent stimulus
19. Preschools in which the teacher structures the program, training children in academic skills

PUZZLE TERM REVIEW

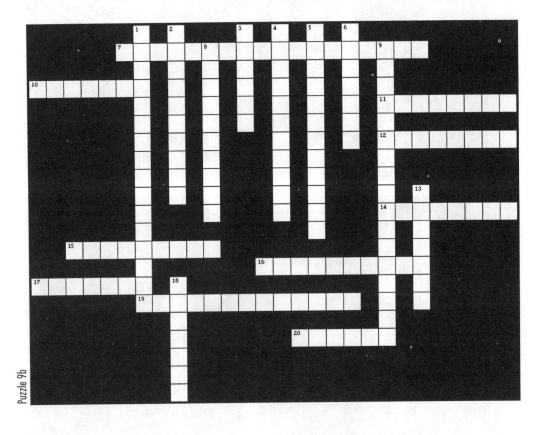

Puzzle 9b

Across

7. Application of regular grammatical rules to words that are exceptions
10. The way words are combined into meaningful phrases and sentences
11. Memory for everyday experiences
12. _____ bootstrapping: Figuring out grammatical rules by relying on word meanings
14. _____ literacy refers to young children's active efforts to construct literacy knowledge through informal experiences
15. _____ bootstrapping: figuring out word meanings by observing how words are used in the structure of sentences
16. The practical, social side of language that is concerned with how to engage in effective and appropriate communication with others
17. _____ speech: self-directed speech that children use to plan and guide their behavior
19. Make-believe play with others
20. _____ strategies: deliberate mental activities that improve the likelihood of remembering

Down

1. _____ theory: theory of problem-solving, which states that children generate a variety of strategies on challenging problems and gradually select those that result in rapid, accurate solutions (2 words)
2. Principle specifying order relationships between quantities
3. Principle of _____ exclusivity: assumption by children in the early stages of vocabulary growth that words mark entirely separate (nonoverlapping) categories
4. Principle stating that the last number in a counting sequence indicates the quantity of items in the set
5. _____ classification: organization of objects into classes and subclasses based on similarities and differences between groups
6. Fast _____ involves connecting a new word with an underlying concept after only a brief encounter.
8. Adult responses that elaborate on a child's utterance, increasing its complexity
9. Process whereby two participants who begin a task with different understandings arrive at a shared understanding
13. Adult responses that restructure children's incorrect speech into a more appropriate form
18. General descriptions of what occurs and when it occurs in a particular situation

SELF-TEST

1. As children move from the sensorimotor to the preoperational stage, the most obvious change is: (324)

   a. an increase in the child's use of senses and movements to explore the world.
   b. development of the capacity for abstract, scientific reasoning.
   c. an increase in mental representation.
   d. more logical, flexible, and organized thought.

2. Sociodramatic play refers to: (325)

   a. make-believe play directed toward the self.
   b. make-believe play with others.
   c. play that is closely linked to the real-life conditions associated with it.
   d. make-believe play involving complex schema combinations.

3. Before age 3, children have difficulty with _____, or viewing a symbolic object as both an object in is own right and a symbol. (326)

   a. dual representation
   b. sensorimotor relations
   c. hypothetical reasoning
   d. objectivity

4. According to Piaget, the most serious deficiency of preoperational thinking is: (327)

   a. egocentrism.
   b. animistic thinking.
   c. centration.
   d. intersubjectivity.

5. Conservation refers to: (328)

   a. children's tendency to focus on one aspect of a situation and neglect other important features.
   b. mental representation of actions that obey logical rules.
   c. the tendency to treat the initial and final states of a problem as completely unrelated.
   d. the notion that certain physical characteristics of objects remain the same, even when their outward appearance changes.

6. Which of the following is NOT true? (334)

   a. If researchers give preschoolers Piaget's original tasks, they perform as poorly as Piaget suggested.
   b. If Piagetian tasks are modified to represent more familiar information, preschoolers demonstrate more advanced cognitive capacities than Piaget predicted.
   c. Research shows that logical operations emerge suddenly when children reach school age.
   d. Preschool children's logical reasoning skills are not as well developed as those of school-age children.

7. A teacher in a Piagetian-based preschool wants to foster her students' cognitive development. Based on the educational principles derived from Piaget's theory, what would she do in order to accomplish this goal? (336)

    a. present verbal lessons on a variety of subject areas
    b. promote children's self-paced discovery by providing a variety of materials and play areas
    c. frequently evaluate children's educational performance through comparison with same-age peers
    d. plan activities for the total class rather than for individuals or small groups in order to minimalize individual differences

8. How did Piaget's view of children's private speech differ from that of Vygotsky? (337)

    a. Piaget thought that private speech resulted from children's inability to take the perspective of others, while Vygotsky reasoned that children use private speech for self-guidance.
    b. Piaget viewed private speech as the foundation for all complex mental activities, while Vygotsky regarded private speech as nonsocial, senseless utterances.
    c. Vygotsky concluded that private speech is ineffective and uncommunicative, and Piaget did not study this phenomenon.
    d. Vygotsky stressed the importance of private speech during early childhood, whereas Piaget discussed the utility of private speech over the course of the lifespan.

9. Scaffolding is: (338)

    a. a concept that calls attention to adult and child contributions to a cooperative dialogue without specifying the precise features of communication.
    b. the process whereby participants who begin a task with different understandings arrive at a shared understanding.
    c. a range of tasks that a child cannot yet perform alone but can do with the assistance of more skilled partners.
    d. a changing quality of social support over the course of a teaching session in which the adult adjusts the assistance provided to fit the child's current level of performance.

10. Vygotskian classrooms promote: (339)

    a. children's self-paced discovery through spontaneous interaction with the environment.
    b. passive student participation in teacher-led activities.
    c. highly structured, large group lessons teaching concrete concepts and skills.
    d. assisted discovery in which teachers guide children's learning.

11. During early childhood, attention becomes more: (341)

    a. planful.
    b. fleeting.
    c. disorderly.
    d. effortful.

12. _____ memory requires that the child generate a mental image of an absent stimulus. (342)

    a. Recognition
    b. Recall
    c. Retrospective
    d. Reflective

13. Preschoolers remember familiar events in terms of _____, or general descriptions of what occurs and when it occurs in a particular situation. (342)

    a. schemas
    b. scripts
    c. plots
    d. recasts

14. Preschoolers' understanding of mental activities is known as: (344)

    a. egocentrism.
    b. reflective thought.
    c. metacognition.
    d. intersubjectivity.

15. Which of the following most accurately describes preschoolers' theory of mind? (346)

    a. Preschoolers understand that people have an internal mental life but view the mind as a passive container of information.
    b. Preschoolers focus on the process of thinking but fail to recognize the outcomes of thought.
    c. Preschoolers view the mind as an active, constructive agent.
    d. Preschoolers do not yet show an understanding of mental activities.

16. Which of the following is true? (346)

    a. Preschoolers do not understand much about written language until they learn to read and write.
    b. Preschoolers have a great deal of understanding about written language long before they learn to read and write.
    c. Since written language lacks meaning for preschool-age children, they typically do not attend to it.
    d. Preschoolers demonstrate a simultaneous understanding of the names of letters and their corresponding sounds.

17. Between ages 4 and 5, children grasp the principle of _____; that is, they understand that the last number in a counting sequence indicates the quantity of items in the set. (349)

    a. cardinality
    b. ordinality
    c. addition
    d. centration

18. Which of the following is NOT true? (350-351)
    a. Early childhood intelligence tests sample both verbal and nonverbal abilities.
    b. By age 5 to 6, children's intelligence test scores are good predictors of later intelligence and academic achievement.
    c. Intelligence tests do not sample the full range of human abilities.
    d. Most intelligence tests are constructed such that culture exerts little influence on performance.

19. Longitudinal studies have found that children who attend Head Start Programs: (352)
    a. do not evidence any gains in IQ or academic achievement when compared to a control group of similar children who did not attend Head Start.
    b. evidence higher IQ and academic achievement during early elementary school when compared to a control group of similar children who did not attend Head Start but show declining test scores after that time.
    c. exhibit permanent gains in IQ and academic achievement.
    d. are just as likely as other low-SES children to be placed in a special education program or to be retained in grade.

20. Research suggests that children who watch *Sesame Street*: (354-355)
    a. score higher on tests designed to measure the program's learning goals.
    b. experience only minimal, short-term gains in academic achievement.
    c. display less elaborate make-believe play.
    d. score significantly higher than other children on childhood intelligence tests.

21. Which of the following is NOT one of the four factors that are especially important in determining child care quality? (355)
    a. group size
    b. home-based versus center-based
    c. caregiver/child ratio
    d. caregiver's educational experience

22. Young children are able to build their vocabularies extremely quickly because they can connect a new word to an underlying concept after only a brief encounter, a process called: (356)
    a. word linking.
    b. conceptual bootstrapping.
    c. fast mapping.
    d. syntactic mapping.

23. Which of the following is NOT true of preschoolers' grammatical development? (357)
    a. Children age 2 to 3 have not yet acquired the subject-object-verb word order used in adult speech.
    b. Once children acquire grammatical rules, they apply them so consistently that they often overextend rules to words that are exceptions.
    c. Preschoolers cling to consistent word order, and, consequently, they have difficulty forming questions and understanding passive sentences.
    d. Children master grammatical rules in a regular sequence, starting with the simple and moving to the complex.

24. The practical, social side of language that is concerned with how to engage in effective and appropriate communication with others is called: (359)

   a. semantics.
   b. syntax.
   c. pragmatics.
   d. grammar.

25. Young Colleen says, "I go school, too." Her mother says, "Yes, you are going to school, too." Her mother's response would be classified as: (360)

   a. repetition and correction.
   b. correction and reflection.
   c. rejection and restatement.
   d. expansion and recast.

CHAPTER 10

EMOTIONAL AND SOCIAL DEVELOPMENT IN EARLY CHILDHOOD

Chapter Summary

Erikson's stage of initiative versus guilt offers an overview of the personality changes of early childhood. During the preschool years, children's self-concepts begin to take shape. Their self-esteem is high, which supports their enthusiasm for mastering new skills. Preschoolers' understanding of emotion, emotional self-regulation, capacity to experience self-conscious emotions, and capacity for empathy and sympathy improve. Cognition, language, and warm, sensitive parenting support these developments.

During the preschool years, peer interaction increases, cooperative play becomes common, and children form first friendships. Preschoolers learn to resolve conflicts with new social problem-solving skills. Peer relations are influenced by parental encouragement quality of sibling ties. Peers provide an important context for the development of a wide range of social skills.

Three approaches to understanding early childhood morality-psychoanalytic, behaviorist and social learning, and cognitive-developmental-emphasize different aspects of moral functioning. While most researchers now disagree with Freud's account of conscience development, the power of inductive discipline is recognized. Social learning theorists believe that children learn to act morally through modeling. A third voice, the cognitive-developmental perspective, regards children as active thinkers about social rules. Hostile family atmospheres, poor parenting practices, and heavy viewing of violent television promote childhood aggression, which can spiral into serious antisocial activity.

Gender typing develops rapidly over the preschool years. Heredity contributes to several aspects of gender-typed behavior, but environmental forces — parents, siblings, teachers, peers, television, and the broader social environment — play powerful roles. Neither cognitive-developmental theory nor social learning theory provides a complete account of the development of gender identity. Gender schema theory is an information-processing approach that shows how environmental pressures and children's cognition combine to affect gender-role development.

Compared to children of authoritarian and permissive parents, children whose parents use an authoritative style are especially well adjusted and socially mature. Warmth, explanations, and reasonable demands for mature behavior account for the effectiveness of the authoritative style. Ethnic groups often have distinct child-rearing beliefs and practices that are adaptive when viewed in light of cultural values and the circumstances in which parents and children live.

Child maltreatment is the combined result of factors within the family, community, and larger culture. Interventions at all of these levels are essential for preventing it.

LEARNING OBJECTIVES

After reading this chapter, you should be able to:

10.1 Describe Erikson's initiative versus guilt stage, noting how this psychological conflict impacts children's emotional and social development. (366-367)

10.2 Discuss preschool children's self-development, including characteristics of self-concept, ability to understand intentions, and emergence of self-esteem. (367-370)

10.3 Describe changes in the understanding of emotion during early childhood, noting achievements and limitations. (370-372)

10.4 Explain how language and temperament contribute to the development of emotional self-regulation during the preschool years, and discuss ways in which adults can help young children manage common fears of early childhood. (372-373)

10.5 Discuss the development of self-conscious emotions, empathy, and sympathy during early childhood, noting how various parenting styles affect emotional development in these areas. (372-374)

10.6 Describe advances in peer sociability over the preschool years, with particular attention to the types of play outlined by Mildred Parten, and discuss cultural variations in peer sociability. (375-376)

10.7 Describe the quality of preschoolers' first friendships, noting how parents and siblings influence early peer relations, and discuss the emergence of social problem solving during early childhood. (377-379)

10.8 Compare psychoanalytic, behaviorist and social learning, and cognitive-developmental perspectives of moral development (380-385)

10.9 Trace milestones in preschoolers' understanding of morality, and discuss the importance of social experience in the development of moral understanding. (380-385)

10.10 Describe the development of aggression in early childhood, noting the influences of family and television, and cite ways to control aggressive behavior. (385-390)

10.11 Describe preschoolers' gender-stereotyped beliefs and behaviors, and discuss genetic and environmental influences on gender-role development. (390-393)

10.12 Describe and evaluate the major theories of gender identity development, and cite ways to reduce gender stereotyping in young children. (393-396)

10.13 Describe the four styles of child rearing, indicating which is most effective, and discuss cultural variations in child-rearing beliefs and practices. (396-398)

10.14 Describe the five forms of child maltreatment, and discuss factors associated with child maltreatment, consequences of child maltreatment, and strategies for the prevention of child maltreatment. (399-402)

STUDY QUESTIONS

Erikson's Theory: Initiative versus Guilt

1. Erikson regarded _____ as the critical psychological conflict of the preschool years. (366)

2. Define *initiative* and describe how it is exhibited in preschoolers. (366)

_____

_____

_____

_____

3. Erikson regarded _____ as the central means through which children find out about themselves and their social world. Explain why this is the case. (366)

_____

_____

_____

4. Compare Erikson's theory of development during the preschool years with that of Freud. (366)

_____

_____

_____

_____

5. According to Erikson, what leads to a negative resolution of the initiative versus guilt stage? (366)

_____

_____

_____

Self-Development

1. What is a *self-concept*? (367)

_____

_____

2. Describe the quality of preschoolers' self-descriptions. (367)

_____

_____

_____

_____

3. Explain the link between preschoolers' self-development and their possessiveness of objects. Given this, how can adults promote friendly peer interaction? (367)

_____

_____

_____

_____

4. Using the following ages as a guide, trace the development of preschoolers' ability to separate intentional from accidental behaviors. (369)

Age 2: _____

_____

Age 2-1/2 - 3: _____

_____

Age 4: _____

_____

Age 5: _____

_____

5. Discuss factors that contribute to the acquisition of preschoolers' understanding of intention. (369)

_____

_____

_____

_____

6. _____ refers to judgments we make about our own worth and the feelings associated with those judgments. (369)

7. True or False: When making self-evaluations, preschoolers tend to rate their own ability as extremely low and often overestimate task difficulty. (369)

8. Discuss at least three ways to foster a healthy self-image in young children. (370)

A. _____

_____

B. _____

_____

C. _____

_____

Cultural Influences: Cultural Variations in Personal Storytelling — Implications for Early Self-Concept

1. Based on the ethnographic research of Peggy Miller, discuss differences in storytelling practices between Chinese and Irish-American parents, and explain the influence on children's self-image. (368)

_____

_____

_____

_____

Emotional Development

1. Early in the preschool years, children refer to _____, _____, and _____ of emotion, and over time their understanding improves in accuracy and complexity. (371)

2. True or False: When explaining emotion, preschoolers are likely to emphasize external factors rather than internal states. (371)

3. Discuss several ways in which preschoolers demonstrate emotional understanding. (371)

_____

_____

_____

_____

4. List two limitations of young children's emotional understanding. (371)

A. _____

_____

B. _____

_____

5. Discussions in which family members (agree/disagree) about their feelings are particularly helpful in improving preschoolers' emotional understanding. Briefly explain your answer. (371)

_____

_____

_____

6. Discuss four factors that affect the development of emotional self-regulation in preschoolers. (372)

A. _____

_____

B. _____

_____

C. _____

_____

D. _____

_____

7. Explain why children experience self-conscious emotions more often during the preschool years than they did as toddlers. (372-373)

_____

_____

_____

8. Beginning in early childhood, _____ is associated with feelings of personal inadequacy and is linked with maladjustment. In contrast, _____, as long as it occurs in appropriate circumstances, is related to positive adjustment, perhaps because it helps children resist harmful impulses. (373)

9. Distinguish between *empathy* and *sympathy*. (373-374)

_____

_____

_____

_____

10. Empathy serves as an important motivator of _____ behavior, or actions that benefit another person without any expected reward for the self. (373)

11. In some children, empathizing with an upset adult or peer escalates into _____. How do these children typically respond? (374)

_____

12. Discuss the impact of parenting on children's development of empathy and sympathy. (374)

_____

_____

_____

_____

Peer Relations

1. Describe Parten's three-step sequence of social development. (375)

   A. _____

   _____

   B. _____

   _____

   C.1 _____

   _____

   C.2 _____

   _____

2. Evaluate the accuracy of this sequence based on current research. (375-376)

   _____

   _____

   _____

3. Recent findings demonstrate that it is the _____, rather than the _____, of solitary and parallel play that change during early childhood. (375)

4. True or False: High rates of nonsocial activity during the preschool years is a sign of maladjustment. (375-376)

5. List three ways in which sociodramatic play contributes to cognitive and social development. (376)

   A. _____

   B. _____

   C. _____

6. Explain how peer sociability in collectivist societies differs from that in Western individualistic cultures. (376)

_____

_____

_____

_____

7. Summarize children's understanding of friendship in early childhood. (377)

_____

_____

_____

8. Summarize the unique quality of preschoolers' interactions with friends. (377)

_____

_____

_____

9. List the six steps in Crick and Dodge's social problem-solving model. (378)

A. _____

B. _____

C. _____

D. _____

E. _____

F. _____

10. Discuss how social problem solving affects peer relations. (378)

_____

_____

_____

11. List three ways that parents influence their children's social relations. (379)

A. _____

B. _____

C. _____

Foundations of Morality

1. State the general direction of moral growth on which most theories agree. (380)

   _____

   _____

2. Match each of the following major theories of moral development with the aspect of moral functioning that it emphasizes: (380-385)

   _____ emotional side of conscience
   _____ ability to reason about justice and fairness
   _____ moral behavior

   1. Behaviorism
   2. Psychoanalytic theory
   3. Cognitive-developmental theory

3. True or False: Most researchers agree with Freud's assertion that fear of punishment and loss of parental love motivates children to behave morally. (380)

4. A special type of discipline called _____ supports conscience formation. Explain how it does so. (380)

   _____

   _____

   _____

5. According to the traditional behaviorist perspective, children start to behave in accord with adult moral standards because parents and teachers _____ "good behavior." (381)

6. Explain why operant conditioning is insufficient for children to acquire moral responses. (381)

   _____

   _____

   _____

7. Social learning theorists believe that children learn to act morally through

_____. (381-382)

8. List three characteristics of models that affect children's willingness to imitate them. (382-383)

A. _____

B. _____

C. _____

9. True or False: Punishment promotes immediate compliance but does not produce long-lasting changes in children's behavior. (383)

10. List three undesirable side effects of harsh punishment. (383)

A. _____

B. _____

C. _____

11. List two alternatives to harsh punishment. (383)

A. _____

B. _____

12. Describe three ways that parents can increase the effectiveness of punishment when they do decide to use it. (383-384)

A. _____

_____

B. _____

_____

C. _____

_____

13. Explain *positive discipline*, noting how it reduces the need for punishment. (384)

_____

_____

_____

14. In what major way does the cognitive-developmental perspective of morality differ from the psychodynamic and behaviorist approaches? (384)

_____

_____

_____

15. Preschoolers are able to distinguish _____, which protect people's rights and welfare, from two other forms of action: _____, or customs such as table manners and dress style, and _____, which do not violate rights and are up to the individual. (384-385)

16. According to cognitive-developmental theorists, how do preschoolers learn to make the distinctions described above in question 15? (385)

_____

_____

_____

_____

17. List three features of parent communication that help children reason about morality. (385)

A. _____

B. _____

C. _____

18. By the end of the preschool years, two general types of aggression emerge. The most common is _____ aggression, aimed at obtaining an object, privilege, or space with no deliberate intent to harm. The other type is _____ aggression, which is intended to hurt another person. (385)

19. Distinguish between overt aggression and relational aggression. (385)

_____

_____

20. Discuss developmental and sex differences in aggression throughout the preschool years. (385-386)

Developmental: _____

_____

_____

Sex: _____

_____

_____

21. Explain how a hostile family atmosphere promotes and sustains high rates of child-hood aggression. (386-387)

_____

_____

_____

_____

_____

22. True or False: Girls are more likely than boys to be targets of harsh physical discipline and parental inconsistency. (386)

23. True or False: Violent content in children's programming occurs at above average rates, and cartoons are the most violent. (387)

24. Explain why young children are especially likely to be influenced by television. (387)

_____

_____

_____

25. Describe the short- and long-term effects of TV violence on children's behavior. (388)

_____

_____

_____

_____

26. List several ways to help parents and children break the cycle of hostilities between family members. (389-390)

A. _____

_____

B. _____

_____

C. _____

_____

Biology and Environment: Temperament and Conscience Development in Young Children

1. Identify parenting practices that best promote moral development in children with the following temperament styles: (382)

Inhibited: _____

_____

Impulsive: _____

_____

2. In nonanxious children, _____ predicts conscience development. (382)

Social Issues: Education Regulating Children's Television

1. _____ has made the federal government reluctant to place limits on television content. Instead of regulatory control, the government now requires at least three hours per week of _____ for children. (388)

2. Why is the V-Chip an incomplete solution for regulating children's TV? (388)

_____

_____

_____

3. List several strategies parents can use to monitor and control children's TV viewing. (389)

A. _____

B. _____

C. _____

Gender Typing

1. Define *gender typing*. (390)

_____

_____

2. Describe preschoolers' gender-stereotyped beliefs and behavior. (391)

_____

_____

_____

_____

3. True or False: Over the preschool years, children's gender-stereotyped beliefs become stronger. (391)

4. True or False: Most preschoolers believe that characteristics associated with each sex (for example, clothes, hairstyles, occupation) determine whether a person is male or female. (391)

5. Discuss Eleanor Maccoby's argument that hormonal differences between males and females have important consequences for gender typing, including play styles evidenced in early childhood. (391)

_____

_____

_____

_____

6. Describe ways in which parents encourage gender-stereotyped beliefs and behavior in their children. (392)

_____

_____

_____

_____

_____

7. True or False: Fathers are more likely to engage in differential treatment of boys and girls than are mothers. (392)

8. Of the two sexes, (girls/boys) are clearly more gender-stereotyped. Why might this be the case? (392)

_____

_____

_____

9. Discuss gender typing in the classroom setting, noting its impact on social behaviors. (392)

_____

_____

_____

10. Describe the influence of peers on preschoolers' gender-stereotyped beliefs and behaviors. (393)

_____

_____

_____

11. True or False: TV gender roles are especially stereotypic in entertainment programs for children and adolescents. (393)

12. Define *gender identity* and indicate how it is measured. (393)

_____

_____

13. _____ refers to a type of gender identity in which the person
    scores highly on both typically masculine and typically feminine personality
    characteristics. (393)

14. How is gender identity related to psychological adjustment? (394)

_____

_____

_____

15. Contrast social learning and cognitive-developmental accounts of the emergence
    of gender identity. (394)

    Social Learning: _____

    _____

    _____

    Cognitive-Developmental: _____

    _____

    _____

16. Discuss the development of gender constancy in young children. (394)

_____

_____

_____

17. _____ theory is an information-processing approach to
    gender typing that combines social learning and cognitive-developmental features.
    (394)

18. What are *gender schemas*? (394)

_____

_____

19. Explain how gender schemas influence gender-typed preferences and behavior. (394-395)

_____

_____

_____

20. Cite several ways that parents can reduce gender stereotyping in young children. (395-396)

_____

_____

_____

_____

Child Rearing and Emotional and Social Development

1. Name and describe the two dimensions of parenting that emerged from Baumrind's observations of parents interacting with their preschoolers. (396)

A. _____

_____

B. _____

_____

2. Describe the four styles of child rearing, and note the relationship of each to child outcomes. (396-397)

Authoritative: _____

_____

_____

_____

Authoritarian: _____

_____

_____

_____

Permissive: _____

_____

_____

_____

Uninvolved: _____

_____

_____

_____

3. _____ child rearing is a rational, democratic approach that recognizes and respects the rights of both parents and children. (396)

4. At its extreme, uninvolved parenting is a form of child maltreatment called _____. (397)

5. Cite four reasons that authoritative parenting is especially effective. (397-398)

A. _____

_____

B. _____

_____

C. _____

_____

D. _____

_____

6. Describe how the parenting practices of the following cultural groups often differ from those of Caucasian Americans. (398)

Chinese: _____

_____

Hispanic and Asian Pacific Island: _____

_____

African-American:_____

_____

7. List and describe five forms of child maltreatment. (399)

   A. _____

   _____

   B. _____

   _____

   C. _____

   _____

   D. _____

   _____

   E. _____

   _____

8. For help in understanding child maltreatment, researchers turned to
   _____ theory. (400)

9. List parent, child, and general family characteristics associated with an increased
   likelihood of abuse. (400)

   Parent: _____

   _____

   _____

   Child: _____

   _____

   _____

   Family: _____

   _____

   _____

10. List two reasons that most abusive parents are isolated from supportive ties to their communities. (401)

A. _____

_____

B. _____

_____

11. Societies that view violence as an appropriate way to solve problems set the stage for child abuse. These conditions (do/do not) exist in the United States. (401)

12. True or False: Over 90 percent of American parents report at least occasional use of slaps and spanking to discipline their children. (401)

13. Summarize the consequences of child maltreatment for abused children. (401)

_____

_____

_____

_____

14. Discuss strategies for preventing child maltreatment. (401-402)

_____

_____

_____

_____

APPLY: Reread the description of Sammy and Mark's argument at the beginning of this chapter. On the basis of what you know about self-development, why was it a good idea for Leslie to resolve the dispute by providing an extra set of beanbags so that both boys could play at once?

_____

_____

_____

_____

CONNECT: Around age 4, children understand intention as a mental state. How is this advance similar to children's mastery of false belief (see Chapter 9, page 346)? Are experiences that promote understanding of intention similar to those that foster a grasp of false belief? Explain.

_____

_____

_____

_____

REVIEW: What do preschoolers understand about emotion, and how do cognition and social experience contribute to their understanding?

_____

_____

_____

_____

APPLY: Four-year-old Tia had just gotten her face painted at a carnival. As she walked around with her mother, the heat of the afternoon caused her balloon to pop. When Tia started to cry, her mother said, "Oh, Tia, balloons aren't such a good idea when it's hot outside. We'll get another on a cooler day. If you cry, you'll mess up your beautiful face painting." What aspect of emotional development is Tia's mother trying to promote, and why is her intervention likely to help Tia?

_____

_____

_____

_____

CONNECT: Explain why good emotional self-regulation is vital for empathy to result in sympathetic concern and prosocial behavior. How can parents promote emotional self-regulation, empathy, and sympathy at the same time?

_____

_____

_____

_____

REVIEW: Among children who spend much time playing alone, what factors distinguish those who are more likely to have adjustment difficulties from those who are well-adjusted and socially skilled?

_____

_____

_____

_____

APPLY: Three-year-old Bart lives in the country, with no other preschoolers nearby. His parents wonder whether it is worth driving Bart into town once a week to play with his 3-year-old cousin. What advice would you give Bart's parents, and why?

_____

_____

_____

_____

CONNECT: Illustrate the influence of temperament on social problem solving by explaining how an impulsive child and a shy, inhibited child might respond at each social problem-solving step in Figure 10.1 on page 378.

_____

_____

_____

_____

REFLECT: Think back to your earliest friendship. How old were you? What did you and your friend like to do, and how would you describe the quality of your relationship?

_____

_____

_____

_____

REVIEW: Cite a major difference between the cognitive-developmental and the psychoanalytic and behaviorist perspectives on moral development. How do preschoolers distinguish between moral imperatives, social conventions, and matters of personal choice? Why are these distinctions important for moral development?

_____

_____

_____

_____

APPLY: Nanette told her 3-year-old son Darren not to go into the front yard without asking, since the house faces a very busy street. Darren disobeyed several times, and now Nanette thinks it's time to punish him. How would you recommend that Nanette discipline Darren, and why?

_____

_____

_____

_____

REFLECT: Did you display a strong, internalized conscience as a child? How do you think temperament, parenting practices, and TV viewing affected your childhood moral maturity?

_____

_____

_____

_____

REVIEW: Cite biological, social, and cognitive influences on sex segregation in children's peer associations.

_____

_____

_____

_____

APPLY: When 4-year-old Roger was in the hospital, he was cared for by a male nurse named Jared. After Roger recovered, he told his friends about Dr. Jared. Using gender schema theory, explain why Roger remembered Jared as a doctor, not a nurse.

_____

_____

_____

_____

REFLECT: Think back to storybooks you read and TV shows you watched as a child. Was their content gender stereotyped? Examine children's books at your local bookstore and watch some children's TV shows. Do you think portrayals of gender have changed? Cite examples.

_____

_____

_____

_____

REVIEW: Summarize findings on ethnic variations in child-rearing styles. Is the concept of authoritative parenting useful for understanding effective parenting across cultures? Explain.

_____

_____

_____

_____

APPLY: Chandra heard a news report that ten severely neglected children, living in squalor in an inner-city tenement, were discovered by Chicago police. Chandra thought to herself, "What could possibly lead parents to mistreat their children so badly?" How would you answer Chandra's question?

_____

_____

_____

_____

CONNECT: Which child-rearing style is most likely to be associated with use of inductive discipline, and why?

_____

_____

_____

_____

REFLECT: How would you classify your parents' child-rearing styles? What factors might have influenced their approach to child rearing?

_____

_____

_____

_____

SUGGESTED STUDENT READINGS

Berk, L. E. (Ed.). (1999). *Landscapes of development: An anthology of readings.* Belmont, CA: Wadsworth. A collection of current reviews of research and essays by internationally recognized scholars and expert practitioners, each of which discusses applications to children's lives. An especially strong section on early childhood emotional and social development includes such topics as intersubjectivity in caregiver-child communication, young children's understanding of everyday emotions, discipline, bicultural development, and parent involvement in child protection programs.

Harris, J. R. (1998). *The nurture assumption: Why children turn out the way they do.* New York: The Free Press. Provides an alternative account of childhood personality development, maintaining that a child's personality is shaped, not by his or her parents, but by experiences outside of the home. The author carefully focuses on the influence of peer interactions in the development of personality.

Hoffman, M. L. (2000). *Empathy and moral development: Implications for caring and justice.* New York: Cambridge University Press. Presents a comprehensive approach to studying and understanding moral development in young children. The author also examines the psychological processes involved in the development of empathy and altruism across a variety of situations.

Wolfe, D. A. (1999). *Child abuse: Implications for child development and psychopathology* (2nd Ed.). Thousand Oaks, CA: Sage Publications, Inc. Drawing on current research, the author discusses the long-term consequences of child abuse, particularly the impact of different types of child abuse on emotional, cognitive, academic, and social development.

Yelland, N. (Ed.). (1998). *Gender in early childhood.* New York: Routledge. For those interested in early childhood education, this book explores the development of gender identity and its impact on peer relations. Also reviews the influence of popular culture on children's perceptions of themselves and others.

PUZZLE TERM REVIEW

Puzzle 10a

Across

6. Aggression aimed at obtaining an object, privilege, or space with no intent to harm
8. Judgments we make about our own self-worth and the feeling associated with those judgments (2 words)
10. Gender _____: understanding that sex remains the same even if outward appearance changes
12. Play with others directed toward a common goal
14. A form of hostile aggression that does damage to another's peer relationships
16. _____ problem solving: resolving conflicts in ways that are both acceptable to others and beneficial to the self

Down

1. Aggression intended to harm another person
2. Moral _____ protect people's rights and welfare.
3. Social _____ are customs such as table manners and dress styles.
4. A form of hostile aggression that harms another through physical injury or the threat or such injury
5. _____ theory: approach to gender typing that combines social learning and cognitive-developmental features (2 words)
7. Play involving separate activities but exchange of toys and comments
9. Set of attributes, abilities, attitudes, and values that individuals believe define who they are (2 words)
11. Activity involving unoccupied, onlooker behavior and solitary play
13. Play that occurs near other children with similar materials but involves no interaction
15. Type of discipline communicating the effects of the child's misbehavior on others

Puzzle 10b

244

Across

1. Mild punishment involving removal of the child from the immediate setting until he/she is ready to behave appropriately (2 words)
4. Physical _____: living conditions in which the child does not receive enough food, clothing, medical attention, or supervision
11. Gender identity in which the person scores high on both masculine and feminine personality traits
15. Child rearing style that is demanding and responsive
16. _____ abuse: assaults on children that produce pain and injury
17. _____ abuse: fondling, intercourse, and other forms of exploitation involving a child

Down

2. Child rearing style that is both undemanding and unresponsive
3. Gender _____: image of oneself as relatively masculine or feminine in characteristics
5. Child rearing style that is responsive but not demanding
6. Feeling with another person and responding emotionally in a similar way
7. Actions that benefit another person without any expected reward for the self are known as _____, or altruistic, behaviors.
8. _____ abuse: actions, such as ridicule, humiliation, scapegoating, or terrorizing, that damage children's cognitive, emotional, or social functioning
9. Child rearing style that is demanding but not responsive
10. Erikson regarded _____ *versus guilt* as the critical psychological conflict of the preschool years.
12. _____ neglect: failure to meet child's needs for affection and support
13. Feelings of concern or sorrow for another's plight
14. Gender _____: process of developing gender roles

SELF-TEST

1. According to Erikson, the critical psychological conflict of the preschool years is: (366)

    a. autonomy versus shame and doubt.
    b. trust versus mistrust.
    c. initiative versus guilt.
    d. industry versus inferiority.

2. Erikson regarded _____ as the central means through which children find out about themselves and their social world. (366)

    a. conflicts with peers
    b. interaction with adults
    c. play
    d. modeling

3. Preschoolers' self-concepts are: (367)

    a. concrete, typically focused on observable characteristics.
    b. abstract, usually centered on their unique psychological characteristics.
    c. internalized, since they cannot yet talk about their own subjective experiences.
    d. based on stable personality traits.

4. The high self-esteem characteristic of most preschoolers contributes to their developing sense of: (369)

    a. initiative.
    b. empathy.
    c. altruism.
    d. androgyny.

5. Which of the following is true with regard to emotional understanding in preschoolers? (371)

    a. Preschoolers emphasize internal states rather than external events when explaining another's emotions.
    b. Preschoolers are good at predicting what a playmate who is expressing a certain emotion might do next.
    c. Preschoolers are able to reconcile conflicting cues about how a person is feeling.
    d. Preschoolers recognize that people can experience more than one emotion at a time.

6. Empathy: (374)

    a. always promotes sympathetic, prosocial responding.
    b. is equally likely in all children, regardless of parental influence.
    c. leads to personal distress and self-focused responding in some children.
    d. is expressed more often by abused children than by their nonabused agemates.

7. In _____ play, a child plays near another child, with similar materials, but they do not interact. (375)

    a. nonsocial
    b. parallel
    c. associative
    d. cooperative

8. Recent research on peer interaction indicates that: (375)

   a. it is the *type*, rather than the *amount*, of play that changes during early childhood.
   b. Parten's play types emerge in a developmental sequence, with later-appearing ones replacing earlier ones.
   c. nonsocial activity among preschoolers is a sign of maladjustment.
   d. sociodramatic play declines during the preschool years.

9. Which of the following is NOT true of preschoolers' first friendships? (377)

   a. Preschoolers perceive friendship in concrete, activity-based terms such as pleasurable play and sharing of toys.
   b. During the preschool years, friends are more emotionally expressive with each other than with nonfriends.
   c. Preschoolers give much more reinforcement to children they identify as friends.
   d. Preschool-age children already have a notion of friendship as a long-term relationship based on mutual trust.

10. During the early school years, social problem solving: (378)

    a. is deficient in most children.
    b. is directed exclusively toward the child's own needs rather than the mutual needs of the self and others.
    c. is unrelated to socially competent behavior.
    d. profoundly affects peer relations.

11. A form of discipline known as _____ supports conscience formation by pointing out the effects of the child's misbehavior on others. (380)

    a. positive discipline
    b. induction
    c. punishment
    d. time out

12. Modeling of prosocial behavior: (383)

    a. is less effective than reinforcement in helping children acquire moral responses.
    b. has no long-term effects on children's behavior.
    c. exerts the greatest influence on children's behavior during the preschool years.
    d. is equally effective regardless of the model's characteristics.

13. The most effective form of discipline is: (384)

    a. withdrawal of privileges.
    b. time out.
    c. rewarding good conduct.
    d. punishment.

14. The _____ view of morality regards children as active thinkers about social rules. (384)

    a. psychoanalytic
    b. cognitive-developmental
    c. behaviorist
    d. social learning

15. _____ aggression, aimed at obtaining an object, privilege, or space with no deliberate intent to harm another person, is the most common form of aggression exhibited during the preschool years. (385)
    a. Hostile
    b. Overt
    c. Instrumental
    d. Relational

16. During the preschool years: (386)
    a. boys and girls display the same type and amount of aggression.
    b. girls are less aggressive than are boys.
    c. boys are more overtly aggressive, whereas girls are more relationally aggressive.
    d. aggressive behavior is highly atypical and is cause for great concern.

17. TV violence: (388)
    a. hardens children to aggression, making them more willing to tolerate it in others.
    b. teaches children that violence is socially unacceptable and has harsh negative consequences.
    c. is unlikely to increase violent behavior, even among highly aggressive children.
    d. is uncommon in children's programming, particularly cartoons.

18. The process of developing gender-linked preferences and behaviors valued by the larger society is called: (390)
    a. gender typing.
    b. gender intensification.
    c. gender identification.
    d. gender constancy.

19. Which of the following is NOT true of familial influences on gender typing? (392)
    a. Parents tend to reward active, assertive behavior in sons and dependent behavior in daughters.
    b. Mothers and fathers are equally likely to show differential treatment of boys and girls.
    c. Parents with nonstereotyped gender beliefs and behaviors have less gender-stereotyped children.
    d. Parents are less tolerant of cross-gender behavior in their sons than in their daughters.

20. Individuals who are androgynous: (393)
    a. display highly gender-stereotyped behavior.
    b. demonstrate mostly cross-gender behaviors.
    c. score highly on both masculine and feminine personality characteristics.
    d. have a poorly developed gender identity.

21. Gender schema theory: (394)
    a. stresses genetic influences on gender typing.
    b. emphasizes development of gender-stereotyped beliefs through identification with the same-sex parent.
    c. focuses on the role of modeling and reinforcement in gender identity development.
    d. emphasizes how environmental pressures and children's cognitions work together to shape gender-role development.

22. _____ child-rearing is marked by a rational, democratic approach that recognizes and respects the rights of both parents and children. (396)
    a. Authoritative
    b. Authoritarian
    c. Permissive
    d. Uninvolved

23. Which of the following outcomes are typically associated with children exposed to permissive parenting? (397)
    a. positive mood, high self-confidence and self-control, superior academic achievement
    b. anxiety, withdrawal, unhappiness
    c. immaturity, rebelliousness, dependence on adults, low persistence
    d. low tolerance for frustration, poor emotional control, school achievement difficulties, delinquency in adolescence

24. Which form of abuse is likely to be the most common, since it also accompanies most other types? (399)
    a. physical abuse
    b. psychological abuse
    c. emotional neglect
    d. physical neglect

25. Child maltreatment: (401)
    a. is rare in large, industrialized nations and has declined in recent years.
    b. is rooted in adult psychological disturbance, and therefore, abusers demonstrate an easily identifiable abusive personality type.
    c. is best understood from a social learning perspective.
    d. is associated with peer difficulties, academic failure, depression, substance abuse, and delinquency.

CHAPTER 11

PHYSICAL DEVELOPMENT IN MIDDLE CHILDHOOD

Chapter Summary

The slow gains in body growth that took place during the preschool years continue in middle childhood. Large individual differences in body size that are the combined result of heredity and environment remain apparent. Bones of the body lengthen and broaden, and primary teeth are replaced with permanent ones. Because of better nutrition and health care, children in industrialized nations are growing larger and reaching physical maturity earlier than they did in previous generations.

Although many children are at their healthiest in middle childhood, health problems do occur. Vision and hearing difficulties, malnutrition, obesity, nighttime bedwetting, asthma, and unintentional injuries are among the most frequent health concerns of the school years. School-age children can learn a wide range of health information, but it has little impact on their everyday behavior. Interventions must also provide them with healthier environments and consistently reward good health practices.

Growth in body size and muscle strength supports the refinement of many gross motor capacities in middle childhood. Gains in flexibility, balance, agility, force, and reaction time underlie improvements in children's gross motor skills. Fine motor coordination also increases. Children's writing becomes more legible, and their drawings show greater organization, more detail, and the addition of the depth dimension.

The physical activities of school-age children reflect advances in the quality of their play. Child-organized games with rules become common. These games support emotional and social development. Increasingly, children are participating in adult-oriented youth sports. Some researchers are concerned that this trend may have an adverse effect on development. Rough-and-tumble play and dominance hierarchies are features of children's interaction that reflect our evolutionary past. Wide individual differences in athletic performance exist that are influenced by both genetic and environmental factors. Physical education classes help ensure that all children have access to the benefits of regular exercise and play.

LEARNING OBJECTIVES

After reading this chapter, you should be able to:

11.1 Describe changes in body size, body proportions, and skeletal maturity during middle childhood, noting secular trends in physical growth. (410-413)

11.2 Describe brain development in middle childhood, including the influence of neurotransmitters and hormones. (413)

11.3 Identify common health problems in middle childhood, discuss their causes and consequences, and cite ways to alleviate them. (414-421)

11.4 Summarize findings on school-age children's concepts of health and illness, and indicate ways that parents and teachers can foster healthy lifestyles in school-age children. (422-424)

11.5 Cite major milestones of gross and fine motor development during middle childhood. (425-426)

11.6 Describe individual and group differences in motor performance during middle childhood. (427-428)

11.7 Describe qualities of children's play during middle childhood, including participation in adult-organized youth sports and engagement in rough-and-tumble play. (428-431)

11.8 Describe the state of physical education programs in most American schools, and discuss the importance of high-quality physical education during the school years. (431-432)

STUDY QUESTIONS

Body Growth

1. During middle childhood, children continue to add _____ inches in height and _____ pounds in weight each year. However, rather than occurring steadily, growth occurs in _____. (410)

2. Describe sex differences in body growth and proportions during middle childhood. (410)

_____

_____

_____

_____

3. Discuss factors that account for the vast differences in physical size among children around the world. (411)

_____

_____

_____

4. _____ trends in physical growth refer to changes in body size from one generation to the next. (412)

5. Research on secular growth patterns reveals that the larger size of today's children, as compared to children of previous generations, is mostly due to

_____

(412)

6. Cite factors that contribute to current secular growth patterns. (412)

_____

_____

_____

7. During middle childhood, the bones of the body _____ and _____. However, _____ are not yet firmly attached to bones. This, combined with increasing muscle strength, grants children

_____.

(412)

8. Between the ages of _____ and _____, all primary teeth are replaced by permanent ones, with _____ losing their teeth slightly earlier than _____. (412)

9. One-third of school-age children suffer from _____, a condition in which the upper and lower teeth do not meet properly. (413)

10. List two causes of malocclusion. (413)

A. _____

B. _____

11. List four advances in brain development that occur in middle childhood. (413)

A. _____

B. _____

C. _____

D. _____

12. Chemicals that permit neurons to communicate across synapses are called _____. (413)

13. Summarize changes in neurotransmitters and hormones during middle childhood, including their effects on brain functioning. (413)

Neurotransmitters: _____

_____

_____

Hormones: _____

_____

_____

_____

Common Health Problems

1. List three factors that lead many children to be at their healthiest in middle childhood. (414)

   A. _____

   B. _____

   C. _____

2. Many health problems are more prevalent among _____ children. (414)

3. The most common vision problem of middle childhood is _____, or nearsightedness. (414)

4. Cite evidence indicating that myopia is related to both heredity and environmental factors. (414)

   Heredity:_____

   _____

   _____

   _____

Environment: _____

_____

_____

_____

5. True or False: If left untreated, chronic ear infections can lead to permanent hearing loss. (414)

6. Summarize the effects of prolonged malnutrition that become apparent by middle childhood. (415)

_____

_____

_____

7. Over _____ percent of American children suffer from obesity, a greater than _____ percent increase over average body weight based on the child's age, sex, and physical build. About _____ percent of obese children retain their overweight status into adulthood. (415-416)

8. (Low-SES/Middle-SES) children are more likely to be overweight. Cite three factors that contribute to this trend. (417)

A. _____

B. _____

C. _____

9. Describe parenting practices that contribute to obesity, along with their consequences for children's eating habits. (417)

_____

_____

_____

10. Describe evidence of the relationship between TV viewing and obesity. (417-418)

_____

_____

_____

11. Summarize the effects of childhood obesity on emotional and social development. (418)

_____

_____

_____

12. The most effective interventions for treating childhood obesity are _____ based and focus on _____. Furthermore, weight loss is greater when treatments focus on both _____ and _____ changes. (418-419)

13. Ten percent of American school-age children suffer from _____ _____, or bedwetting during the night. (419)

14. In the majority of cases, nocturnal enuresis is caused by (biological/ environmental) factors. (419)

15. Describe the most effective treatment for enuresis. (419)

_____

_____

_____

16. The most common chronic illness during childhood is _____. (420)

17. Describe the characteristics of children who are at greatest risk for asthma. (420)

_____

_____

_____

18. List five interventions for chronically ill children and their families that foster improvements in family interactions and child adjustment. (420-421)

A. _____

B. _____

C. _____

D. _____

E. _____

19. The frequency of injury fatalities (increases/decreases) from middle childhood into adolescence. (421)

20. What is the leading cause of injury during the school years? (421)

_____

21. Describe components of school-based safety programs which have longer-lasting effects on children's behavior. (421)

_____

_____

_____

_____

22. Parents can reduce children's risk of head injuries when bicycling, rollerblading, skateboarding, or using scooters by
_____. (421)

23. Explain why boys have a higher injury rate than girls during the school years. (421)

_____

_____

_____

24. Why is the school-age period especially important for fostering healthy lifestyles? (422)

_____

_____

_____

25. List three reasons why efforts to impart health concepts to school-age children often have little impact on their behavior. (423)

A. _____

B. _____

C. _____

26. Discuss at least four strategies for fostering healthy lifestyles in school-age children. (424)

A. _____

_____

B. _____

_____

C. _____

_____

D. _____

_____

Biology and Environment: Growth Stunting Due to Early Malnutrition — Risk Factor for Childhood Obesity

1. Cite two physiological consequences of malnutrition that may explain why growth-stunted children are at increased risk for obesity. (416)

A. _____

_____

B. _____

_____

Social Issues: Education — Children's Understanding of Health and Illness

1. Trace changes in children's understanding of health and illness from preschool into adolescence. (422)

Preschool and early school-age (4- to 8-year-olds): _____

_____

Older school-age (9- to 10-year-olds): _____

_____

Early Adolescence: _____

_____

2. Describe factors that affect children's understanding of health and illness. (422-423)

_____

_____

_____

Motor Development and Play

1. Describe gains in four basic motor capacities that support improvements in gross motor skills during middle childhood. (425-426)

A. _____

_____

B. _____

_____

C. _____

_____

D. _____

_____

2. Explain how more efficient information processing contributes to the improved motor performance of school-age children. (426)

_____

_____

3. Gains in fine motor skills are especially evident in children's _____ and _____. Summarize changes in these areas. (426)

_____

_____

_____

_____

4. Discuss the influence of socioeconomic status on children's motor development. (427)

_____

_____

_____

5. Summarize sex differences in motor skills, and explain how environmental factors contribute to these differences. (427-428)

_____

_____

_____

_____

6. Discuss ways to increase girls' participation, self-confidence, and sense of fair treatment in athletics. (428)

_____

_____

_____

_____

_____

7. Gains in _____ permit the transition to rule-oriented games during middle childhood. (428)

8. Explain how child-invented games contribute to emotional and social development. (428-429)

_____

_____

_____

9. List four arguments in favor of and four arguments against adult-organized youth sports. (429)

   In favor:

   A. _____

   B. _____

   C. _____

   D. _____

   Against:

   A. _____

   B. _____

   C. _____

   D. _____

10. Cite several ways that parents and/or coaches can make participation in adult-organized sports a more positive experience for children. (429)

    A. _____

    B. _____

    C. _____

11. _____ play is a form of peer interaction involving friendly chasing and play-fighting. (430)

12. In our evolutionary past, rough-and-tumble play may have been important for the development of _____. Another possibility is that rough-and-tumble play assists children in establishing _____, a stable ordering of group members that predicts who will win when conflict arises. (431)

13. Describe the state of physical education programs in most American schools, and discuss the impact that this has on children. (431)

_____

_____

_____

14. List three strategies for improving physical education in American schools. (431-432)

A. _____

B. _____

C. _____

ASK YOURSELF . . .

REVIEW: What aspects of physical growth account for the long-legged appearance of many 8- to 12-year-olds?

_____

_____

_____

_____

APPLY: Joey complained to his mother that it wasn't fair that his younger sister Lizzie was almost as tall as he was. He worried that he wasn't growing fast enough. How should Rena respond to Joey's concern?

_____

_____

_____

_____

CONNECT: Relate secular trends in physical growth to the concept of _cohort effects_, discussed on page 44 of Chapter 1.

_____

_____

_____

_____

REFLECT: In your family, how do members of your generation compare with members of your parents' generation in height and weight? How about your grandparents' generation? Do your observations illustrate secular trends?

_____

_____

_____

_____

REVIEW: Select one of the following health problems of middle childhood: myopia, obesity, bedwetting, asthma, or unintentional injuries. Explain how both genetic and environmental factors contribute to it.

_____

_____

_____

APPLY: Nine-year-old Talia is afraid to hug and kiss her grandmother, who has cancer. What explains Talia's mistaken belief that the same behaviors that cause colds to spread might lead her to catch cancer? What would you do to change her thinking?

_____

_____

_____

_____

CONNECT: How does the link between early malnutrition and later obesity, described in the Biology and Environment box on page 416, illustrate the concept of epigenesis, described on page 91 of Chapter 2.

_____

_____

_____

_____

REFLECT: List unintentional injuries that you experienced as a child. Were you injury-prone? Why or why not?

_____

_____

_____

_____

REVIEW: Explain the adaptive value of rough-and-tumble play and dominance hierarchies among children.

_____

_____

_____

_____

APPLY: Alex thinks he isn't good at sports and doesn't like physical education. Suggest some strategies his teacher can use to improve his enjoyment and involvement in physical activity.

_____

_____

_____

_____

CONNECT: On Saturdays, 8-year-old Gina gathers with friends at a city park to play kickball. Besides improved ball skills, what else is she learning?

_____

_____

_____

_____

REFLECT: Did you participate in adult-organized sports as a child? If so, what kind of climate for learning did coaches and parents create? How do you think your experience affected your development?

_____

_____

_____

_____

SUGGESTED STUDENT READINGS

Drotar, D. (Ed.). (2000). *Promoting adherence to medical treatment in chronic childhood illness: Concepts, methods, and interventions.* Mahwah, NJ: Lawrence Erlbaum Associates, Inc., Publishers. A collection of chapters highlighting the physical and psychological benefits to chronically ill children who adhere to their medical regiments. Also includes recommendations for promoting treatment adherence in pediatric patients.

Elder, J. P. (2001). *Behavior change & public health in the developing world.* Thousand Oaks, CA: Sage Publications, Inc. A comprehensive approach to understanding universal public health issues. An excellent resource for those interested in health psychology, health education, and other health-related specialties.

Singer, D. G., & Singer, J. L. (2000). *Make-believe: Games and activities for imaginative play: A book for parents, teachers, and the young children in their lives.* Washington, DC: Magination Press/American Psychological Association. Presents over 100 games and activities specially designed to foster self-confidence and the development of cognitive, social, physical, and creative skills. Also provides a reference list for parents and educators who wish to research the benefits of make-believe and sociodramatic play.

PUZZLE TERM REVIEW

Puzzle 11

Across

2. A condition in which the upper and lower teeth do not meet properly
3. _____ trends in physical growth refer to changes in body size from one generation to the next.
4. Chemicals that permit neurons to communicate across synapses
6. A form of peer interaction involving friendly chasing and play-fighting
7. An illness in which highly sensitive bronchial tubes fill with mucus, leading to episodes of coughing, wheezing, and breathing difficulties
9. A greater than 20-percent increase over average body weight, based on the child's age, sex, and physical build.

Down

1. A stable ordering of group members that predicts who will win when conflict arises (2 words)
5. Nocturnal _____: repeated bedwetting during the night
8. Nearsightedness

SELF-TEST

1. Body growth in middle childhood tends to be: (410)
   a. characterized by slight spurts followed by lulls.
   b. faster than during toddlerhood.
   c. very irregular.
   d. fast for boys, slow for girls.

2. Cross-cultural research on children's physical size reveals that: (411)
   a. growth norms are highly consistent from one culture to the next.
   b. there are wide cultural variations in children's body size.
   c. children in the United States tend to be shorter, on average, than children in most other countries around the world.
   d. growth norms based largely on Caucasian children are universally applicable.

3. Changes in body size from one generation to the next are known as _____ in physical growth. (412)
   a. secular trends
   b. cohort effects
   c. genetic trends
   d. temporal patterns

4. One-third of school-age children suffer from malocclusion, a condition in which: (413)
   a. the adaptation of muscles to children's enlarging skeleton causes stiffness and aches in the legs.
   b. children repeatedly wet the bed at night.
   c. children lose their upper and lower front teeth, giving them a "toothless" smile.
   d. the child's upper and lower teeth do not meet properly.

5. The trend toward more efficient and flexible thinking and behavior during the school years may be affected by: (413)
   a. an increased secretion of androgens.
   b. the increasingly selective response of neurons to only certain neuro-transmitters.
   c. declines in synaptic pruning.
   d. reduced communication between the two hemispheres of the brain.

6. The most common vision problem in middle childhood is: (414)
   a. astigmatism.
   b. hyperopia, or farsightedness.
   c. myopia, or nearsightedness.
   d. lack of eye muscle control.

266

7. Which of the following is NOT true with regard to nutrition during middle childhood? (415)

   a. Growth-stunted children who experience improvements in diet decrease their risk for childhood obesity.
   b. The percentage of children eating dinner with their families drops sharply between 9 and 14 years.
   c. Readily available, healthy snacks, such as cheese, fruit, and vegetables, help meet school-age children's nutritional needs.
   d. By middle childhood, prolonged malnutrition is associated with negative consequences, including retarded physical growth, low intellectual test scores, poor motor coordination, and inattention.

8. Obese children: (418)

   a. rarely maintain their overweight status into adulthood.
   b. most often come from middle- or high-SES families.
   c. are more responsive to internal hunger cues than are normal-weight children.
   d. report greater feelings of depression and display more behavior problems than their normal-weight agemates.

9. Research indicates that the best treatment for childhood obesity is: (418-419)

   a. placing the child on a strict, low-calorie diet.
   b. daily exercise for the child.
   c. behavior modification plans which reinforce exercise and punish inactivity.
   d. family-based interventions that focus on changing behavior.

10. Nocturnal enuresis, or nighttime bedwetting: (419)

    a. typically results from underlying psychological problems.
    b. has a biological basis in most cases.
    c. is problematic for approximately 43 percent of school-age children.
    d. is most effectively treated with antidepressant drugs.

11. The most common childhood chronic illness is: (420)

    a. allergies.
    b. diabetes.
    c. asthma.
    d. cancer.

12. Risk of unintentional injuries increases during middle childhood because: (421)

    a. young children often do not think before they act.
    b. school-age children do not yet understand the consequences of risky behaviors.
    c. school-age children lack safety knowledge.
    d. young school-age children become increasingly involved in adult-organized sports.

13. Parents often: (421)

    a. underestimate their children's safety knowledge and behavior.
    b. overestimate their children's safety knowledge and behavior.
    c. increase their children's risk-taking behavior by being overly worried about safety.
    d. can increase children's safe behavior by simply rewarding it for a short period of time.

14. Which of the following is NOT a reason for the gap between health knowledge and practice in school-age children? (422-423)
    a. Health is usually not an important goal for children.
    b. Children do not yet have an adult-like time perspective, which makes engaging in preventive behaviors difficult.
    c. Much of the health information that children receive is contradicted by other sources.
    d. Children do not yet have a sense of physical well-being.

15. Improvements in motor skills during the school years reflect gains in all of the following EXCEPT: (425-426)
    a. force.
    b. balance.
    c. muscle control.
    d. agility.

16. Increasingly efficient information processing allows for steady improvements in _____, which is crucial for effective motor performance. (426)
    a. hand-eye coordination
    b. reaction time
    c. physical reasoning
    d. physical strength

17. Gains in fine motor development are especially evident in children's: (426)
    a. writing and drawing.
    b. running.
    c. jumping.
    d. ball skills.

18. Which of the following is true of children's drawings in middle childhood? (426)
    a. Drawings are usually very unorganized.
    b. It is difficult for them to copy two-dimensional shapes.
    c. Little detail is used.
    d. Depth cues begin to appear.

19. During middle childhood: (427)
    a. girls show advanced gross motor performance, while boys are better at fine motor skills.
    b. girls are ahead of boys in fine motor skills, whereas boys outperform girls on most gross motor tasks.
    c. boys outperform girls in both gross and fine motor skill areas.
    d. gender differences in motor development become less pronounced.

20. Recent findings indicate that: (428)
    a. boys' superiority in gross motor skills can be entirely attributed to a genetic advantage in muscle mass.
    b. girls' sports involvement now equals that of boys.
    c. among young children, both boys and girls view sports in a gender-stereotyped fashion, believing sports are more important for boys.
    d. girls view themselves as having as much athletic talent as boys.

21. School-age children's participation in rule-oriented games is attributable to: (428)
    a. gains in perspective taking.
    b. gains in agility.
    c. physical maturation.
    d. improvements in fine motor skills.

22. Which of the following is NOT an advantage of adult-organized sports in middle childhood? (429)
    a. Adult-structured athletics prepare children for realistic competition.
    b. Regularly scheduled games and practices ensure that children get plenty of exercise.
    c. Adult-organized games typically provide children with abundant opportunities to learn about leadership, followership, and fair play.
    d. Children get instruction in physical skills necessary for future success in athletics.

23. Rough-and-tumble play: (430)
    a. cannot be distinguished from aggressive fighting.
    b. is characterized by friendly chasing and play fighting.
    c. takes the same form for boys and girls.
    d. is an important indicator of social skills deficits.

24. Dominance hierarchies among children serve the adaptive function of: (431)
    a. limiting aggression among group members.
    b. promoting fairness among group members.
    c. promoting leadership skills in physically weaker children.
    d. assuring leadership by the most intelligent group members.

25. Research findings on the status of physical education in the United States indicate that: (431)
    a. the majority of American children and adolescents have daily physical education classes.
    b. children get most of their exercise in the school setting.
    c. physical education programs tend to emphasize informal games instead of competitive sports.
    d. American schools need to adjust the frequency and content of their physical education programs.

270

CHAPTER 12

COGNITIVE DEVELOPMENT IN MIDDLE CHILDHOOD

Chapter Summary

During Piaget's concrete operational stage, thought becomes more logical, flexible, and organized. However, children cannot yet think abstractly. Cross-cultural findings raise questions about whether mastery of Piagetian tasks emerges spontaneously in all children. The gradual development of operational reasoning challenges Piaget's assumption of an abrupt, stagewise transition to logical thought.

Brain development leads to gains in information-processing capacity and cognitive inhibition, which facilitate diverse aspects of thinking. Information-processing research reveals that attention becomes more controlled, adaptable, and planful, and memory strategies become more effective. By the end of the school years, knowledge acquisition and use of memory strategies are intimately related and support one another. Metacognition moves from a passive to an active view of mental functioning. Still, school-age children have difficulty regulating their progress toward a goal and redirecting unsuccessful efforts. Academic instruction that combines an emphasis on meaning and understanding with training in basic skills may be most effective in reading and mathematics.

Intelligence tests for children measure overall IQ as well as a variety of separate intellectual factors. Sternberg's triarchic theory of intelligence extends our understanding of the determinants of IQ scores. Gardner's theory of multiple intelligences highlights several intelligences not measured by IQ scores. Heritability and adoption research shows that both genetic and environmental factors contribute to individual differences in intelligence. Because of different language customs and lack of familiarity with test content, IQ scores of low-SES, ethnic minority children often do not reflect their true abilities. Supplementing IQs with measures of adaptive behavior and adjusting testing procedures to take cultural differences into account are ways of reducing test bias.

Language development continues during the school years, although changes are less dramatic than they were during early childhood. Vocabulary increases rapidly, and pragmatic skills are refined. Bilingual children are advanced in cognitive development and metalinguistic awareness.

Schools are powerful forces in children's development. Class size, the school's educational philosophy, teacher-pupil interaction, grouping practices, and the way computers are integrated into classroom learning experiences affect motivation and achievement in middle childhood. Teachers face special challenges in meeting the needs of children who have learning difficulties or special intellectual strengths. American pupils have fared unevenly in recent international comparisons of academic achievement. Efforts are currently underway to upgrade the quality of American education.

After reading this chapter, you should be able to:

12.1 Describe the major characteristics of concrete operational thought, including limitations of cognition during this stage. (438-440)

12.2 Discuss recent research on concrete operational thought, noting the implications of recent findings for the accuracy of Piaget's concrete operational stage. (440-442)

12.3 Describe two basic changes in information processing which occur during middle childhood. (442-443)

12.4 Describe changes in attention and memory during middle childhood, and discuss the role of knowledge in memory performance. (443-448)

12.5 Describe the school-age child's theory of mind and capacity to engage in cognitive self-regulation. (448-449)

12.6 Discuss the application of information-processing research to children's learning in the areas of reading and mathematics, noting current controversies as to how to teach children in these areas. (449-452)

12.7 Describe the Stanford-Binet Intelligence Scale and the Wechsler Intelligence Scale for Children-III, the two scales most commonly used to assess intelligence in school-age children. (453-454)

12.8 Discuss recent developments in defining intelligence, including Sternberg's triarchic theory of intelligence and Gardner's theory of multiple intelligences. (454-457)

12.9 Discuss evidence indicating that both heredity and environment contribute to intelligence. (457-458)

12.10 Describe cultural influences on intelligence test performance, and discuss efforts to reduce cultural bias in intelligence testing. (458-460)

12.11 Describe changes in metalinguistic awareness, vocabulary, grammar, and pragmatics during middle childhood. (461-462)

12.12 Discuss the major issues surrounding bilingual development and bilingual education. (462-463)

12.13 Discuss the impact of class size, educational philosophy, teacher-student interaction, and grouping practices on student motivation and academic achievement. (464-469)

12.14 Describe learning advantages of and concerns about computers in classrooms. (469-470)

12.15 Explain issues surrounding the educational placement of students with learning disabilities, noting the effectiveness of mainstreaming and full inclusion. (470-472)

12.16 Describe the characteristics of gifted children, and discuss current efforts to meet their educational needs. (472-474)

12.17 Compare the American cultural climate for academic achievement with that of Asian nations. (474-476)

Piaget's Theory: The Concrete Operational Stage

1. As children enter Piaget's concrete operational stage, thought becomes more
_____, _____, and _____ than it was
during early childhood. (438)

2. The ability to pass _____ tasks provides clear evidence of
operations. Name and describe two characteristics of thought which illustrate
this ability. (438)

A. _____

_____

B. _____

_____

3. Between ages 7 and 10, children pass Piaget's _____
problem, indicating that they are more aware of _____ hierarchies and can focus on _____ between a general category and
two specific categories at the same time. Explain how this ability is evidenced in
children's play activities. (438)

_____

_____

_____

4. Define the terms *seriation* and *transitive inference*, and distinguish the
performance of a concrete operational child from that of a preoperational child
on these two types of problems. (438-439)

A. Seriation: _____

_____

_____

B. Transitive inference: _____

_____

_____

5. Advances in spatial reasoning are evidenced by children's understanding of _____ and ability to give _____. Summarize changes in these two areas as children move from preoperational thought to concrete operational thought. (439)

A. _____

_____

_____

_____

B. _____

_____

_____

_____

6. Describe the major limitation of concrete operational thought. (439)

_____

_____

7. Explain what is meant by *horizontal décalage*. (439-440)

_____

_____

8. Discuss recent research indicating that specific cultural practices and school experiences affect children's mastery of Piagetian tasks, and explain how such findings challenge Piaget's theory. (440)

Cultural practices: _____

_____

_____

_____

School experiences: _____

_____

_____

Challenge: _____

_____

9. The horizontal décalage suggests that logical understanding improves (gradual-ly/suddenly) over the school years. Consequently, some neo-Piagetian theorists argue that the development of operational thinking can best be understood in terms of gains in _____ capacity rather than a sudden shift to a new stage. (441)

10. Summarize Case's information-processing view of cognitive development. (441)

_____

_____

_____

_____

11. What are *central conceptual structures*? (441)

_____

_____

12. Cite two reasons why children show a horizontal décalage. (441)

A. _____

_____

B. _____

_____

13. Many researchers believe that both _____ improvements in logical skills and _____ restructuring of children's think-ing contribute to cognitive development during childhood. (442)

Information Processing

1. Discuss two ways in which brain development contributes to changes in information processing. (442-443)

A. •_____

_____

B. _____

_____

2. During middle childhood, attention becomes more _____,
   _____, and _____. (443)

3. List and describe the four-step sequence of attentional strategy development. (443)

   A. _____

   _____

   B. _____

   _____

   C. _____

   _____

   D. _____

   _____

4. Trace the development of planning as it relates to the solution of multi-step
   problems. (444)

   _____

   _____

   _____

5. Explain how children typically learn planning skills, and discuss what parents
   can do to foster the development of planning in their children. (444)

   _____

   _____

   _____

6. List and describe three memory strategies that emerge during middle childhood.
   (444-445)

   A. _____

   _____

B. _____

_____

C. _____

_____

7. Because the strategies of organization and elaboration combine items into _____, they permit children to hold on to much more information, thus expanding working memory. (445)

8. Discuss the relationship between knowledge and memory. (445-446)

_____

_____

_____

9. Discuss how culture and schooling are related to the development of memory strategies. (447-448)

Culture: _____

_____

_____

Schooling: _____

_____

_____

10. Describe how a school-age child's theory of mind differs from that of a preschooler. (448)

_____

_____

_____

11. List three experiences which may promote the school-age child's reflective, process-oriented view of the mind. (448)

A. _____

_____

B. _____

_____

C. _____

_____

12. True or False: School-age children can differentiate memory techniques based on their effectiveness. (448)

13. Cognitive _____ refers to the process of continually monitoring progress toward a goal, checking outcomes, and redirecting unsuccessful efforts. (449)

14. Explain how cognitive self-regulation relates to academic success. (449)

_____

_____

_____

15. Discuss ways that parents and teachers can foster self-regulation. (449)

_____

_____

_____

16. List the diverse information-processing skills that contribute to the process of reading. (450)

_____

_____

_____

_____

17. The two sides in the great debate about how to teach beginning reading are the
_____ approach and the _____
approach. Contrast these two perspectives. (450)

_____

_____

_____

_____

18. True or False: Research clearly demonstrates that the basic skills approach is superior to the whole language approach. (450)

19. Why might combining phonics with whole language be the most effective strategy? (450)

_____

_____

_____

_____

20. Encouraging students to _____and making sure that they
_____ are vital for solid mastery of basic math. (451)

21. True or False: Drill-oriented math instruction provides students with the greatest opportunities for conceptual understanding and exploration of problem-solving strategies. (452)

Biology and Environment: Children with Attention-Deficit Hyperactivity Disorder

1. Describe typical characteristics of children with attention-deficit hyperactivity disorder (ADHD). (446)

_____

_____

_____

2. True or False: The intelligence of ADHD children is normal, and they show no signs of serious emotional disturbance. (446)

3. Discuss hereditary and environmental contributions to ADHD. (446-447)

Hereditary: _____

_____

_____

Environmental: _____

_____

_____

4. Discuss three ways to treat ADHD, noting which method is the most common and which method is the most effective. (447)

A. _____

_____

B. _____

_____

C. _____

_____

Individual Differences in Mental Development

1. Virtually all intelligence tests provide an overall score that represents
   _____, or reasoning ability, and an array of separate scores
   measuring _____. (453)

2. Test designers use a statistical technique called _____
   to identify the various abilities that intelligence tests measure. (453)

3. Distinguish between group and individually administered intelligence tests,
   and cite the advantages of each. (453)

Group administered: _____

_____

_____

Individually administered: _____

_____

_____

4. Match the following intelligence tests with the appropriate descriptions: (453-454)

_____ Appropriate for individuals age 6-16

_____ Appropriate for individuals between 2 years of age and adulthood

_____ Assess two broad intellectual factors: verbal and performance

_____ Assess four broad intellectual factors: verbal reasoning, quantitative reasoning, abstract/visual reasoning, and short-term memory

_____ First test to be standardized on samples representing the total population of the United States, including ethnic minorities

1. Stanford-Binet Intelligence Scale

2. Wechsler Intelligence Scale for Children-III

5. Researchers conduct _____ analysis of children's mental test scores in order to look for relationships between aspects of _____ and children's IQ. (454)

6. What is the major shortcoming of the componential approach? (455)

_____

_____

7. Sternberg's _____ theory of intelligence is made up of three interacting subtheories. Name and describe each of the three subtheories. (455)

A. _____

_____

B. _____

_____

C. _____

_____

8. Explain how Sternberg's theory is relevant to the controversy surrounding cultural bias in intelligence testing. (455)

_____

_____

_____

9. State how Gardner defines intelligence, and list Gardner's eight intelligences. (455-456)

_____

_____

A. _____   B. _____

C. _____   D. _____

E. _____   F. _____

G. _____   H. _____

10. True or False: Because it is not firmly grounded in research, Gardner's theory has not been especially helpful in efforts to understand and nurture children's special talents. (456-457)

11. True or False: On average, African-American children score 15 points below Caucasian-American children on IQ tests. (457)

12. Evidence from kinship studies suggests that about _____ of the differences in IQ among children can be traced to their genetic makeup. (457)

13. Describe evidence from adoption research indicating that both heredity and environment affect IQ scores. (457-458)

Heredity: _____

_____

Environment: _____

_____

14. True or False: When African-American children are placed in economically advantaged white homes during the first two years of life, they show significantly higher mean IQ scores than those of children growing up in low-income black communities. (458)

15. Compare traditional language customs in middle-income white homes, low-income black homes, and homes of Hispanic immigrants. (458-459)

Middle-income white homes: _____

_____

_____

Low-income black homes: _____

_____

_____

Homes of Hispanic immigrants: _____

_____

_____

16. How might fixed instructions and lack of feedback undermine minority students' performance on intelligence tests? (459)

_____

_____

17. Describe evidence indicating that intelligence test performance is influenced by learning opportunities. (459)

_____

_____

_____

_____

18. True or False: IQ scores often underestimate the intelligence of minority children. (459)

19. Describe *dynamic testing*, and discuss its effectiveness for reducing cultural bias in testing. (459-460)

_____

_____

_____

_____

Language Development

1. School-age children develop _____ awareness, the ability to think about language as a system. (461)

2. True or False: The rate of vocabulary growth during the school years exceeds that of early childhood. (461)

3. Describe changes in children's word definitions between the beginning and end of middle childhood. (461)

_____

_____

_____

4. Cite two gains in grammatical construction that emerge during the school years. (461-462)

A. _____

_____

B. _____

_____

5. Describe evidence indicating that school-age children have an improved ability to adapt to the needs of listeners in complex communicative situations. (462)

_____

_____

_____

6. Cite two examples of gains in conversational strategies during middle childhood. (462)

   A. _____

   B. _____

7. Cite two ways in which children can become bilingual, and discuss children's development in each instance. (462-463)

   A. _____

   _____

   _____

   B. _____

   _____

8. True or False: There is a sensitive period for second language development. (463)

9. List the cognitive benefits of bilingualism. (463)

   _____

   _____

   _____

10. Discuss the current controversy surrounding the education of American ethnic minority children with limited English proficiency, and describe educational outcomes associated with each perspective. (463)

   _____

   _____

   _____

   _____

11. _____ refers to inadequate proficiency in both languages. (463)

Children's Learning in School

1. Discuss the benefits of small class size. (464)

_____

_____

_____

2. List and describe at least four characteristics of high-quality education in elementary school. (465)

   A. _____

   _____

   B. _____

   _____

   C. _____

   _____

   D. _____

   _____

3. Distinguish between traditional and open classrooms, citing outcomes associated with each. (465-466)

   Traditional: _____

   _____

   _____

   _____

   _____

   Open: _____

   _____

   _____

   _____

4. True or False: Kindergartners placed in traditional classrooms exhibit advanced academic achievement and increased motivation toward learning when compared with students placed in open classrooms. (466)

5. List and describe three educational themes that were inspired by Vygotsky's emphasis on the social origins of learning. (466)

   A. _____

   _____

   B. _____

   _____

   C. _____

   _____

6. _____ refers to a method of learning in which a teacher and 2 to 4 students form a cooperative group and take turns leading dialogues on the content of a text passage. List four cognitive strategies that group members apply during these dialogues. (466-467)

   A. _____

   B. _____

   C. _____

   D. _____

7. Describe the main features of the *Kamehameha Elementary Education Program* (KEEP), and state whether or not research supports the effectiveness of this model. (468)

   _____

   _____

   _____

   _____

   _____

8. Research suggests that students are more attentive when teachers encourage _____ thinking, such as analyzing, synthesizing, and applying ideas and concepts, rather than _____. (468)

9. Describe how teachers interact differently with high-achieving students versus low-achieving, disruptive students. (468)

_____

_____

_____

_____

10. What is an *educational self-fulfilling prophecy*, and how does it affect students' motivation and performance? (468-469)

_____

_____

_____

_____

11. True or False: Ability grouping widens the performance gap between high- and low-achievers. (469)

12. True or False: Self-esteem and attitudes toward school are more positive in multigrade classrooms than in single-grade classrooms. (469)

13. Define *cooperative learning*. (469)

_____

_____

_____

14. List three ways in which computers are used in classrooms, and describe the benefits of each. (469-470)

A. _____

_____

_____

B. _____

_____

_____

C. _____

_____

_____

15. Cite two common concerns about use of computers in the classroom. (470)

A. _____

_____

B. _____

_____

16. Distinguish between *mainstreaming* and *full inclusion*. (471)

Mainstreaming: _____

_____

Full inclusion: _____

_____

17. Describe characteristics of a learning disability. (471)

_____

_____

_____

18. Discuss findings on the effectiveness of mainstreaming and full inclusion. (471)

_____

_____

_____

_____

19. Special-needs children placed in regular classrooms often do best when they receive instruction in a _____ room for part of the day and in the regular classroom for the remainder of the day. (471)

20. Discuss ways in which teachers can promote peer acceptance of mainstreamed children. (471-472)

_____

_____

_____

21. Define *giftedness*. (472)

_____

_____

22. _____ refers to the ability to produce work that is *original* yet *appropriate*. (472)

23. Distinguish between convergent and divergent thinking. (472)

Convergent: _____

_____

Divergent: _____

_____

24. _____ refers to outstanding performance in a particular field. (473)

25. Describe family characteristics that foster talent. (473)

_____

_____

_____

26. True or False: Gifted children report more emotional and social difficulties than do their ordinary agemates. (473)

27. List three models for educating gifted children. (473)

A. _____

B. _____

C. _____

28. Describe the findings of international studies comparing the achievement of American children with that of children in other industrialized nations. (474-476)

_____

_____

_____

29. True or False: Research shows that Asian children are high achievers because they are smarter, and they start school with cognitive advantages over their American peers. (475)

Social Issues: Education — When Are Children Ready for School? Academic Redshirting and Early Retention

1. Define *academic redshirting*, and discuss student outcomes associated with this practice. (467)

_____

_____

_____

_____

2. True or False: Children retained in kindergarten show many learning benefits, as well as other positive consequences in motivation, self-esteem, and attitudes toward school. (467)

3. _____ classes, or way stations between kindergarten and first grade, are a form of homogeneous grouping and have the same implications for teacher-student interactions as other "low-ability" groups. (467)

Cultural Influences: Education in Japan, Taiwan, and the United States

1. Describe five cultural conditions in Japan and Taiwan that support high academic achievement, noting how this compares to conditions in the United States. (474-475)

A. _____

_____

_____

B. _____

_____

_____

C. _____

_____

_____

D. _____

_____

_____

E. _____

_____

_____

ASK YOURSELF . . .

REVIEW: Mastery of conservation provides one illustration of Piaget's horizontal décalage. Review the preceding sections. Then list additional examples showing that operational reasoning develops gradually during middle childhood.

_____

_____

_____

_____

APPLY: Nine-year-old Adrienne spends many hours helping her father build furniture in his woodworking shop. Explain how this experience may have contributed to her advanced performance on Piagetian seriation problems.

_____

_____

_____

_____

CONNECT: Examine the children's drawings on pages 314 and 427-the first by a 6-year-old, the second by an 8-year-old, and the third by a 10-year-old. Explain how the drawings illustrate Case's information-processing view of the development of operational thought.

_____

_____

_____

_____

REVIEW: Cite evidence indicating that school-age children view the mind as an active, constructive agent.

_____

_____

_____

_____

APPLY: One day, the children in Lizzie and Joey's school saw a slide show about endangered species. They were told to remember as many animal names as they could. Fifth and sixth graders recalled considerably more than did second and third graders. What factors might account for this difference?

_____

_____

_____

_____

APPLY: Lizzie knows that if you have difficulty learning part of a task, you should devote most of your attention to that aspect. But she plays each of her piano pieces from the beginning to end instead of picking out the hard parts for extra practice. What explains Lizzie's failure to apply what she knows?

_____

_____

_____

_____

REFLECT: Describe the relative emphasis on computational practice and understanding of concepts in your elementary-school math education. How do you think that balance affected your interest and performance in math?

_____

_____

_____

_____

REVIEW: Using Sternberg's triarchic theory and Gardner's theory of multiple intelligences, explain the limitations of current mental tests in assessing the complexity of human intelligence.

_____

_____

_____

_____

APPLY: Desiree, an African-American child, was quiet and withdrawn while taking an intelligence test. Later she remarked to her mother, "I can't understand why that lady asked me all those questions, like what a ball and stove are for. She's a grownup. She must know what a ball and stove are for!" Using Sternberg's triarchic theory, explain Desiree's reaction to the testing situation. Why is Desiree's score likely to underestimate her intelligence?

_____

_____

_____

_____

CONNECT: Referring to Chapter 2, pages 87-88, and evidence in this chapter, summarize the limitations of heritability estimates. Cite concepts discussed in Chapter 2 that support the position that heredity and environment cannot be divided into separate influences.

_____

_____

_____

_____

REFLECT: Do you think intelligence tests are culturally biased? What evidence and observations influenced your conclusion?

_____

_____

_____

_____

REVIEW: Cite examples of language progress that benefit from school-age children's metalinguistic awareness.

_____

_____

_____

_____

APPLY: Ten-year-old Shana arrived home from school after a long day, sank into the living room sofa, and commented, "I'm totally wiped out!" Megan, her 5-year-old sister, looked puzzled and asked, "What did'ya wipe out, Shana?" Explain Shana and Megan's different understanding of the meaning of this expression.

_____

_____

_____

_____

REFLECT: Did you acquire a second language at home or study one in school? If so, when did you begin? Considering what you now know about bilingual development and education, what changes would you make in your second-language learning, and why?

_____

_____

_____

_____

REVIEW: List teaching practices that foster children's academic achievement and those that undermine it. For each practice, provide a brief explanation.

_____

_____

_____

_____

APPLY: Ray is convinced that his 5-year-old son Tripper would do better in school if only Tripper's kindergarten would provide more teacher-directed lessons and worksheets and reduce the time devoted to learning-center activities. Is Ray correct? Explain.

_____

_____

_____

_____

APPLY: Sandy, a parent of a third grader, wonders whether she should support her school board's decision to teach first, second, and third graders together, in a mixed-age classrooms. How would you advise Sandy, and why?

_____

_____

_____

_____

CONNECT: Relate _genetic-environmental correlation_, discussed in Chapter 2, pages 89-91, to the development of gifted children. Which parenting and teaching practices can enhance that correlation, and which ones can undermine it?

_____

_____

_____

_____

SUGGESTED STUDENT READINGS

Barkley, R. A. (1998). *Attention-deficit hyperactivity disorder: A handbook for diagnosis and treatment (2nd Edition).* New York: The Guilford Press. Written primarily for clinicians and those interested in working with school-age children, this book presents current literature on the diagnosis, assessment, and treatment of ADHD.

Meichenbaum, D., & Biemiller, A. (1998). *Nurturing independent learnings: Helping students take charge of their learning.* Cambridge, MA: Brookline Books. Discusses the development of cognitive self-regulation in school-age children. Considers factors that distinguish children who falter in school from those who thrive, how and when differences emerge between these groups, and how teachers can foster the development of both types of learners. Drawing on a wealth of research evidence, presents practical advice on how teachers can promote active, self-directed learning.

Sternberg, R. J. (Ed.). (2000). *Handbook of intelligence.* New York: Cambridge University Press. A collection of chapters examining the development and assessment of intelligence. Other topics include group and cultural differences in intelligence, biological influences, and the relationship between intelligence and information processing.

Topping, K., & Stewart, E. (Eds.). (1998). *Peer-assisted learning.* Mahwah, NJ: Lawrence Erlbaum Associates, Inc. A unique approach to classroom instruction, this book explores the various techniques involved in peer-assisted learning. The authors argue that peer tutoring promotes learning and is applicable for students of all ability levels.

Zentella, A. C. (1997). *Growing up bilingual: Puerto Rican children in New York.* Cambridge, MA: Blackwell. Walks readers through an urban disadvantaged community and illustrates its bilingual and multi-dialectical communication patterns. Describes differences in language development of five childhood friends as they grow into adulthood.

PUZZLE TERM REVIEW

Puzzle 12a

Across

1. Gardner's theory of _____ intelligences proposes at least eight independent intelligences.

7. The ability to order items along a quantitative dimension, such as length or weight

8. _____ deficiency: inability to improve performance even with consistent use of a mental strategy

9. _____ deficiency: inability to consistently execute a mental strategy

11. The ability to focus on several aspects of a problem at once and to relate them

13. In _____ classrooms, children are passive learners who acquire information presented by teachers.

15. A childhood disorder involving inattentiveness, impulsivity, and excessive motor activity (abbr.)

16. Educational ___-_____ prophecy: children may adopt teachers' positive or negative attitudes toward them and start to live up to these expectations

17. An individually administered intelligence test measuring general intelligence and four factors

Down

2. _____ strategy use: consistent use of a mental strategy that leads to improved performance

3. Piaget's _____ operational stage is marked by logical, flexible, and organized thought.

4. _____ deficiency: failure to produce a mental strategy when it could be helpful

5. Generation of a single correct answer to a problem is known as _____ thinking.

6. Generation of multiple and unusual possibilities when faced with a problem is referred to as _____ thinking.

7. Cognitive ___-____: process of continually monitoring progress toward a goal, checking outcomes, and redirecting unsuccessful efforts

10. Sternberg's _____ theory of intelligence suggests that information-processing skills, ability to learn efficiently in novel situations, and contextual factors interact to determine intelligent behavior.

12. Cognitive _____: ability to resist interference from distracting stimuli

14. _____-III: Individually administered IQ test measuring verbal & performance skills (abbr.)

18. Classrooms in which teachers share decision making with students, and students are evaluated in relation to their own prior development

PUZZLE TERM REVIEW

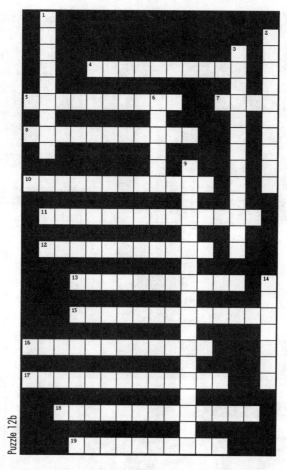

Puzzle 12b

Across

4. _____ inference: ability to mentally order items along a quantitative dimension
5. The ability to produce work that is original yet appropriate
7. An educational reform effort based on Vygotsky's theory; designed to enhance teacher–child and child–child interaction and to be culturally responsive (abbr.)
8. Approach to beginning reading that emphasizes training in phonics and simplified reading materials (2 words)
10. Memory strategy of grouping together related items
11. The ability to think about language as a system is known as _____ awareness.
12. Memory strategy of creating a relation between two or more items that are not members of the same category
13. _____ learning: collaboration on a task by a small group of students who resolve differences of opinion, share ideas, consider one another's ideas, and work toward common goals
15. Placement of pupils with learning difficulties in regular classrooms for the entire school day
16. Learning _____: specific learning disorders leading to poor academic achievement despite average or above-average IQ
17. Approach to beginning reading that parallels children's natural language learning (2 words)
18. Placement of pupils with learning difficulties in regular classrooms for part of the school day
19. Exceptional intellectual strengths; includes high IQ, creativity, and talent

Down

1. Memory strategy of repeating information
2. Vygotsky-inspired method of teaching in which a teacher and 2 to 4 students form a cooperative learning group
3. Ability to mentally go through a series of steps in a problem and then reverse direction, returning to the starting point
6. Outstanding performance in a particular field
9. Development within a Piagetian stage (2 words)
14. _____ testing: individualized teaching is introduced into the testing situation to see what the child can attain with social support

SELF-TEST

1. The ability to pass conservation tasks provides clear evidence of
   _____ -mental actions that obey logical rules. (438)
   a. transitive inference
   b. classification
   c. operations
   d. metacognitive awareness

2. Nadia can sort sticks of varying length into a sequence from shortest to longest. However, she cannot mentally infer that stick A is longer than stick C given that A is longer than B and that B is longer than C. Which of the following abilities does Nadia lack? (438-439)

   a. decentration
   b. seriation
   c. class inclusion
   d. reversibility

3. Horizontal décalage refers to: (440)
   a. consistent use of a mental strategy that leads to improvements in performance.
   b. patterns of development across the Piagetian stages.
   c. development within a Piagetian stage.
   d. the generation of a single correct answer to a problem.

4. According to the information-processing perspective proposed by Robbie Case, the development of operational thinking results from: (441)

   a. automation of cognitive schemas, which frees up space in working memory, thus allowing children to focus on combining old schemas and creating new ones.
   b. gains in long-term memory and increasingly efficient retrieval processes.
   c. a sudden shift to a new stage of cognitive processing.
   d. children's interactions with adults.

5. During middle childhood, attention changes in all of the following ways EXCEPT: (443-444)

   a. children become better at selectively attending to only those aspects of a situation that are relevant to their task goals.
   b. attention becomes a more automatic process, therefore requiring less cognitive effort on the part of the child.
   c. children are better able to adapt their attention to current situational demands.
   d. attentional strategies become more planful, as evidenced by school-age children's ability to follow a sequence of steps in order to solve complex tasks.

6. Failure to use an attentional strategy in situations in which it could be helpful is indicative of a: (443)

   a. control deficiency.
   b. utilization deficiency.
   c. performance deficiency.
   d. production deficiency.

7. When trying to remember the words book and monkey, Jordan creates a mental image of a monkey reading a book. This is an example of: (445)

    a. organization.
    b. rehearsal.
    c. elaboration.
    d. planning.

8. Which of the following is NOT true of the school-age child's theory of mind? (448)

    a. School-age children view the mind as a passive container of information.
    b. School-age children understand the process of thinking and the impact of psychological factors on performance.
    c. School-age children grasp the interrelatedness of memory and understanding (i.e., that memory is essential for understanding and that understanding strengthens memory).
    d. School-age children regard the mind as an active, constructive agent.

9. Parents and teachers can foster cognitive self-regulation in children by doing all of the following EXCEPT: (449)

    a. pointing out the special demands of a task.
    b. encouraging the use of strategies and explaining why these strategies are effective.
    c. emphasizing the value of self-correction.
    d. telling children how to complete a task but letting them figure out on their own why particular strategies are effective.

10. The _____ approach to beginning reading instruction emphasizes training in phonics and use of simplified reading materials. (450)

    a. whole language
    b. basic skills
    c. dynamic systems
    d. sequential

11. Math instruction is most effective when it focuses on: (451)

    a. drill and repetition.
    b. automatic retrieval of math facts.
    c. formal computational techniques.
    d. both computational strategies and conceptual understanding.

12. Both the WISC-III and the WPPSI-R measure: (454)

    a. verbal reasoning, quantitative reasoning, abstract/visual reasoning, and short-term memory.
    b. verbal and performance abilities.
    c. information-processing capacity.
    d. sensorimotor skills.

13. In Sternberg's triarchic theory of intelligence, which subtheory states that highly intelligent individuals process information more skillfully in novel situations than do less intelligent individuals? (455)

    a. componential subtheory
    b. experiential subtheory
    c. contextual subtheory
    d. pragmatical subtheory

14. Kinship studies reveal that: (457)

    a. heredity is the primary determinant of IQ.
    b. environment is the primary determinant of IQ.
    c. both heredity and environment contribute significantly to IQ.
    d. individuals possess many different independent intelligences rather than one general intelligence.

15. The _____ testing approach introduces teaching into the testing situation to see what kids can attain with social support. (459-460)

    a. dynamic
    b. microgenetic
    c. standardized
    d. individualized

16. School-age children show noticeable gains in pragmatics by: (462)

    a. learning two languages at a time.
    b. using metaphors.
    c. adapting to the needs of listeners.
    d. using more precise word definitions.

17. Which of the following statements is TRUE? (463)

    a. When bilingual parents try to teach their children both languages during early childhood, the children often experience severe problems in language development.
    b. Parents and teachers should be concerned if bilingual children start mixing the two languages.
    c. Recent research refutes the notion of a sensitive period for second language learning.
    d. Bilingual children evidence advances in cognitive development.

18. Which of the following is NOT true of traditional classrooms? (465)

    a. In traditional classrooms, children are passive learners who acquire information presented by teachers.
    b. Traditional classrooms are still prevalent today.
    c. Compared to open classrooms, traditional classrooms are associated with advanced critical thinking skills and more positive student attitudes toward school.
    d. Traditional classrooms may increase the incidence of grade retention.

19. The term *educational self-fulfilling prophecy* refers to the idea that: (468)

    a. children may adopt teachers' positive or negative attitudes toward them and start to live up to these expectations.
    b. students' self-esteem and attitudes toward school are enhanced by placement in a multigrade classroom.
    c. high-achieving students typically experience more positive interactions with teachers than do low-achieving students.
    d. students with learning disabilities should be placed in regular classrooms for part of the day in order to better prepare them for participation in society.

20. Which of the following is true of computers in classrooms? (470)

    a. Computer-assisted instruction promotes active experimentation and increased conceptual understanding.
    b. The use of computers for word processing results in shorter, lower quality written products.
    c. It is recommended that word-processing replace other classroom writing experiences.
    d. Computer programming is associated with improvements in problem solving and creativity.

21. Mainstreaming refers to: (471)

    a. full-time placement of students with disabilities in regular classrooms.
    b. placement of students with disabilities in regular classrooms for part of the school day.
    c. homogeneous grouping of students with disabilities in a self-contained classroom.
    d. full-time placement of students with disabilities in a resource room, where they work with a special education teacher on an individual and small group basis.

22. Research on the educational placement of students with disabilities reveals that: (471)

    a. mainstreaming and full inclusion provide all students with the greatest academic benefit.
    b. mainstreamed students are usually well-accepted by regular classroom peers.
    c. students with disabilities do best when placed in a resource room for part of the day and in a regular classroom for the remainder of the day.
    d. mainstreaming and full inclusion do not have any benefit for students with disabilities.

23. Current conceptualizations of giftedness focus on: (472-473)

    a. intelligence.
    b. creativity on measures of divergent thinking.
    c. talent in a particular area.
    d. intelligence, creativity, and talent.

24. Gifted children: (473)

    a. spend as much time interacting with peers as do nongifted agemates.
    b. report higher levels of emotional and social difficulties.
    c. tend to have parents who are driven and overly ambitious.
    d. often have higher self-esteem than ordinary peers.

25. Which of the following factors is NOT important in the superior academic performance of Asian as compared to American children? (475)

    a. Academic achievement is highly encouraged and supported by Asian parents.
    b. Asian students are smarter and start school with cognitive advantages over their American peers.
    c. Asian parents and teachers place greater emphasis on effort than on innate ability.
    d. There is no ability grouping in Japanese elementary schools; all children receive the same high-quality education.

CHAPTER 13

EMOTIONAL AND SOCIAL DEVELOPMENT IN MIDDLE CHILDHOOD

Chapter Summary

Erikson's stage of industry versus inferiority captures the school-age child's capacity for productive work and new feelings of competence and mastery. During middle childhood, psychological traits and social comparisons appear in children's self-concepts, and a hierarchically organized self-esteem emerges. Attribution research has identified adult communication styles that affect children's explanations for success and failure and, in turn, their academic self-esteem, motivation, and task performance. Self-conscious emotions become clearly governed by personal responsibility, and both emotional understanding and emotional self-regulation improve. Perspective taking undergoes major advances, and moral understanding expands.

By the end of middle childhood, children form peer groups. Friendships change, emphasizing mutual trust and assistance. Researchers have identified four categories of social acceptance: popular, rejected, controversial, and neglected children. Peer acceptance is a powerful predictor of current and future psychological adjustment. The antisocial behavior of rejected children leads to severe dislike by age-mates. During the school years, boys' masculine gender identities strengthen, whereas girls' identities become more flexible. However, cultural values and practices can modify these trends.

In middle childhood, child rearing shifts toward coregulation. Parents exercise general oversight while granting children more decision-making power. Sibling rivalry tends to increase, and siblings often take steps to reduce it by striving to be different from one another. Only children are just as well developed as children with siblings, and they are advantaged in self-esteem and achievement motivation. Children of gay and lesbian parents are well adjusted, and the large majority are heterosexual. The situations of children in never-married, single-parent families can be improved through strengthening social support, education, and employment opportunities for parents.

Large numbers of American children experience the divorce and remarriage of their parents. Child, parent, and family characteristics influence how well they fare. Maternal employment can lead to many benefits for school-age children, although outcomes vary with the child's sex and SES, the demands of the mother's job, the father's participation in child rearing, and the availability of high quality after-school programs as an alternative to self-care.

Fears and anxieties change during middle childhood as children experience new demands in school and begin to understand the realities of the wider world. Child sexual abuse, a serious problem in the United States, has devastating consequences for children and is especially difficult to treat. Personal characteristics of children, a warm, well-organized home life, and social supports outside the family are related to children's ability to cope with stressful life conditions.

LEARNING OBJECTIVES

After reading this chapter, you should be able to:

13.1 Explain Erikson's stage of industry versus inferiority, noting major personality changes. (482-483)

13.2 Describe the development of the self during middle childhood, noting changes in self-concept and self-esteem, as well as factors that influence children's self-evaluations. (483-488)

13.3 Describe changes in self-conscious emotions, understanding of emotional states, and emotional self-regulation in middle childhood. (489-491)

13.4 Trace the development of perspective taking, and discuss the relationship between perspective taking and social skills. (491-492)

13.5 Describe changes in moral understanding during middle childhood, and discuss the debate over moral education in the schools, including Narvaez's four-component model of moral education. (492-495)

13.6 Describe changes in peer relations during middle childhood, including characteristics of peer groups and friendships and the contributions of each to social development. (495-497)

13.7 Describe the four categories of peer acceptance, noting how each is related to social behavior, and discuss ways to help rejected children. (497-501)

13.8 Describe changes in gender-stereotyped beliefs and gender identity during middle childhood, noting sex differences and cultural influences. (501-502)

13.9 Discuss changes in the parent-child relationship during middle childhood, including new issues confronting parents and changes in parent-child communication. (503)

13.10 Describe changes in sibling relationships during middle childhood, noting the impact of birth order on sibling experiences, and compare the experiences and developmental outcomes of only children with those of children with siblings. (503-504)

13.11 Describe gay and lesbian families, and discuss the developmental outcomes of children raised in such families. (504-505)

13.12 Describe the characteristics of never-married, single-parent families, and explain how living in a single-parent household affects children. (505)

13.13 Discuss children's adjustment to divorce and blended families, noting the influence of parent and child characteristics and social supports within the family and surrounding community. (505-510)

13.14 Discuss the impact of maternal employment and dual-earner families on school-age children's development, noting the influence of social supports within the family and surrounding community, and explain issues regarding child care for school-age children. (510-512)

13.15 Discuss common fears and anxieties in middle childhood, with particular attention to school phobia. (513)

13.16 Discuss factors related to child sexual abuse, its consequences for children's development, and ways to prevent and treat it. (513-516)

13.17 Cite factors that foster resilience in middle childhood, and describe the RCCP program, a school-based program aimed at reducing violence and antisocial behavior. (516, 518)

Erikson's Theory: Industry versus Inferiority

1. Erikson's theory of personality change during the school years builds upon
   Freud's _____ stage. (482)

2. According to Erikson, the combination of _____
   and _____ sets the stage for the psychologi-
   cal conflict of middle childhood, *industry versus inferiority*. Explain the meaning of
   industry. (482)

   _____

3. List two ways in which a sense of inferiority can develop during middle
   childhood. (482)

   A. _____

   B. _____

Self-Development

1. List four changes in self-concept that occur during middle childhood. (483)

   A. _____

   B. _____

   C. _____

   D. _____

2. Cognitive development affects the changing _____ of the self,
   while both cognitive capacities and feedback from others produce changes in the
   _____ of self-concept. (483-484)

3. Discuss the relationship between perspective-taking skills and self-concept
   development. (484)

   _____

   _____

   _____

   _____

4. True or False: Beginning in middle childhood, peers become more important than parents in children's self-definitions. (484)

5. True or False: Self-concept development follows the same pattern in all societies. (484)

6. How does self-esteem change from the preschool years to the school years, and what accounts for these changes? (484)

_____

_____

_____

7. List four self-esteems that children form by the age of 7 or 8. (484)

A. _____

B. _____

C. _____

D. _____

8. As children begin to combine their separate self-evaluations into a general psychological image of themselves, self-esteem takes on a _____ structure. (485)

9. True or False: Separate self-evaluations contribute equally to general self-esteem. (485)

10. Self-esteem (rises/drops) during the early elementary school years. Explain why this is the case. (485)

_____

_____

_____

11. True or False: The role of social comparison in self-concept development varies from culture to culture. (486)

12. Describe child-rearing practices associated with high self-esteem in middle childhood. (486)

_____

_____

_____

13. _____ are our common, everyday explanations for the causes of behavior. (486)

14. Distinguish between mastery-oriented attributions and learned helplessness. (487)

Mastery-oriented attributions: _____

_____

_____

Learned helplessness: _____

_____

_____

15. Mastery-oriented children focus on _____ goals, whereas learned-helpless children focus on _____ goals. (487)

16. Discuss the role of adult communication in accounting for children's development of mastery-oriented and learned-helpless attributions. (487)

_____

_____

_____

17. True or False: Girls and low-income ethnic minority children are especially vulnerable to learned helplessness. (487)

18. _____ is an intervention that encourages learned-helpless children to believe that they can overcome failure by exerting more effort. Briefly describe this technique. (488)

_____

_____

_____

19. Discuss four ways to foster a mastery-oriented approach to learning and to prevent learned helplessness in middle childhood. (489)

A. _____

_____

B. _____

_____

C. _____

_____

D. _____

_____

Emotional Development

1. As children integrate _____ standards into their self-definitions, a sense of personal responsibility clearly governs the self-conscious emotions of _____ and _____. Discuss changes in how children experience these emotions during middle childhood. (489)

_____

_____

_____

_____

2. Profound feelings of _____ are particularly destructive because they involve taking a single unworthy act to be the whole of self-worth. (490)

3. List three advances in school-age children's understanding of emotions. (490)

   A. _____

   B. _____

   C. _____

4. What factors underlie the rise in empathy during middle childhood? (490-491)

   _____

   _____

   _____

5. By age 10, most children have an adaptive set of techniques for regulating emotion. In situations where they have some control over the outcome, they view _____ and _____ as the best strategies. When outcomes are beyond their control, they opt for _____ or _____. Compared with preschoolers, school-age children more often us these _____ strategies to manage emotions. (491)

6. Define *emotional self-efficacy*. (491)

   _____

   _____

7. List characteristics of emotionally well-regulated children and children with poor emotional regulation. (491)

   Well-regulated: _____

   _____

   Poorly-regulated: _____

   _____

Understanding Others: Perspective Taking

1. Name and briefly describe Selman's five stages of perspective taking. (492)

   A. _____

   _____

B. _____

_____

C. _____

_____

D. _____

_____

E. _____

_____

2. What factors contribute to individual differences in perspective-taking skill? (492)

_____

_____

_____

Moral Development

1. True or False: School-age children continue to be heavily dependent on adult oversight, modeling, and reinforcement for engaging in good conduct. (492)

2. Define distributive justice. (493)

_____

_____

3. Trace the development of children's concepts of distributive justice during middle childhood. (493)

A. _____

B. _____

C. _____

4. True or False: Peer interaction is particularly important in the development of standards of justice. (493)

5. Describe three changes in moral and social-conventional understanding during middle childhood. (494)

A. _____

_____

B. _____

_____

C. _____

_____

6. True or False: Children in Western and non-Western cultures use the same criteria to distinguish moral and social-conventional concerns. (494)

7. Describe Narvaez's four-component model of morality education. (495)

A. _____

_____

B. _____

_____

C. _____

_____

D. _____

_____

Peer Relations

1. Describe the characteristics of a peer group. (496)

_____

_____

_____

2. Describe the positive functions of children's peer groups. (496)

_____

_____

_____

_____

3. How do school-age boys and girls express hostility toward the "outgroup" differently? (496)

_____

_____

_____

_____

4. Describe changes in children's concepts of friendship during middle childhood. (497)

_____

_____

_____

_____

5. True or False: New ideas about the meaning of friendship lead school-age children to be more selective in their choice of friends than they were at younger ages. (497)

6. Friendships (do/do not) tend to remain stable over middle childhood. (497)

7. Discuss the qualities of aggressive children's friendships. (497)

_____

_____

_____

8. Researchers usually assess peer acceptance with self-report measures called _____. (498)

9. Name and describe four categories of peer acceptance. (498)

A. _____

B. _____

C. _____

D. _____

10. True or False: All school-age children fit into one of the four categories of peer acceptance described above in Question 9. (498)

11. Discuss emotional and social outcomes associated with peer rejection. (498)

_____

_____

_____

12. Identify and describe two types of peer popularity. (498)

A. _____

_____

_____

B. _____

_____

_____

13. Describe the social behavior of rejected-aggressive and rejected-withdrawn children. (499)

Aggressive: _____

_____

Withdrawn: _____

_____

14. True or False: Controversial children are hostile and disruptive but also engage in high rates of positive, prosocial acts. (499)

15. True or False: Controversial children have as many friends as do popular children. (499)

16. Describe the social behavior and adjustment of neglected children. (499)

_____

_____

_____

17. Describe four interventions designed to help rejected children. (499-501)

A. _____

B. _____

C. _____

D. _____

Biology and Environment: Bullies and Their Victims

1. _____ is a form of interaction in which certain children become frequent targets of verbal and physical attacks or other forms of abuse. (500)

2. Describe characteristics common to victimized children. (500)

_____

_____

_____

3. List adjustment difficulties associated with victimization by peers. (500)

_____

_____

_____

4. Children who emerge as aggressive bully/victims often experience
_____ parenting, including _____. (500)

5. Discuss individual and school-based interventions for peer victimization. (500)

_____

_____

_____

_____

Gender Typing

1. Describe ways in which children extend their gender-stereotyped beliefs during middle childhood. (501)

_____

_____

_____

2. True or False: School-age children adopt a biological perspective of gender typing, and consequently, regard gender as a certain predictor of personality traits, activities, and behaviors. (501)

3. Contrast the gender identity development of boys and girls during middle childhood, and note implications for behavior. (502)

_____

_____

_____

_____

4. Briefly describe cultural influences on gender typing. (502)

_____

_____

_____

5. True or False: Research overwhelmingly suggests that boys benefit from assignment of "cross-gender" tasks. (502)

Family Influences

1. True or False: In middle childhood, the amount of time that children spend with their parents declines dramatically. (503)

2. During the school years, child rearing becomes easier for those parents who established a(n) _____ style during the early years.

   Explain why this is the case. (503)

   _____

   _____

   _____

3. What is *coregulation*? (503)

   _____

   _____

4. Why does sibling rivalry tend to increase in middle childhood? (503-504)

   _____

   _____

5. When siblings are _____ and _____ parental comparisons are more frequent, resulting in more quarreling and antagonism. (504)

6. Siblings often try to reduce sibling rivalry by _____ (504)

7. Discuss the impact of birth order on sibling experiences. (504)

   _____

   _____

   _____

8. Discuss the adjustment of only children. (504)

   _____

   _____

   _____

9. Compare and contrast gay and lesbian families with heterosexual families. (505)

_____

_____

_____

_____

10. About _____ percent of American children have parents who have never married. (505)

11. The largest group of never-married parents are _____. (505)

12. Cite outcomes associated with children raised in never-married, single-parent families. (505)

_____

_____

_____

13. Between 1960 and 1985, the divorce rate in the United States _____. (505)

14. True or False: Currently, the United States has the highest divorce rate in the world. (506)

15. About _____ of American marriages end in divorce; _____ of these involve children. (506)

16. About _____ of divorced parents marry a second time, and _____ of these marriages end in divorce. (506)

17. Summarize ways in which divorce has an immediate impact on the home environment. (506)

_____

_____

_____

_____

18. Discuss how children's ages affect their reactions to divorce, noting differences between younger and older children. (506-507)

_____

_____

_____

_____

19. True or False: Temperament affects children's adjustment to stressful life events, including divorce. Briefly explain your answer. (507)

_____

_____

_____

20. Girls sometimes respond to divorce with internalizing reactions, such as
_____, _____, and _____. More often, they show _____ behavior. (507)

21. True or False: In mother custody families, girls experience more serious adjustment difficulties than do boys. Explain your response. (507)

_____

_____

_____

22. Boys of divorcing parents receive (more/less) emotional support from mothers, teachers, and peers than do girls. (507)

23. True or False: Parental divorce typically has no impact on school achievement, particularly for boys. (507)

24. Most children show improved adjustment by _____ years after divorce. (507)

25. (Boys/Girls) and children with _____
are especially likely to drop out of school and display antisocial behavior in adolescence following a parental divorce. (507)

26. For both sexes, divorce is linked to problems with _____
and with the development of _____. (507)

27. What is the overriding factor in positive adjustment following divorce? (507)

_____

28. Explain why a good father-child relationship is important for both boys and girls following divorce. (508)

Girls: _____

_____

Boys: _____

_____

29. True or False: Making the transition to a low-conflict, single-parent household is better for children than staying in a stressed intact family. (508)

30. Describe divorce mediation, and explain why it is likely to have benefits for children. (508)

_____

_____

_____

_____

31. In _____, the court grants the mother and father equal say in important decisions regarding the child's upbringing. Describe common living arrangements associated with this option, noting their impact on children's adjustment. (508)

_____

_____

_____

_____

32. List at least four suggestions for helping children adjust to their parent's divorce. (509)

A. _____

_____

B . _____

_____

C. _____

_____

D. _____

_____

33. When single parents remarry or cohabitate, the parent, stepparent, and children form a new family structure called the _____, or _____, family. (509)

34. List two reasons why blended families present adjustment difficulties for most children. (509)

A. _____

_____

B . _____

_____

35. The most frequent form of blended family is a _____ arrangement. Contrast boys' and girls' adjustment in this family arrangement. (509)

Boys: _____

_____

Girls: _____

_____

36. (Older/Younger) school-age children are more likely to display adjustment problems following parental remarriage. Explain why this is the case. (510)

_____

_____

_____

37. Remarriage of noncustodial fathers often leads to (reduced/increased) contact with children, particularly if they have (sons/daughters). (510)

38. Cite two reasons why children tend to react negatively to the remarriage of custodial fathers. (510)

A. _____

B. _____

39. (Girls/Boys) have an especially hard time getting along with stepmothers. Briefly explain your response. (510)

_____

_____

_____

40. Explain how family life education and therapy can help parents and children in blended families adapt to the complexities of their new circumstances. (510)

_____

_____

_____

_____

41. _____ percent of employed mothers have children between the ages of 6 and 13 years. (510)

42. Differentiate between self-care children who fare well and those who fare poorly. (510-511)

_____

_____

_____

_____

43. List at least four signs of readiness for self-care. (511)

A. _____

B. _____

C. _____

D. _____

44. Discuss ways to help children manage on their own in self-care situations. (511)

_____

_____

_____

_____

45. List several factors that affect the impact of maternal employment on child outcomes. (511-512)

_____

_____

_____

46. Describe potential benefits of maternal employment for school-age children, and note the circumstances under which such outcomes are achieved. (511-512)

_____

_____

_____

47. List four supports which help parents juggle the demands of work and child-rearing. (512)

A. _____

B. _____

C. _____

D. _____

Some Common Problems of Development

1. Summarize new fears and anxieties that emerge in middle childhood. (513)

_____

_____

_____

2. Describe typical child characteristics associated with school phobia, and cite symptoms of the disorder. (513)

Child characteristics: _____

Symptoms: _____

_____

_____

3. Distinguish common causes of school phobia in early childhood from those in later childhood and adolescence, noting implications for treatment. (513)

Early childhood: _____

_____

_____

Later childhood and adolescence: _____

_____

_____

4. Sexual abuse is committed against children of both sexes, but more often against (girls/boys). (513)

5. Describe typical characteristics of sexual abusers. (514-515)

_____

_____

_____

_____

6. Abusers often pick out child victims who are _____

_____. (515)

7. Discuss the adjustment problems of sexually abused children, noting differences between younger children and adolescents. (515)

_____

_____

_____

_____

8. Describe common behavioral characteristics of sexually abused girls as they move into young adulthood. (515)

_____

_____

_____

9. Why is it difficult to treat victims of child sexual abuse? (516)

_____

_____

_____

10. Discuss the role of educational programs in preventing child sexual abuse. (516)

_____

_____

_____

11. List three broad factors that help children cope with stress and protect against maladjustment. (516)

A. _____

_____

B. _____

_____

C. _____

_____

12. The _____, or RCCP, is an effective school-based program designed to reduce violence and other anti-social acts by fostering _____. (518)

Cultural Influences: The Impact of Ethnic and Political Violence on Children

1. Discuss children's adjustment to ethnic and political violence, noting differences between situations involving temporary crises and those involving chronic danger. (514)

_____

_____

_____

2. What is the best safeguard against lasting problems? (514)

_____

Social Issues: Health: Children's Eyewitness Testimony

1. True or False: Children as young as age 3 are frequently asked to provide testimony in court cases involving child abuse and neglect. (517)

2. Summarize age differences in children's ability to provide accurate testimony. (517)

_____

_____

_____

_____

3. When adults lead children by suggesting _____,
   they (increase/decrease) the likelihood of incorrect reporting among preschool
   and school-age children alike. (517)

4. True or False: Special interviewing methods involving the use of anatomically
   correct dolls have been successful in prompting more accurate recall of sexual
   abuse experiences, particularly among preschoolers. (517)

5. Discuss three interventions that can be used to assist child witnesses. (517)

   A. _____

   _____

   B. _____

   _____

   C. _____

   _____

ASK YOURSELF . . .

REVIEW: How does level of self-esteem change in middle childhood, and what accounts for those changes?

_____

_____

_____

_____

APPLY: Should parents try to promote children's self-esteem by telling them they're "smart" and "wonderful"? Is it harmful if children do not feel good about everything they do? Why or why not? How would you recommend that parents foster children's self-esteem?

_____

_____

_____

_____

CONNECT: What cognitive changes, described in Chapter 12, support the transition from a self-concept consisting of a collection of behaviors and internal states to a self-concept emphasizing competencies, personality traits, and social comparisons?

_____

_____

_____

_____

REFLECT: Describe your attributions for academic successes and failures during childhood. What are those attributions like now? What experiences do you think contributed to your attributions?

_____

_____

_____

_____

REVIEW: How does emotional self-regulation improve in middle childhood? Do gains in emotional self-regulation have implications for children's self-esteem? Explain.

_____

_____

_____

_____

APPLY: Joey's fourth-grade class participated in a bowl-a-thon to raise money for a charity serving children with cancer. Explain how activities like this one can foster emotional development, perspective taking, and moral understanding.

_____

_____

_____

_____

CONNECT: Describe how older children's capacity to take more information into account affects each of the following: self-concept, emotional understanding, perspective taking, and moral understanding.

_____

_____

_____

_____

REVIEW: Return to Chapter 10, page 393, and review the concept of _androgyny_. Which of the two sexes is more androgynous in middle childhood, and why?

_____

_____

_____

_____

APPLY: Apply your understanding of attributions to rejected children's social self-esteem. How are rejected children likely to explain their failure to gain peer acceptance? What impact on future efforts to get along with agemates will those attributions have?

_____

_____

_____

_____

CONNECT: Cite similarities in school-age children's more mature self-concept and understanding of friendship.

_____

_____

_____

_____

REFLECT: Recall a popular child, a rejected child, a bully, and a victim from your own childhood. Describe the social behavior of each, and indicate whether it is consistent with research findings on peer acceptance.

_____

_____

_____

_____

REVIEW: List findings from our discussion of the family that highlight the influence of fathers on children's development.

_____

_____

_____

_____

APPLY: "How come you don't study hard and get good grades like your sister?" a mother exclaimed in exasperation after seeing her son's poor report card. What impact do remarks like this have on sibling interaction, and why?

_____

_____

_____

_____

APPLY: Steve and Marissa are in the midst of an acrimonious divorce. Their 9-year-old son Dennis has become hostile and defiant. How can Steve and Marissa help Dennis adjust?

_____

_____

_____

_____

CONNECT: How does each level in Bronfenbrenner's ecological system theory-microsystem, mesosystem, exosystem, and macrosystem-contribute to the effects of maternal employment on children's development?

_____

_____

_____

_____

REVIEW: What can legal professionals do to increase the chances of accurate reporting when children must testify in court cases?

_____

_____

_____

_____

APPLY: Claire told her 6-year-old daughter to be very careful never to talk to or take candy from strangers. Why will Claire's directive not protect her daughter from sexual abuse?

_____

_____

_____

_____

CONNECT: Explain how the three factors that protect against maladjustment, listed in the previous section, help account for variations in children's adjustment following divorce.

_____

_____

_____

_____

SUGGESTED STUDENT READINGS

Adler, P. A., & Adler, P. (1997). *Peer power: Preadolescence culture and identity.* New Brunswick, NJ: Rutgers University Press. Based on 8 years of research, this book explores the role of peers in childhood identity development. Among the topics addressed are: popularity, friendships, social isolation, bullying, boy-girl relationships, and the influence of cliques.

Drucker, J. (1998). *Families of value: Gay and lesbian parents and their children speak out.* New York: Insight Books/Plenum Press. A collection of personal accounts by gay and lesbian families regarding the unique roles and challenges associated with raising children in a homophobic society. The author maintains that a nurturing environment contributes to healthy child development, regardless of the gender or sexual orientation of the caregivers.

Garbarino, J., Dubrow, N., Kostelny, K., & Pardo, C. (1998). *Children in danger: Coping with the consequences of community violence.* San Francisco, CA: Jossey-Bass. Illustrates how living in many of today's violent communities affects various aspects of development. Useful for teachers, counselors, and other professionals who are interested in helping children who reside in a dangerous environment.

Hetherington, E. M. (1999). *Coping with divorce, single parenting, and remarriage: A risk and resiliency perspective.* Mahwah, NJ: Erlbaum. Examines family functioning and child adjustment in different kinds of families. Discusses interactions among individual, familial, and extrafamilial risk and protective factors associated with different kinds of experiences related to marriage, divorce, single parenting, and remarriage.

Nyman, A., & Svensson, B. (1997). *Boys: Sexual abuse and treatment.* Bristol, PA: Kingsley. Using a number of case studies, discusses procedures followed by the Swedish Save the Children's Boys' Clinic over 5-year period. Offers useful advice for those working with victims of sexual abuse.

333

PUZZLE TERM REVIEW

Puzzle 13a

Across

3. Children who are seldom chosen, either positively or negatively, on sociometric measures of peer acceptance
5. Children who are actively disliked and get many negative votes on sociometric measures of peer acceptance
6. Social unit with shared values and behavioral standards and a social structure of leaders and followers (2 words)
11. Judgments of appearance, abilities, behavior, and other characteristics in relation to those of others (2 words)
12. Children who get many positive votes on sociometric measures of peer acceptance

Down

1. Common, everyday explanations for the causes of behavior
2. Supervision in which parents exercise general oversight but permit children to manage moment-to-moment decisions
4. Children who get a large number of positive and negative votes on sociometric measures of peer acceptance
7. Erikson's psychological conflict of middle childhood is known as industry vs. _____.
8. An arrangement following divorce in which both parents are granted equal say in important decisions regarding the child's upbringing (2 words)
9. _____ techniques: self-report measures that ask peers to evaluate one another's likability.
10. Divorce _____ attempts to settle disputes of divorcing adults while avoiding legal battles that intensify family conflict.

PUZZLE TERM REVIEW

Puzzle 13b

Across

3. Rejected-_____ children are a subgroup of rejected children who are passive and socially awkward.
5. Attribution _____ is an intervention in which the attributions of learned-helpless children are modified.
7. Beliefs about how to divide up material goods fairly is known as _____ justice.
8. Rejected-_____ children are a subgroup of rejected children who engage in high rates of conflict, hostility, hyperactivity, inattention, and impulsivity.
9. Severe apprehension about attending school, often accompanied by physical complaints that disappear once the child is allowed to remain home (2 words)
11. _____ taking: the capacity to imagine what others may be thinking and feeling
12. Learned _____: attributions that credit success to luck and failure to low ability

Down

1. Popular-_____ children: highly aggressive, yet viewed by peers as "cool"
2. _____ children look after themselves while their parents are at work.
4. Popular-_____ children: good students who communicate with peers in sensitive, friendly, and cooperative ways
6. _____ attributions credit success to high ability and failure to insufficient effort.
10. Family structure resulting from cohabitation or remarriage that includes parent, child, and steprelatives

SELF-TEST

1. By developing competencies at useful skills and tasks, elementary school children show evidence of _____ in the fourth stage of Erikson's theory. (482)

   a. initiative
   b. autonomy
   c. identity
   d. industry

2. Which of the following is NOT one of the changes in self-understanding that takes place during middle childhood? (483)

   a. Children start to compare their own characteristics to those of their peers.
   b. Children start to focus on either all positive or all negative attributes when providing self-descriptions.
   c. Children begin to describe themselves in terms of psychological traits rather than specific behaviors.
   d. Children begin to speculate about the causes of their strengths and weaknesses.

3. Based on George Herbert Mead's concept of self, the ability to _____ is critical to the development of self-concept during middle childhood. (484)

   a. become introspective
   b. compare one's own abilities and behaviors to those of others
   c. imagine what others think about oneself
   d. resolve the Oedipal and Electra conflicts

4. During middle childhood: (484)

   a. children form at least four separate self-esteems.
   b. self-evaluations across multiple domains contribute equally to general self-esteem.
   c. children's overall sense of self-esteem is replaced by their separate self-evaluations regarding academic, social, and athletic competence and physical appearance.
   d. most children experience a steady increase in self-esteem.

5. Children who develop learned helplessness: (487)

   a. have an incremental view of ability; that is, they think that ability can be altered.
   b. tend to attribute their failures, but not their successes, to ability.
   c. often persevere on difficult tasks in an effort to gain a sense of mastery and competence.
   d. focus on learning goals rather than performance goals.

6. Which of the following is NOT among the changes in self-conscious emotions that take place during middle childhood? (490)

   a. A sense of personal responsibility governs the self-conscious emotions of pride and guilt.
   b. School-age children experience self-conscious emotions in the absence of adult monitoring.
   c. Feelings of shame become adaptive for modifying children's undesirable behavior.
   d. School-age children report guilt only for intentional wrongdoing and not for accidental misdeeds.

7. Which of the following is NOT true of emotional understanding in school-age children? (490)

   a. They explain emotions in terms of internal states rather than physical events.
   b. They recognize that people can experience more than one emotion at a time.
   c. They consider more information when interpreting the emotions of others, including facial expressions and situational cues.
   d. They cannot yet appreciate that emotional reactions may not reflect a person's true feelings.

8. During which of Selman's stages of perspective taking can children "step into another person's shoes" and view their feelings and behavior from the other person's perspective? (492)

   a. self-reflective perspective taking
   b. third-party perspective taking
   c. societal perspective taking
   d. undifferentiated perspective taking

9. By around 8 years of age, children view morality in terms of _____. They recognize that special consideration should be given to those at a disadvantage, such as the needy or the disabled. (493)

   a. equality
   b. merit
   c. benevolence
   d. empathy

10. Which component of Narvaez's moral education model pertains to the evaluation of moral values above personal values? (495)

    a. moral sensitivity
    b. moral motivation
    c. moral judgment
    d. moral character

11. Which of the following is NOT true of school-age children's peer relations? (496)

    a. Trust becomes a defining feature of friendships during middle childhood.
    b. School-age children are more selective about their friendships than are preschoolers.
    c. Children's peer groups tend to organize on the basis of proximity (such as, being in the same classroom) and similarity in gender, ethnicity, and popularity.
    d. Peer groups are highly stable, even when children experience a change in classroom setting.

12. Research on peer acceptance indicates that: (498)

    a. all children fit into one of the four categories of peer acceptance — popular, rejected, neglected, or controversial.
    b. rejected children are at greatest risk for poor school performance, delinquency, and dropping out.
    c. peer status during the school years is unrelated to adjustment problems later in life.
    d. controversial children have few friends and are typically unhappy with their peer relationships.

13. Which of the following is NOT true of gender typing in middle childhood? (501)

    a. During middle childhood, children extend their gender-stereotyped beliefs and begin to label certain personality traits as either masculine or feminine.
    b. School-age children regard gender typing as biologically rather than socially based, and therefore, believe that a person's sex is a certain predictor of personality traits, activities, and behaviors.
    c. In middle childhood, boys strengthen their identification with the "masculine" role, while girls begin to describe themselves as having some "other-gender" characteristics.
    d. Wide cultural variation exists with regard to children's gender-stereotyped beliefs and behaviors.

14. A transitional form of supervision in which parents exercise general oversight while permitting children to be in charge of moment-by-moment decision making is called: (503)

    a. permissive parenting.
    b. cooperative parenting.
    c. coregulation.
    d. self-regulation.

15. During middle childhood, sibling rivalry: (503)

    a. tends to decrease.
    b. tends to increase.
    c. is very rare.
    d. is more common when siblings are far apart in age.

16. Only children: (504)

    a. are typically spoiled and selfish.
    b. tend to exhibit higher self-esteem and achievement motivation.
    c. have more distant relationships with parents.
    d. are less socially competent than children with siblings.

17. Gay and lesbian families: (505)

    a. often experience strain due to the ineffective parenting skills adopted by many homosexual parents.
    b. are commonly associated with poor parent-child relationships.
    c. often produce children with long-term adjustment difficulties.
    d. are very similar to heterosexual families.

18. The disorganized family situation often seen immediately following a divorce is called: (506)

    a. optimal parenting.
    b. minimal parenting.
    c. reconstruction.
    d. divorce mediation.

19. Which of the following is NOT true with regard to the influence of children's age on adjustment to parental divorce? (506)

    a. Younger children often blame themselves for the marital breakup.
    b. School-age children and adolescents are more likely than are preschoolers to fantasize that their parents will get back together.
    c. Older children often react strongly to parental divorce, engaging in problem behaviors such as running away, truancy, early sexual behavior, and delinquency.
    d. For some older children, divorce can trigger more mature behavior.

20. Research suggests that, in the long run, divorce: (508)

    a. is better for children than is remaining in a high-conflict intact family.
    b. has no impact on children's behavior and adjustment.
    c. is often associated with serious difficulties which persist into adulthood.
    d. is linked with more detrimental effects for girls than for boys.

21. Which of the following is true of blended families? (510)

    a. Girls are especially likely to experience positive adjustment in mother-stepfather families.
    b. Older school-age children and adolescents of both sexes display more irresponsible and antisocial behavior than do their agemates in nonblended families.
    c. Remarriage of a noncustodial father often leads to increased contact with children.
    d. Both boys and girls react more positively to the remarriage of a custodial father than a custodial mother.

22. Childhood self-care: (511)

    a. is consistently linked with adjustment problems, including low self-esteem, anti-social behavior, and poor academic achievement.
    b. is associated with worse outcomes for older children than for younger children.
    c. is inappropriate for children under the age of 9.
    d. is associated with positive outcomes for children who have a history of permissive parenting.

23. Maternal employment: (511)

    a. is linked with more positive outcomes for sons than for daughters.
    b. results in a decline in the amount of time that children spend on homework and household chores.
    c. results in a decline in the amount of time that fathers devote to child care and household duties.
    d. is associated with positive adjustment for children as long as the mother remains committed to her role as a parent.

24. School phobia: (513)
    a. is most commonly evidenced by low-SES children with below-average achievement.
    b. most often results from a troubled parent-child relationship.
    c. is most common among elementary-age children and is rarely exhibited by older children and adolescents.
    d. is often accompanied by physical complaints.

25. Which of the following is NOT true of the characteristics of child sexual abusers and their victims? (514)
    a. The majority of victims experience only a single episode of abuse.
    b. The abuser is generally a male.
    c. Sexual abuse is committed more often against girls than boys.
    d. Abusers tend to select victims who are physically weak, emotionally deprived, and socially isolated.

CHAPTER 14

PHYSICAL DEVELOPMENT IN ADOLESCENCE

Chapter Summary

Adolescence is a time of dramatic physical change leading to an adult-sized body and sexual maturity. Although early biologically-oriented theories viewed puberty as a period of storm and stress, recent research shows that serious psychological disturbance is not a common feature of the teenage years. Adolescent development and adjustment are products of both biological and social forces.

The physical changes of puberty are regulated by growth and sex hormones. On the average, girls experience puberty 2 years earlier than do boys, although there are wide individual differences. Regional and SES differences also exist, along with a secular trend toward earlier maturation in industrialized nations. Most teenagers greet the beginning of menstruation and the first ejaculation of seminal fluid with mixed feelings. Puberty is related to increased moodiness and a mild rise in conflict between parents and children. Timing of pubertal maturation affects adolescent adjustment in an opposite way for girls than for boys, and the effects of maturational timing involve a complex blend of biological, social, and cultural factors.

The arrival of puberty is accompanied by new health concerns. For some teenagers, the cultural ideal of thinness combines with family and psychological problems to produce the serious eating disorders of anorexia nervosa and bulimia nervosa. Teenage sexual activity in the United States has increased over several decades but recently declined slightly. Sexual orientation is affected strongly by heredity but also by a variety of biological and environmental combinations. Adolescents have the highest rate of sexually transmitted disease of any age group. Sexual activity is accompanied by high rates of adolescent pregnancy and parenthood. Although most teenagers engage in some experimentation with alcohol and drugs, a worrisome minority make the transition from use to abuse. Unintentional injuries increase in adolescence, largely due to motor vehicle collisions-the leading killer of American teenagers. Firearm injuries and deaths are also high in the United States.

During adolescence, both sexes improve in gross motor performance, although boys show much larger gains than girls. Girls continue to receive less encouragement and recognition for athletic skill during the teenage years. Overall, they are also less physically active than are boys.

After reading this chapter, you should be able to:

14.1 Discuss changing conceptions of adolescence over the twentieth century, and identify the three phases of adolescence recognized in modern industrialized nations. (526-527)

14.2 Describe physical changes associated with puberty, including hormonal changes, changes in body size, body proportions, and muscle-fat makeup, and sexual maturation. (528-531)

14.3 Cite factors that influence the timing of puberty. (531-532)

14.4 Discuss adolescents' reactions to the physical changes of puberty, noting factors that influence their feelings and behavior. (533-536)

14.5 Discuss the impact of maturational timing on adolescent adjustment, noting sex differences, as well as immediate and long-term consequences. (536-539)

14.6 Describe the nutritional needs of adolescents. (540)

14.7 Describe the symptoms of anorexia nervosa and bulimia nervosa, and cite factors within the individual, the family, and the larger culture that contribute to these disorders. (540-542)

14.8 Discuss personal, familial, and cultural influences on adolescent sexual attitudes and behavior. (542-545)

14.9 Discuss biological and environmental contributions to homosexuality. (545-546)

14.10 Discuss the risk of sexually transmitted diseases in adolescence, particularly AIDS, and cite strategies for STD prevention. (546-548)

14.11 Discuss factors related to adolescent pregnancy, consequences of early childbearing for adolescent parents and their children, and strategies for preventing adolescent pregnancy. (547-552)

14.12 Distinguish between substance use and abuse, describe personal and social factors related to each, as well as consequences of substance abuse, and cite strategies for prevention and treatment. (552-554)

14.13 Cite common unintentional injuries in adolescence. (554-555)

14.14 Describe sex differences in motor development, sports participation, and physical activity during adolescence. (555-556)

Conceptions of Adolescence

1. Explain why theorists such as Rousseau and Freud believed adolescence to be a time of storm and stress. (526)

_____

_____

_____

2. True or False: Rates of psychological disturbance increase dramatically during adolescence, supporting the conclusion that it is a period of storm and stress. (527)

3. Mead's alternative view of adolescence suggests that the _____ is entirely responsible for the range of teenage experiences, from erratic and agitated to calm and stress free. (527)

4. Today we know that adolescence is a product of (biological forces/social forces/both biological and social forces). (527)

5. True or False: Adolescence, as an intervening phase between childhood and full assumption of adult roles, can be found in almost all societies. (527)

6. Name and describe the three phases of adolescence. (527)

A. _____

B. _____

C. _____

Puberty: The Physical Transition to Adulthood

1. On average, girls reach puberty two years (earlier/later) than boys. (528)

2. Increased secretion of the hormones _____ and _____ lead to tremendous gains in body size and attainment of skeletal maturity. (528)

3. During sexual maturation, the boy's testes release large quantities of the androgen _____, which leads to muscle growth, body and facial hair, and other male sex characteristics, as well as contributing to gains in _____. (528)

4. The release of _____ from the girl's ovaries causes the breasts, uterus, and vagina to mature, the body to take on feminine proportions, and fat to accumulate. (528)

5. The first outward sign of puberty is _____. On average, it is underway for North American girls shortly after age _____ and for boys at around age _____. (529)

6. Growth in body size is complete for most girls by age _____ and for boys by age _____. (529)

7. True or False: During puberty, the cephalocaudal trend reverses, with hands, legs, and feet growing first, followed by growth of the torso. (529)

8. Describe sex differences in body proportions and muscle-fat makeup that appear during adolescence. (529)

Boys: _____

_____

Girls: _____

_____

9. Distinguish between primary and secondary sexual characteristics. (530)

Primary: _____

_____

Secondary: _____

_____

10. _____ is the scientific name for first menstruation. (530)

11. Female puberty usually begins with _____ and _____. Menarche takes place (early/late) in the sequence of female pubertal events, typically occurring at around age _____ for North American girls. (530)

12. Explain the adaptive value of the timing of menarche in relation to other pubertal milestones. (530)

_____

13. List early signs of puberty in boys. (531)

_____

_____

14. The growth spurt occurs much (earlier/later) in the sequence of pubertal events for boys than for girls. (531)

15. Around age _____, _____, or first ejaculation, occurs among boys. (531)

16. True or False: Heredity contributes substantially to the timing of puberty. (531)

17. List two factors that appear to be responsible for individual differences in pubertal growth. (531)

_____

18. Describe the secular trend in age of menarche in industrialized nations, noting factors believed to be responsible for it. (532)

_____

_____

_____

19. On average, sleep (increases/declines) from middle childhood into adolescence. Explain why this is the case. (533)

_____

_____

_____

The Psychological Impact of Pubertal Events

1. Discuss two factors that affect girls' reactions to menarche. (533-534)

A. _____

_____

B. _____

_____

2. Overall, boys seem to get (more/less) social support for the physical changes of puberty than do girls. (535)

3. Many tribal and village societies celebrate puberty with a

_____-a community-wide event that marks an important change in privilege and responsibility. Contrast this experience with that of adolescents in Western societies. (535-536)

_____

_____

_____

_____

4. Research shows that adolescents report (more/less) favorable moods than do school-age children and adults. Further, when compared with the moods of adults, adolescents' feelings are less _____. (536)

5. Taken together, research findings suggest that _____ factors combine with _____ influences to affect teenagers' moodiness. (536)

6. Discuss changes in the parent-child relationship that take place during adolescence. (537)

_____

_____

_____

7. _____ between parents and adolescent children, exemplified by increased conflict, may be a modern substitute for the physical departure seen in nonhuman primates and adolescents in nonindustrialized societies. (537)

8. True or False: The increase in parent-child conflict at adolescence is generally severe. (537)

9. Discuss research findings on the effects of maturational timing for the following groups of adolescents: (537-538)

Early maturing boys: _____

_____

Early maturing girls: _____

_____

Late maturing boys: _____

_____

Late maturing girls: _____

_____

10. List two factors that appear to account for trends in the effects of maturational timing. (538)

    A. _____

    B. _____

11. Discuss the impact of maturational timing on adolescents' body images. (538)

    _____

    _____

    _____

    _____

12. Explain how school context can modify the effects of maturational timing. (539)

    _____

    _____

    _____

13. True or False: When long-term outcomes are examined, many of the effects of maturational timing on adjustment appear to reverse themselves. (539)

Cultural Influences: Adolescent Initiation Ceremonies

1. What is the purpose of an *adolescent initiation ceremony*? (534)

   _____

   _____

   _____

2. Describe three features involved in adolescent initiation ceremonies. (534-535)

A. _____

_____

B. _____

_____

C. _____

_____

3. In the simplest societies, adolescent initiation ceremonies are more common for (boys/girls). Why is this the case? (535)

_____

_____

_____

4. As cultures move from simple foraging to _____ communities, rituals for boys (increase/decrease) in frequency. (535)

5. True or False: In more complex cultures, adolescent initiation ceremonies have tremendous importance for teaching adult roles and responsibilities. (535)

Health Issues

1. True or False: Of all age groups, the eating habits of adolescents are the poorest. (540)

2. The most common nutritional problem of adolescence is _____. (540)

3. _____ is the strongest predictor of the onset of an eating disorder in adolescence. The two most serious eating disorders are _____ and _____. (540)

4. Anorexics have an extremely distorted _____, seeing themselves as fat even after they become severely underweight. (541)

5. Describe the physical and behavioral symptoms of anorexia nervosa. (541)

_____

_____

_____

6. Cite cultural, individual, and familial factors related to anorexia nervosa. (541)

Cultural: _____

_____

Individual: _____

_____

Familial: _____

_____

7. Describe three approaches to treating anorexia nervosa, and note which is the most successful. (541)

A. _____

B. _____

C. _____

8. True or False: Almost all anorexics make a full recovery. (541)

9. Bulimia nervosa is an eating disorder in which young people engage in strict dieting and excessive exercise accompanied by _____ _____, typically followed by _____ and _____. (541)

10. Bulimia is (more/less) common than anorexia. (542)

11. How do bulimics tend to differ from anorexics, and what impact does this have for the treatment of the disorder? (542)

_____

_____

_____

_____

12. Contrast the messages that adolescents receive from parents with those that they receive from television with regard to sexual activity, and note the impact on adolescents' understanding of sex. (542-543)

_____

_____

_____

_____

13. The sexual attitudes of American adolescents and adults have become more (conservative/liberal) over the past 30 years. Describe the trends in adolescent sexual behavior over that time period. (543)

_____

_____

_____

14. True or False: Most sexually active teenagers engage in sexual relations with only one partner at a time and engage in relatively low levels of sexual activity. (543)

15. Summarize personal, family, peer, and educational variables that are linked to early and frequent teenage sexual activity. (543-544)

Personal: _____

Family: _____

Peer: _____

Educational: _____

16. Discuss cognitive and social factors that may contribute to adolescents' reluctance to use contraception. (544-545)

Cognitive: _____

_____

_____

Social: _____

_____

_____

17. Cite characteristics of adolescents who are more likely to use contraception. (545)

_____

_____

18. About _____ to _____ percent of teenagers discover that they are lesbian or gay. (545)

19. True or False: Recent research findings indicate that heredity makes a significant contribution to homosexuality. Briefly explain your answer. (546)

_____

_____

_____

20. Describe family factors associated with homosexuality. (546)

_____

_____

21. True or False: Adolescents have the highest incidence of sexually transmitted disease (STD) of any age group. (546)

22. True or False: Nearly all cases of AIDS that appear in young adulthood originate in adolescence. (546)

23. True or False: It is much easier for a female to infect a male with an STD than it is for a male to infect a female. (546)

24. Match each of the following STDs with the correct description. (547)

_____ The most common STD. No symptoms in most cases.

_____ Discharge from the penis or vagina. Can lead to infertility, sterility, and inflammation of the heart.

_____ Blisters on the genitals, fever, aches, and tenderness.

_____ Related to cancer of the cervix.

_____ Discharge from the penis in males; itching, burning, and pelvic pain in females. Can lead to infertility and sterility.

_____ Painless chancre (sore) and swollen glands followed by rash, patchy hair loss, and sore throat. Can lead to damage to brain, heart, and other organs.

1. Gonorrhea
2. Cytomegalovirus
3. Chalmydia
4. Herpes simplex
5. Syphilis
6. Genital warts

25. Discuss at least four ways of preventing STDs. (548)

A. _____

_____

B. _____

_____

C. _____

_____

D. _____

_____

26. The adolescent pregnancy rate in the United States is much higher than that of most other industrialized nations. List three ways in which the United States differs from these nations that may account for this discrepancy. (548)

A. _____

B. _____

C. _____

27. True or False: The United States has one of the highest adolescent abortion rates of any developed country. (548)

28. Why is adolescent parenthood today a much bigger problem than it was 30 years ago? (548)

_____

29. True or False: The percentage of births to unmarried adolescents is fairly consistent across all SES groups. (549)

30. Discuss the consequences of adolescent parenthood in relation to the following areas: (549)

Educational attainment: _____

_____

Marital patterns: _____

_____

Economic circumstances: _____

_____

31. Because many pregnant girls have inadequate diets, smoke and use alcohol and other drugs, and do not receive early prenatal care, their babies often experience _____. Moreover, children of adolescent mothers are also at risk for _____. (550)

32. Cite three maternal factors that are related to better outcomes for teenage mothers and their children. (550)

A. _____

B. _____

C. _____

33. List three components of effective sex education programs. (550)

A. _____

B. _____

C. _____

34. True or False: In European countries where contraception is readily available to teenagers, sexual activity is not higher than in the United States, but pregnancy, childbirth, and abortion rates are much lower. (550)

35. Efforts to prevent adolescent pregnancy and parenthood must go beyond improving sex education and access to contraception to build _____. (550)

36. Discuss three interventions aimed at helping adolescent parents and their children. (552)

A. _____

_____

B. _____

_____

C. _____

_____

37. Discuss the impact of culture on adolescent substance use. (552)

_____

_____

_____

38. True or False: Teenagers who experiment with alcohol, tobacco, and marijuana tend to be seriously maladjusted. (553)

39. Distinguish the characteristics of adolescents who experiment with drugs from those of adolescents who are drug abusers. (553)

_____

_____

_____

_____

40. When adolescents depend on alcohol and hard drugs to deal with daily stress, they fail to learn _____ skills and _____ techniques. (553)

41. Discuss the long-term adjustment of adolescent substance abusers. (553)

_____

_____

_____

42. True or False: School-based programs that "pathologize" adolescent drug use and that employ scare tactics, such as graphic movies showing the dire consequences of addiction, are often most effective in preventing adolescent drug use and abuse. (554)

43. Cite three interventions that help reduce adolescent drug experimentation and help to prevent drug users from endangering themselves and others. (554)

A. _____

_____

B. _____

_____

C. _____

_____

44. Discuss prevention and treatment strategies for drug abuse. (554)

Prevention: _____

_____

_____

Treatment: _____

_____

_____

45. The total rate of unintentional injuries (increases/decreases) during adolescence. Explain why this is the case. (554)

_____

_____

_____

46. _____ are the leading killer of adolescents, accounting for _____ percent of deaths between ages 15 and 19. (554)

47. Outside of automobile accidents, the majority of adolescent deaths are caused by _____. (554)

48. How do coaches often contribute to sports injuries among adolescents? (555)

_____

_____

_____

Biology and Environment: Homosexuality — Coming Out to Oneself and Others

1. Describe the three-phase sequence that homosexual adolescents and adults move through in coming out to themselves and others. (544-545)

    A. _____

    _____

    _____

    B. _____

    _____

    _____

    C. _____

    _____

    _____

2. For homosexual individuals, a first sense of their sexual orientation typically appears between the ages of _____ and _____ and results from

    _____.

    (544)

3. True or False: Most adolescents resolve their feelings of confusion and discomfort at being attracted to same-sex individuals by crystallizing a gay, lesbian, or bisexual identity rather quickly-with a flash of insight into their sense of being different. (544)

4. Discuss the process of coming out, noting factors that are important for reaching this phase of acceptance. (544-545)

    _____

    _____

    _____

    _____

5. True or False: Coming out has the potential to foster many aspects of adolescent development, including self-esteem, psychological well-being, and relationships with family, friends, and co-workers. (545)

Social Issues: Health: Like Mother, Like Child — Intergenerational Continuity in Adolescent Parenthood

1. Based on the research of Janet Hardy, discuss factors that predict the intergenerational continuity of teenage childbearing. (551)

   _____

   _____

   _____

   _____

2. True or False: Hardy found that even when children born to teenage mothers did not repeat the pattern of early childbearing, their development was still compromised. Explain your response. (551)

   _____

   _____

   _____

   _____

Motor Development, Sports Participation, and Physical Activity

1. Describe sex differences in motor development during adolescence. (555)

   _____

   _____

   _____

2. In the United States, about _____ percent of adolescent males and _____ percent of adolescent females take anabolic steroids to boost muscle size and strength. Describe the side effects associated with these drugs. (556)

   _____

   _____

3. True or False: Although high school girls' sports participation has increased dramatically over the past several decades, it still falls far short of boys' participation. (556)

4. Aside from improved motor performance, list benefits of sports participation and exercise. (556)

_____

_____

ASK YOURSELF . . .

REVIEW: Many people believe that the rising sexual passions of puberty cause rebelliousness in adolescents. Where did this belief originate? Explain why it is incorrect.

_____

_____

_____

_____

APPLY: Sabrina, who reached menarche before age 11, was already much taller and heavier than her classmates. She worried that she was going to keep on growing larger and larger. How would you respond to Sabrina's concern?

_____

_____

_____

_____

APPLY: Sixteen-year-old Jonah, who used to go to bed early, stays up until 2 A.M., is often late for school, and dozes in his classes. Why might Jonah's sleep habits have changed, and what can his parents and his school do to help?

_____

_____

_____

_____

REVIEW: List factors that contribute to pubertal timing. Then summarize the consequences of early verses late maturation for adolescent development.

_____

_____

_____

_____

APPLY: After having been home on Friday and Saturday nights for three weekends in a row, 15-year-old Paul was particularly despondent. His parents attributed his gloomy mood to the storm and stress of adolescence. Provide another more likely explanation.

_____

_____

_____

_____

CONNECT: How might adolescent moodiness contribute to the psychological distancing between parents and children that accompanies puberty? (Hint: Think about bidirectional influences in parent-child relationships discussed in previous chapters.)

_____

_____

_____

_____

REFLECT: Think back to your own reactions to the physical changes of puberty. Are they consistent with research findings? Explain.

_____

_____

_____

_____

REVIEW: What unfavorable life experiences do teenagers who engage in early and frequent sexual activity and who abuse drugs have in common? How do those experiences contrast with those of girls at risk for anorexia nervosa?

_____

_____

_____

_____

APPLY: Return to page 548 to review Veronica's life circumstances after becoming a teenage mother. Why are Veronica and her children likely to experience long-term hardships?

_____

_____

_____

_____

CONNECT: Return to Chapter 1, page 10, and Chapter 13, page 516, to review factors that promote resiliency in the face of high life stress. Then list characteristics common to effective pregnancy and substance abuse prevention programs. Are these components well suited to fostering resiliency in at-risk adolescents? Explain.

_____

_____

_____

_____

REFLECT: Describe health education (including drug use prevention) programs that you experienced in secondary school. Did they assist you in resisting peer pressure to engage in sexual activity and alcohol and drug experimentation? Explain.

_____

_____

_____

_____

SUGGESTED STUDENT READINGS

Burt, M. R., Resnick, G., & Novick, E. R. (1998). *Building supportive communities for at-risk adolescents: It takes more than services.* Washington, D. C.: American Psychological Association. Provides new information about how to update and improve community and school-based services for today's adolescents. Stresses prevention, protection, and early detection for behavior problems such as drug abuse, teenage parenthood, and violence.

Johnson, N. G., Roberts, M. C., & Worell, J. P. (Eds.). (1999). *Beyond appearance: A new look at adolescent girls.* Washington, DC: American Psychological Association. An edited volume that explores key topics to understanding girls' adolescent development, including gender-role behaviors, body image issues, relationships with family and friends, sexual decision making, and school- and community-based experiences.

Miller, M. A., Alberts, J. K., Hecht, M. L., Trost, M. R., & Krizek, R. L. (2000). *Adolescent relationships and drug use.* Mahwah, NJ: Lawrence Erlbaum Associates. A collection of chapters exploring the relational features of adolescent drug use, with particular emphasis on risk and protective factors. Other topics include: where drug deals commonly take place, personality characteristics of drug dealers and users, the role of family and peers, and research-based suggestions for drug prevention programs.

Shelley, R. (Ed.). (1997). *Anorexics on anorexia.* Bristol, PA: Kingsley. Individuals from a wide variety of backgrounds who are currently recovering from anorexia nervosa provide descriptions of their experiences. Includes information on the progression of their illness, effects on their families and friends, and effectiveness of treatment.

PUZZLE TERM REVIEW

Puzzle 14

Across

2. An eating disorder in which individuals engage in strict dieting and excessive exercise accompanied by binge eating, often followed by deliberate vomiting or purging with laxatives (2 words)
5. First menstruation
9. Rapid gains in height and weight during adolescence (2 words)
10. Biological changes at adolescence leading to an adult-size body and sexual maturity

Down

1. _____ sexual characteristics are those that directly involve the reproductive organs.
3. Conception of and attitude toward one's physical appearance (2 words)
4. Adolescent _____ ceremony: rite of passage announcing to the community that a young person is making the transition into adolescence or full adulthood
6. _____ sexual characteristics are features visible on the outside of the body but that do not involve the reproductive organs.
7. An eating disorder in which individuals starve themselves due to a compulsive fear of becoming fat and a distorted body image (2 words)
8. First ejaculation of seminal fluid

SELF-TEST

1. Which of the following is currently the most widely accepted view of adolescence? (527)
   a. G. Stanley Hall's view of adolescence as a time of storm and stress
   b. Freud's perspective of adolescence as a period in which instinctual drives reawaken, resulting in psychological conflict and volatile, unpredictable behavior
   c. Margaret Mead's perspective, in which the social environment is entirely responsible for the range of teenage experiences
   d. a balanced perspective that emphasizes both internal stresses and social expectations

2. Sexual maturation in males results from the release of large quantities of _____ from the testes. (528)
   a. estrogen
   b. adrenal androgens
   c. testosterone
   d. thyroxine

3. Physical growth in adolescence: (529)
   a. occurs at a slow, steady pace.
   b. follows the cephalocaudal trend that is also characteristic of infancy and childhood.
   c. leads to large differences in the body proportions of boys and girls.
   d. begins at the same age for both boys and girls.

4. Menarche is the scientific name for: (530)
   a. first ejaculation in males.
   b. first menstruation in females.
   c. maturation of the reproductive organs.
   d. outward signs of sexual maturity, including breast development in females and the appearance of underarm and pubic hair in both sexes.

5. The first sign of puberty in boys is: (531)
   a. spermarche.
   b. the appearance of pubic hair.
   c. enlargement of the testes.
   d. deepening of the voice.

6. Which of the following is true with regard to secular trends in industrialized nations? (532)
   a. Secular trends show a steady decline in age of menarche.
   b. The secular trend in pubertal timing suggests that biological factors play a key role in adolescent growth.
   c. Secular gains in height have increased dramatically over the past several decades.
   d. Secular trends show a decline in rates of overweight and obesity.

7. Boys and girls reactions to pubertal changes are: (533-534)

   a. overwhelmingly positive.
   b. similar in all cultures around the world.
   c. dependent upon age of pubertal onset.
   d. dependent upon prior knowledge of such changes.

8. Compared to school-age children and adults, adolescents: (536)

   a. experience decreased moodiness.
   b. report less favorable moods.
   c. have more stable moods.
   d. are more likely to report negative mood during times of
      day which are spent with friends.

9. Conflict in the parent-child relationship during adolescence: (537)

   a. serves the function of cognitive distancing, a modern substitute
      for physical departure from the family.
   b. is typically severe in nature.
   c. occurs with variable frequency across American subcultures.
   d. continually increases in intensity, resulting in particularly heated
      arguments in late adolescence.

10. Which of the following groups are likely to have positive self-images
    during adolescence? (537-538)

    a. late maturing boys and girls
    b. early maturing boys and girls
    c. late maturing boys and early maturing girls
    d. early maturing boys and late maturing girls

11. Research on the consequences of maturational timing shows that: (539)

    a. early maturing adolescents tend to seek out younger companions in
       an effort to better fit in with peers.
    b. school context (such as, grade and sex composition of the school) has
       little or no impact on maturational timing effects.
    c. maturational timing effects seen in adolescence tend to reverse in
       the long-term (i.e., early maturing boys and late maturing girls show
       a decline in adjustment, whereas late maturing boys and early maturing
       girls show improved adjustment).
    d. maturational timing has no long-term consequences.

12. A tired, listless, irritable adolescent may be suffering from a deficiency
    of what nutrient, rather than from unhappiness? (540)

    a. calories
    b. protein
    c. iron
    d. fat

13. Which of the following is NOT a risk factor for the development of eating
    problems in adolescence? (540)

    a. overweight and obesity in early childhood
    b. early pubertal maturation
    c. dissatisfaction with body image
    d. a home environment marked by a high degree of concern
       with weight and thinness.

14. Anorexia nervosa: (541)

    a. is more common among girls from middle-SES families than among girls from low-SES families.

    b. is characterized by a loss of 25 to 50 percent of one's body weight.

    c. is more prevalent among girls with serious adjustment problems, particularly school failure.

    d. is fairly easy to treat, resulting in a full recovery in most cases.

15. Which of the following is NOT true? (542)

    a. Bulimia nervosa is more common than anorexia nervosa.

    b. Bulimia nervosa is characterized by strict dieting and excessive exercise accompanied by binge eating, often followed by deliberate vomiting and purging with laxatives.

    c. Some bulimics lack self-control not only in eating, but in other areas of their lives as well, engaging in behaviors such as shoplifting and alcohol abuse.

    d. Bulimics tend to deny their eating problems and are often resistant to getting treatment.

16. Which of the following is NOT true? (543)

    a. Most adolescents engage in high levels of sexual activity, often with more than one partner at a time.

    b. Early sexual activity is more common among early maturing adolescents.

    c. Teenagers from low-SES homes are more likely to engage in early sexual activity.

    d. The rate of teenage sexual activity in the United States is about the same as in Western European nations.

17. According to research, which of the following factors is linked with increased contraceptive use among sexually active adolescents? (545)

    a. sexual contact with multiple partners

    b. imitation of the sexually-responsible role-models seen in most prime-time TV shows

    c. having a good relationship with parents and being able to talk openly with them about sex and contraceptives

    d. participation in sex education courses

18. Homosexuality: (546)

    a. results entirely from hereditary causes, most notably the level and impact of prenatal sex hormones.

    b. is caused by growing up with a same-sex parent who is cold, rejecting, or distant.

    c. likely results from a variety of biological and environmental combinations.

    d. has a prevalence rate of approximately 15 percent in the adolescent population.

19. Which of the following is NOT true? (546)

    a. Adolescents have the highest incidence of STD of any age group.

    b. The United States has a much higher rate of STD among the adolescent population than that of other industrialized nations.

    c. One-fifth of the AIDS cases in the United States occur between the ages of 20 and 29, and nearly all of those originate in adolescence.

    d. Over 90 percent of high school students do not even know the basic facts about AIDS.

20. Adolescent mothers: (550)

    a. are as likely as other adolescent girls to finish high school.

    b. usually have a good understanding of child development.

    c. tend to have children who achieve poorly in school and who engage in disruptive social behavior.

    d. rarely experience pregnancy and birth complications.

21. The most effective aspect of sexual education programs for preventing adolescent pregnancy involves: (550)

    a. teaching sexual facts.

    b. providing information about and ready access to contraceptives.

    c. teaching skills for handling sexual situations through creative discussion and role plays.

    d. promoting the value of abstinence.

22. Research on adolescent drug use and abuse shows that: (553)

    a. the majority of adolescents completely abstain from using alcohol and drugs.

    b. adolescents who experiment with alcohol and drugs are psychologically healthy, sociable, and curious individuals.

    c. experimentation with drugs often leads to long-term abuse and dependency.

    d. drug experimentation should be taken lightly by parents and teachers because it is a normal part of adolescent development.

23. Long-term consequences of adolescent drug abuse include all of the following EXCEPT: (553)

    a. failure to learn responsible decision-making skills.

    b. depression and antisocial behavior.

    c. premature entry into marriage and childbearing.

    d. development of alternative coping patterns.

24. The leading killer of adolescents is: (554)

    a. drug overdose.

    b. AIDS.

    c. automobile collisions.

    d. injury related to firearms.

25. The social importance of athletic competence during adolescence is: (556)

    a. strongly linked with peer admiration among girls.

    b. associated with the use of anabolic steroids to increase motor skills.

    c. a result of undue parental pressure.

    d. unrelated to sports participation among female adolescents.

CHAPTER 15

COGNITIVE DEVELOPMENT IN ADOLESCENCE

Chapter Summary

During Piaget's formal operational stage, adolescents' abstract reasoning abilities become well developed. However, cross-cultural research challenges Piaget's view of formal operations as a universal change in cognition that results from adolescents' independent efforts to make sense of their world. Instead, it may be a culturally transmitted way of reasoning specific to literate societies and fostered by school experiences. According to the information-processing perspective, abstract, scientific reasoning is fostered by greater information-processing capacity, years of schooling, and increasingly sophisticated metacognition. Scientific reasoning develops gradually out of many specific experiences. The dramatic cognitive changes of adolescence are reflected in many aspects of everyday behavior, including argumentativeness, self-consciousness and self-focusing, idealism and criticism, and difficulties with planning and decision making.

By adolescence, boys are ahead of girls in mathematical performance, a difference related to biology, experience, social attitudes, and self-esteem. However, these sex differences appear only on some types of test items, such as complex word problems. Language continues to develop in subtle ways. For example, vocabulary expands, the grammatical complexity of speech increases, and communicative competence improves. School transitions create new adjustment problems for adolescents. Timing of school transitions, child-rearing practices, parent involvement in school, the peer culture, and characteristics of the learning environment affect school achievement during the teenage years. Although graduation rates have improved over the last half century, dropping out of school remains high in the United States and is related to a variety of family background and school variables that undermine life success.

During late adolescence, young people face a major life decision: the choice of an occupation. Factors that influence adolescents' vocational decisions include personality, family background, teachers, and gender stereotypes in the larger social environment, and access to vocational information. Compared to young people in European nations, American adolescents who terminate their education with a high school diploma have a more difficult time making the transition from school to a challenging, well-paid career.

369

After reading this chapter, you should be able to:

15.1 Describe the major characteristics of formal operational thought. (562-564)

15.2 Discuss recent research on formal operational thought and its implications for the accuracy of Piaget's formal operational stage. (564-566)

15.3 Explain how information-processing theorists account for cognitive change during adolescence. (566)

15.4 Summarize the development of scientific reasoning during adolescence. (566-568)

15.5 Describe cognitive and behavioral consequences of adolescents' newfound capacity for abstract reasoning. (569-572)

15.6 Describe sex differences in mental abilities during adolescence, along with factors that influence such differences. (573-574)

15.7 Describe changes in vocabulary, grammar, and pragmatics during adolescence. (575-576)

15.8 Discuss the impact of school transitions on adolescent adjustment, and cite ways to ease the strain of these changes. (577-579)

15.9 Discuss family, peer, and school influences on academic achievement during adolescence. (579-584)

15.10 Describe personal, familial, and school factors related to dropping out, and cite ways to prevent early school leaving. (584-587)

15.11 Summarize the phases of vocational development, and discuss factors that influence vocational choice. (588-591)

15.12 Describe the impact of part-time work on adolescents' adjustment, and discuss the problems faced by American non-college bound youths in making the transition from school to work, along with ways to help them. (592, 594)

Piaget's Theory: The Formal Operational Stage

1. Summarize the basic difference between concrete and formal operational reasoning. (562)

   _____

   _____

   _____

2. Name and describe two features of formal operational reasoning. (562-564)

   A. _____

   _____

   _____

   B. _____

   _____

   _____

3. Although Piaget did not view _____ as playing a central role in cognitive development, he acknowledged that it is more important during adolescence. Briefly explain why this is the case. (564)

   _____

   _____

   _____

4. True or False: School-age children have the capacity for hypothetico-deductive reasoning and propositional thought; however, it is inferior to that of adolescents in terms of depth, complexity, and abstractness. (564)

5. Explain why many college students and adults are not yet fully formal operational. (565)

   _____

   _____

   _____

6. True or False: Rather than being situation- or task-specific, formal operations emerge in all contexts at the same time. (565)

7. How does the apparent lack of formal operational reasoning in some village and tribal societies pose a challenge to Piaget's theory? (565-566)

_____

_____

_____

An Information-Processing View of Adolescent Cognitive Development

1. Based on information-processing theory, cite five mechanisms of cognitive change in adolescence, and note which of these is central to the development of abstract thought. (566)

   A. _____

   B. _____

   C. _____

   D. _____

   E. _____

2. As individuals move from childhood into adolescence, they are better able to distinguish _____ from _____ and use _____ to examine their relationship in complex multi-variable situations. (567)

3. Describe the relationship between metacognitive understanding and scientific reasoning ability. (567-568)

   _____

   _____

   _____

4. True or False: Adolescents develop formal operational abilities in a similar step-by-step fashion on different kinds of tasks. (568)

5. True or False: Information-processing research corroborates Piaget's belief that scientific reasoning results from an abrupt, stagewise change. (568)

6. Researchers who study _____ thought have shown that cognitive development is not complete at adolescence. (568)

7. Explain the concept of *relativistic reasoning*. (569)

_____

_____

Consequences of Abstract Thought

1. The acquisition of formal operational thought contributes to greater _____ in adolescence. However, as long as parent-child disagreements remain focused on _____ and do not deteriorate into meaningless battles, they can promote development. (570)

2. Name and describe two distorted images of the relation between self and others that appear at adolescence, and state which of these distortions is the strongest. (570-571)

   A. _____

   _____

   _____

   B. _____

   _____

   _____

3. Explain how the emergence of formal operations leads to idealism and criticism in adolescence. (571-572)

   _____

   _____

   _____

4. Adolescents become better at _____-planning what to do first and what to do next, monitoring progress toward a goal, and redirecting actions that prove unsuccessful. They also show improvements in _____ _____, meaning that they continually evaluate how well they understand while reading and listening. (572)

Sex Differences in Mental Abilities

1. Although boys and girls do not differ in _____ intelligence, they do vary in _____. (573)

2. Girls tend to have an advantage on tests of _____, although the sex differences in this area are slight, whereas boys show advanced performance in the area of _____ ability. (573)

3. The gender gap in mathematics is related to student _____ and _____. Explain how these factors influence girls' math performance. (573)

    _____

    _____

    _____

4. Sex differences in cognitive abilities have (increased/declined) steadily over the past several decades. Cite the primary factor responsible for this change. (573)

    _____

5. Cite ways in which parents and teachers can promote girls' interest in and confidence at math and science. (573-574)

    _____

    _____

    _____

    _____

6. True or False: Girls show better math and science achievement in single-sex secondary schools, where they encounter fewer gender-biased stereotypes and more same-sex role models. (574)

Biology and Environment: Sex Differences in Spatial Abilities

1. Clear sex differences in some spatial reasoning tasks exist by age _____. From middle childhood on, the gender gap favoring males is larger for _____ _____ tasks, in which individuals must rotate a three-dimensional figure rapidly and accurately inside their heads. Males also perform better on _____ tasks, in which people determine spatial relationships by considering the orientation of the surrounding environment. (574)

374

2. Sex differences on _____ tasks, involving analysis of complex visual forms, are weak or nonexistent. (574)

3. True or False: Sex differences in spatial abilities persist throughout the lifespan. (574)

4. Summarize biological and environmental factors that may contribute to sex differences in spatial abilities. (574-575)

Biological: _____

_____

_____

Environmental: _____

_____

_____

Language Development

1. Adolescents add a variety of _____ words to their vocabularies, and abstract thinking permits them to master _____ and _____. Further, adolescents' gain a better grasp of _____ language, including proverbs. (575-576)

2. List two ways in which grammar changes during adolescence. (576)

   A. _____

   B. _____

3. Adolescents show an improved capacity to vary their language style according to the situation. Summarize factors that contribute to this change. (576)

   _____

   _____

   _____

4. Explain the social function of teen slang. (576)

   _____

   _____

Learning in School

1. With each school transition, adolescents' course grades (improve/decline). Cite two reasons for this occurrence. (577)

   A. _____

   B. _____

2. Contrast adolescents' adjustment to school transitions in districts with a 6-3-3 grade organization to those having an 8-4 grade organization. (577-578)

   6-3-3: _____

   _____

   _____

   8-4: _____

   _____

   _____

3. Overall, findings show that the (earlier/later) the school transition occurs, the more dramatic and long-lasting its impact on psychological well-being, especially for (boys/girls). Explain why this is the case. (578)

   _____

   _____

   _____

   _____

4. List three ways of helping adolescents adjust to school transitions. (578-579)

   A. _____

   B. _____

   C. _____

5. _____ parenting is linked to higher academic achievement in adolescence, while _____ parenting, on the other hand, predicts the poorest grades, along with worsening performance over time. (579)

6. Parenting that is especially high in _____ is often linked with better grades among Asian and African-American adolescents. Explain why this is the case. (579)

_____

_____

_____

7. Discuss four factors that enhance academic achievement during adolescence. (580)

A. _____

_____

B. _____

_____

C. _____

_____

_____

_____

8. Discuss the association between parent school involvement and adolescent achievement. (580)

_____

_____

_____

_____

9. List five ways in which schools can increase parental involvement. (580-581)

A. _____

B. _____

C. _____

D. _____

E. _____

10. Summarize peer influences on adolescent academic achievement, noting how both family and the overall climate of the peer culture affect these influences. (581)

_____

_____

_____

_____

11. Describe changes in classroom learning experiences that often coincide with school transitions, noting the impact on student motivation and achievement. (581)

_____

_____

_____

12. True or False: Mixed-ability rather than tracked classes are desirable into the early years of secondary school. (583)

13. True or False: A good student from a disadvantaged family is just as likely to be placed in an academically-oriented, college-bound track as a student of equal ability from a middle-SES background. What affect does this have on student achievement? (584)

_____

_____

_____

14. True or False: High school students are separated into academic and vocational tracks in virtually all industrialized nations. (584)

15. Explain how the system of educational placement in the United States differs from that in Japan, China, and many European nations, and note the impact of these differences on student outcomes. (584)

_____

_____

_____

_____

16. _____ percent of American young people drop out of high school by the age of 18. The dropout rate is particularly high among _____ youths. (584)

17. Summarize personal, familial, and school characteristics related to dropping out. (585)

Personal: _____

_____

_____

Familial: _____

_____

_____

School: _____

_____

_____

18. Discuss four strategies for the prevention of early school leaving. (586-587)

A. _____

_____

B. _____

_____

C. _____

_____

D. _____

_____

19. True or False: Over the past half century, the percentage of adolescents completing high school has more than doubled. (587)

Social Issues: Education: Dispositions Toward Collective Struggle — Highly Achieving, Optimistic African-American High School Students

1. Adolescents' recognition of limited opportunities promotes a
   _____ outlook, which increases the likelihood of
   _____ from school. (582)

2. Explain the collective struggle orientation adopted by some high achieving, optimistic African-American students. (582-583)

   _____

   _____

   _____

3. Discuss the relationship between African-American students' disposition toward the collective struggle and their aspirations for the future. (583)

   _____

   _____

   _____

4. True or False: High achieving African-American students often succeed academically at the expense of connecting with their African-American heritage. (583)

Vocational Development

1. Summarize characteristics of each of the following phases of vocational development. (588)

   Fantasy period: _____

   _____

   Tentative period: _____

   _____

   Realistic period: _____

   _____

2. Match each of the following personality types that affect vocational development with the appropriate description. (589)

_____ Likes well-structured tasks and values social status; tends to choose business occupations

_____ Prefers real-world problems and work with objects; tends toward mechanical occupations

_____ Adventurous, persuasive, and a strong leader; drawn toward sales and supervisory positions

_____ Enjoys working with ideas; likely to select scientific occupations

_____ Has high need for emotional and individual expression; drawn toward fields such as writing, music, and the visual arts

_____ Likes interacting with people; gravitates toward human service occupations

1. Investigative
2. Social
3. Realistic
4. Artistic
5. Conventional
6. Enterprising

3. Explain why personality is only a modest predictor of vocational choice. (589)

_____

_____

_____

4. Adolescents' vocational aspirations tend to show a (weak/strong) correlation with the jobs of their parents. Cite two reasons why this may be. (589)

A. _____

_____

B. _____

_____

5. True or False: When asked who had the greatest impact on their choice of a field of study, college freshmen most often mentioned high school teachers. (590)

6. True or False: Over the past 30 years, boys' career preferences have remained strongly gender stereotyped, whereas girls have shown increasing interest in careers commonly dominated by men. (590)

7. In virtually all fields, the achievements of women (lag behind/far surpass) those of men. _____ play a key role in accounting for these dramatic sex differences. (590-591)

8. Cite two ways in which girls can be encouraged to maintain high career aspirations. (591)

   A. _____

   _____

   B. _____

   _____

9. What type of student is at-risk for becoming a "dreaming drifter", and how can schools better help these students to select an occupational goal that interests them and that fits with their personal attributes? (591)

   _____

   _____

   _____

   _____

10. Identify three reasons why college graduates have an easier time gaining employment in their chosen field than do non-college-bound high school graduates. (592)

    A. _____

    B. _____

    C. _____

11. Describe the nature of most jobs held by adolescents, and discuss the impact of heavy job commitment on adolescents' attitudes and behaviors. (592)

    _____

    _____

    _____

12. When work experiences are specially designed to meet _____ and _____ goals and involve _____ and _____, outcomes are different. Participation in _____ programs is related to positive school and work attitudes, improved academic achievement, lower dropout rates, and continued work in the occupational area after high school graduation. (592)

13. True or False: Like some European nations, the United States has a widespread training system designed to prepare youth for skilled business and industrial occupations and manual trades. (592)

Cultural Influences: Work-Study Apprenticeships in Germany

1. Summarize the features of Germany's work-study apprenticeship system, and explain how it creates a smooth transition from school to work. (593)

_____

_____

_____

_____

2. True or False: Two-thirds of adolescents participate in Germany's apprenticeship system, making it the most common form of secondary education. (593)

3. Identify three major challenges to the implementation a national apprenticeship program in the United States. (593)

A. _____

B. _____

C. _____

ASK YOURSELF . . .

REVIEW: Describe and cite examples of the role of metacognition in adolescent cognitive development.

_____

_____

_____

_____

APPLY: Louis suggested that Franca and Antonio vote for a certain candidate in the upcoming election, offering many good reasons. Franca and Antonio countered with reasons that Louis's favored candidate might not be best, but Louis insisted that his view was right. What aspects of adolescent cognition may have prevented Louis from seeing beyond his own perspective?

_____

_____

_____

_____

CONNECT: What questions raised about Piaget's formal operational stage are similar to those raised about the concrete operational stage? (See Chapter 12, page 440.)

_____

_____

_____

_____

REFLECT: Can you recall displaying the imaginary audience, the personal fable, and idealistic thinking when you were a young teenager? Cite examples of each.

_____

_____

_____

_____

REVIEW: What steps can schools take to help ensure that adolescents' occupational choices match their interests, personality dispositions, and abilities?

_____

_____

_____

_____

APPLY: In high school, Valerie wanted to become an astronomer. By her second year in college, she continued to excel in physics classes, but she gave up her dream of becoming a research scientist. What factors may have led Valerie to change her mind?

_____

_____

_____

_____

CONNECT: Review the discussion of achievement-related attributions on pages 486-487 of Chapter 13. Why are mastery-oriented attributions vital for optimum vocational development in adolescence? What steps can parents and teachers take to promote a mastery-oriented approach and, thereby, foster occupational choice and decision making at later ages?

_____

_____

_____

_____

REFLECT: Describe the career guidance you received from your family, school, and community. Which relationships and experiences were most influential? What assistance would you have liked that was not available?

_____

_____

_____

_____

SUGGESTED STUDENT READINGS

Barling, J., & Kelloway, K. E. (Eds.). (1999). *Young workers: Varieties of experience.* Washington, DC: American Psychological Association. Presents the various nuances and complexities associated with the adolescent's transition from school to the workforce. Topics include: the young worker's first job, attitudes and beliefs about work, the costs and benefits of part-time employment, young people's salary expectations, and the experience of unemployment.

Freedman, M. (1998). *The kindness of strangers: Adult mentors, urban youth and the new volunteerism.* San Francisco: Jossey-Bass. A realistic examination of the mentoring process based on interviews with over 300 mentors, adolescents, and school officials. Vivid illustrations of how adults around the country are trying to help youths turn their lives around.

Johnson, D. (1997). *Minorities and girls in schools: Effects on performance and achievement.* Thousand Oaks, CA: Sage. Four psychologists present their views on what helps and hinders academic success for minority students and girls. Information on how knowledge can be used to change public policy is also presented.

Jones, B. F., Rasmussen, C. M., & Moffitt, M. C. (1997). *Real-life problem solving: Collaborative approach to interdisciplinary learning.* Washington, DC: American Psychological Association. Useful for teachers and students alike, this book illustrates a classroom approach in which open-ended, authentic problems with clear relevance to real-world experiences are used to help students set goals, take control of their learning, and build knowledge from a variety of sources. Includes lesson plans and inspiring case studies.

PUZZLE TERM REVIEW

Puzzle 15

387

Across

1. _____ thought: evaluating the logic of verbal statements without referring to real-world circumstances
6. Comprehension _____: sensitivity to how well one understands a spoken or written message
7. Period of vocational development in which adolescents focus on a general career category and then settle on a single occupation
9. The personal _____ refers to adolescents' belief that they are special and unique.
10. Period of vocational development in which children explore career options through make-believe play
11. _____ operational stage: Piaget's final stage, in which adolescents develop the capacity for abstract, scientific thinking
12. Hypothetico-_____ reasoning begins with a theory of all possible factors that could affect an outcome and inferences of specific hypotheses, which are then tested in a systematic fashion.

Down

2. Reasoning that views all knowledge as embedded in a framework of thought and that accepts the existence of multiple truths
3. _____ thought: cognitive development beyond Piaget's formal operational stage
4. Adolescents' belief that they are the focus of everyone's attention and concern is referred to as the _____ audience.
5. _____ necessity: specifies that the accuracy of conclusions drawn from premises rests on the rules of logic, not on real-world confirmation
8. Period of vocational development in which adolescents weigh vocational options against their interests, abilities, and values

SELF-TEST

1. When faced with a problem, adolescents begin with a general theory, deduce from it specific predictions about outcomes, and then test the predictions — a process Piaget called: (562)

    a. hypothetico-deductive reasoning.
    b. horizontal décalage.
    c. transitive inference.
    d. inductive reasoning.

2. An experimenter hides a poker chip in her hand and asks participants to indicate whether the following statement is true, false, or uncertain: "Either the chip in my hand is green or it is not green." A concrete operational child will indicate uncertainty, whereas a formal operational adolescent will respond "true." This response reflects the formal operational child's understanding of: (563-564)

    a. causal reasoning.
    b. concrete thought.
    c. propositional thought.
    d. relativistic reasoning.

3. Development of formal operations seems to be: (565)

    a. rather sudden, occurring in all contexts at once.
    b. gradual and situation- and task-specific.
    c. unrelated to language processes.
    d. a universal phenomenon.

4. Which of the following mechanisms of cognitive change do researchers believe to be central to the development of abstract thought? (566)

    a. knowledge
    b. metacognition
    c. attention
    d. processing capacity

5. Which of the following is NOT true with regard to the development of scientific reasoning? (568)

    a. The capacity to reason scientifically improves with age.
    b. Scientific reasoning is strongly influenced by years of schooling.
    c. Even after the development of scientific reasoning, adolescents and adults continue to demonstrate a self-serving bias in their thinking, evidenced by the fact that they apply logic more effectively to ideas they doubt than to ones they favor.
    d. Scientific reasoning appears to result from an abrupt, stagewise change, much as Piaget believed.

6. Argumentativeness during adolescence seems to be due to: (570)

    a. general disagreeableness.
    b. the exercising of new reasoning powers.
    c. intense self-reflection.
    d. improvements in self-regulation.

7. Adolescents' belief that they are the focus of everyone else's attention and concern is referred to as: (570)

    a. the imaginary audience.
    b. the personal fable.
    c. narcissism.
    d. social phobia.

8. The personal fable contributes to: (571)

    a. risk-taking.
    b. disengagement from others.
    c. poor school work.
    d. peer conformity.

9. Teenage idealism often leads to a disparity between adults' and teenagers' world views, which is called: (571)

    a. adolescent egocentrism.
    b. the generation gap.
    c. attitudinal asymmetry
    d. cohort bias

10. Which of the following is NOT true of sex differences in mental abilities? (574)

    a. Girls demonstrate an advantage on tests of verbal ability, whereas boys show an advantage in mathematical ability.
    b. Sex differences are greatest among academically talented students.
    c. Sex differences in cognitive abilities of all kinds have declined steadily over the past several decades.
    d. Girls show better math and science achievement in same-sex secondary schools, where they encounter fewer gender-biased messages and more same-sex role models.

11. Gains in language development during adolescence are largely due to: (575)

    a. the memorization of vocabulary lists in school.
    b. the reading of adult literary works.
    c. an improved capacity for reflective thought and abstraction.
    d. enrollment in high school foreign language courses.

12. Teenagers' use of slang reflects: (576)

    a. their inability to develop a vocabulary of abstract words.
    b. their difficulty in grasping figurative language.
    c. a desire to distinguish themselves from adults.
    d. poor development of social perspective-taking skills.

13. Research on school transitions shows that: (578)

    a. the earlier the transition occurs, the more dramatic and long-lasting its negative impact on psychological well-being, especially for girls.
    b. earlier transitions are associated with negative outcomes for boys, whereas girls fare worse with later transitions.
    c. the transition from junior high to high school is relatively problem-free for most adolescents and rarely has an affect on academic achievement.
    d. young people identified as "multiple problem" youths tend to show improved adjustment following the transition to high school.

14. Which of the following is an effective way to ease the strain of school transition in adolescence? (579)

    a. reorganizing schools into 6-3-3 arrangements rather than 8-4 arrangements
    b. making sure that academic expectations in junior high are tougher than those in elementary school
    c. assigning students to classes with several familiar peers or a constant group of new peers
    d. reducing the number of extracurricular activities available in high school so that students have more time to focus on academic work

15. One factor that supports high academic achievement during adolescence is (580)

    a. authoritative parenting.
    b. a strict, rule-oriented classroom structure.
    c. departmentalized school organization whereby students are placed in separate classes for each subject so that they can be taught by experts in each area.
    d. a strong commitment to a part-time job, which fosters a sense of responsibility.

16. Parent-school involvement: (580)

    a. increases as children get older.
    b. is less important at the junior and senior high school levels than it was during elementary school.
    c. has been shown to predict student grade point average beyond the influence of SES and previous academic achievement.
    d. has no impact on student outcomes once they reach the high school level.

17. Research on ability grouping shows that: (583)

    a. students in low-ability groups evidence gains in academic achievement since instruction is adapted to meet their needs.
    b. mixed-ability classes are preferable, at least into the early years of secondary school.
    c. good students from low-SES families are just as likely to be placed in academically oriented, college-bound tracks as are students of equal ability from middle-SES homes.
    d. mixed-ability groups stifle high-achieving students and provide few, if any, intellectual or social benefits to low-achieving students.

18. Which of the following is NOT one of the factors associated with dropping out of high school? (585)

    a. poor school attendance
    b. enrollment in a general education or vocational track
    c. parents who punish their adolescents for low grades
    d. attending a high school with a small student body

19. Potential dropouts benefit from: (586)

    a. remedial instruction in small classes.
    b. decreased emphasis on vocational training.
    c. reduced participation in extracurricular activities.
    d. transferring to a large high school.

20. During which phase of vocational development do adolescents evaluate vocational options in terms of their interests, values, and abilities? (588)

   a. fantasy period
   b. tentative period
   c. realistic period
   d. exploratory period

21. Which of the following is NOT true? (589-590)

   a. Personality is not a strong predictor of vocational choice.
   b. Adolescents' vocational aspirations are strongly correlated with the jobs of their parents.
   c. Peers have the greatest influence on adolescents' career decisions.
   d. Parenting practices play a role in determining adolescents' choice of a career.

22. Which of the following is NOT true? (590)

   a. Over the past 30 years, high school boys' career preferences have remained strongly gender-stereotyped, whereas girls have become increasingly interested in occupations typically dominated by men.
   b. Women's progress in entering and excelling in male-dominated fields has been extremely rapid, and few women now remain in the less well-paid traditionally female professions.
   c. In virtually all fields, women's achievements lag behind those of men.
   d. During the college years, the career aspirations of academically talented females tend to decline.

23. The term "dreaming drifters" is used to refer to adolescents who: (591)

   a. are at high risk for dropping out of high school.
   b. opt to enter the work force after high school rather than pursuing a college education.
   c. remain stuck in the fantasy phase of vocational development.
   d. are highly ambitious with regard to vocational development but who lack knowledge of their preferred vocation and the educational requirements to enter their chosen field.

24. Teenagers who do not plan to go to college after high school graduation: (592)

   a. have a much easier time finding employment than do many college graduates.
   b. are typically limited to low-paid, unskilled jobs.
   c. often have high-quality vocational preparation, which enables them to enter high-paying, high-skill occupations.
   d. do not have well-developed career aspirations.

25. High school students who work more than 15 hours per week: (592)

   a. develop a sense of responsibility which often leads to improved academic performance.
   b. develop many job skills that help them find employment after high school.
   c. have poor school attendance and lower grades.
   d. develop positive attitudes about work life.

CHAPTER 16

EMOTIONAL AND SOCIAL DEVELOPMENT IN ADOLESCENCE

Chapter Summary

Erikson's stage of identity versus identity confusion recognizes the formation of a coherent set of values and life plans as the major personality achievement of adolescence. An organized self-concept and a more differentiated sense of self-esteem prepare the young person for constructing an identity. Adolescents vary in their degree of progress toward developing a mature identity. Identity achievement and moratorium are adaptive statuses associated with positive personality characteristics, parents who offer a "secure base" from which teenagers can confidently move out into the wider world, and schools and communities offering rich and varied opportunities for exploration. Teenagers who remain in identity foreclosure or identity confusion tend to have adjustment difficulties.

Piaget's theory of moral development served as the inspiration for Kohlberg's expanded cognitive-developmental perspective. According to Kohlberg, from late childhood into adulthood, morality changes from concrete, externally controlled reasoning to more abstract, principled justifications for moral choices. Although Kohlberg's theory emphasizes a "masculine" morality of justice rather than a "feminine" morality of care, it does not underestimate the moral maturity of females. A broad range of experiences, including personality, family, school, peer, and cultural factors, fosters moral development. As individuals advance through Kohlberg's stages, moral reasoning becomes better related to behavior.

Biological, social, and cognitive forces combine to make early adolescence a period of gender intensification. Over the adolescent years, relationships with parents and siblings change as teenagers strive to establish a healthy balance between family connection and separation. As adolescents spend more time with peers, intimacy and loyalty become central features of friendship. Adolescent peer groups are organized into tightly knit groups called cliques. Sometimes several cliques with similar values form a crowd, which grants the adolescent an identity within the larger social structure of the school. Although dating relationships increase in intimacy with age, they lag behind same-sex friendships. Peer pressure rises in adolescence, but most teenagers do not blindly conform to the dictates of agemates.

Depression is the most common psychological problem of the teenage years, resulting from a diverse combination of biological and environmental factors. When it is severe, it often leads to suicidal thoughts. The suicide rate increases dramatically at adolescence. Although many teenagers become involved in some delinquent activity, only a few are serious and repeat offenders. Personal, family, school, peer, and neighborhood factors are related to delinquency.

LEARNING OBJECTIVES

After reading this chapter, you should be able to:

16.1 Discuss Erikson's theory of identity development. (600-601)

16.2 Describe changes in self-concept and self-esteem during adolescence. (601-603)

16.3 Describe the four identity statuses, noting how each is related to psychological adjustment, and describe the factors that influence identity development. (603-605, 607)

16.4 Describe Piaget's theory of moral development and Kohlberg's extension of it, noting research that evaluates the accuracy of each. (608-613)

16.5 Discuss sex differences in moral reasoning, with particular attention to Gilligan's argument. (613)

16.6 Describe the factors that influence moral reasoning, and discuss the relationship between moral reasoning and behavior. (613-615)

16.7 Explain why early adolescence is a period of gender intensification, and cite factors that promote the development of an androgynous gender identity. (616-618)

16.8 Discuss familial influences on adolescent development, including the impact of the parent-child relationship, family circumstances, and sibling interaction. (619-622)

16.9 Describe the characteristics of adolescent friendships and peer groups, and discuss the contributions of each to emotional and social development. (622-626)

16.10 Describe adolescent dating relationships. (626)

16.11 Discuss the influence of peer pressure during adolescence, noting how parental behavior is related to adolescent conformity. (627)

16.12 Discuss factors related to adolescent depression and suicide, along with approaches for prevention and treatment. (628-632)

16.13 Discuss factors related to delinquency, and cite strategies for prevention and treatment. (632-636)

STUDY QUESTIONS

Erikson's Theory: Identity versus Identity Confusion

1. Erikson was the first to recognize the formation of a(n) _____ as the major personality achievement of adolescence. (600)

2. Constructing an identity involves defining _____, _____, and _____. (600)

3. True or False: Erikson believed that identity development occurs independently of the outcome of early stages of development. (600)

4. According to Erikson, in complex societies, teenagers experience an _____ — a temporary period of confusion and distress as they experiment with alternatives before settling on a set of values and goals. Teenagers who go through a process of _____ eventually arrive at a mature identity. (600)

5. Explain why current theorists no longer refer to the process of identity development as a "crisis." (601)

_____

_____

_____

6. Describe the negative outcome of Erikson's psychological conflict of adolescence — *identity confusion*. (601)

395

_____

_____

_____

Self-Development

1. List four changes in self-concept that take place during middle and late adolescence. (601-602)

A. _____

B. _____

C. _____

D. _____

2. Self-esteem continues to _____ during the teenage years. To the self-evaluations of middle childhood-academic competence, social competence, physical/athletic competence, and physical appearance-are added several new dimensions, which reflect important concerns of the adolescent period; these include _____, _____, and _____. (602)

3. Except for temporary declines associated with _____ _____, self-esteem rises among most adolescents. (602)

4. Of those young people whose self-esteem declines during adolescence, most are (girls/boys). (602-603)

5. Summarize factors that influence self-esteem during adolescence. (602-603)

_____

_____

_____

_____

6. Match each of the following identity statuses with the appropriate description. (603)

_____ Committed to values and goals without taking time to explore alternatives

_____ Have not yet made definite commitments and are still exploring alternatives

_____ Committed to self-chosen values and goals after having already explored alternatives

_____ Lack clear direction; are not committed to values and goals and are not actively seeking them

1. Identity achievement
2. Moratorium
3. Identity foreclosure
4. Identity diffusion

7. Most adolescents start out at "lower" statuses, such as _____ and _____, but by late adolescence, they have moved toward "higher" statuses, including _____ and _____. (603)

8. True or False: Most adolescent girls follow a different path to identity formation than do boys: They postpone the task of establishing an identity, focusing instead on intimacy development. (603-604)

9. True or False: Research supports the conclusion that identity achievement and moratorium are healthy routes to a mature self-definition, whereas identity foreclosure and identity diffusion are maladaptive. (604)

10. Summarize personality characteristics associated with each identity status. (604-605)

Identity achievement and moratorium: _____

_____

_____

Identity foreclosure: _____

_____

_____

_____

Identity diffusion: _____

_____

_____

11. Match the following identity statuses with the appropriate description of associated personality, familial, school, community, and larger cultural factors. Descriptions may apply to more than one identity status. (605)

_____ Assume that absolute truth is always attainable

_____ Lack confidence in the prospect of ever knowing anything with certainty

_____ Appreciate that they can use rational criteria to choose among alternatives

_____ Feel attached to parents but are also free to voice their own opinions

_____ Have close bonds with parents but lack healthy separation

_____ Report the lowest levels of warm, open communication at home

_____ Fostered by classrooms that promote high-level thinking, as well as extracurricular and community activities that permit teens to take on responsible roles

1. Identity achievement
2. Moratorium
3. Identity foreclosure
4. Identity diffusion

12. Discuss four ways in which adults can support healthy identity development in adolescents. (607)

A. _____

_____

B. _____

_____

C. _____

_____

D. _____

_____

Cultural Influences: Identity Development Among Ethnic Minority Adolescents

1. What is an *ethnic identity*? (606)

_____

_____

2. Explain why ethnic minority adolescents often experience unique problems in developing a sense of identity. (606)

_____

_____

_____

3. Many minority high school students are _____ or _____ on ethnic identity issues. (606)

4. List four ways in which minority adolescents can be helped to resolve identity conflicts constructively. (606)

A. _____

B. _____

C. _____

D. _____

5. What is a *bicultural identity*, and how does it benefit minority adolescents? (606)

_____

_____

_____

Moral Development

1. Describe the main characteristics of Piaget's heteronomous and autonomous stages of moral development. (608-609)

Heteronomous: _____

_____

_____

Autonomous: _____

_____

_____

2. True or False: Although Piaget underestimated children's moral capacities, his account of morality does describe the general direction of moral development. (609)

3. Kohlberg used a _____ procedure to study moral development. He gave children, adolescents, and adults _____-stories that present a genuine conflict between two moral values-and asked them what the main character should do and why. (609)

4. True or False: Kohlberg emphasized that it is the *way an individual reasons* about a dilemma, not the *content of the response*, which determines moral maturity. (609)

5. List two factors that Kohlberg believed to promote moral understanding. (610)

A. _____

B. _____

6. Explain the basic characteristics of moral reasoning at each of Kohlberg's three levels: (610-611)

Preconventional: _____

_____

Conventional: _____

_____

Postconventional: _____

_____

7. Match each of the following moral orientations with the appropriate description. (610-612)

_____ Laws must be obeyed under all circumstances, rules must be enforced in the same even-handed manner for everyone, and each member of society has a personal duty to uphold them

_____ Right action is defined by self-chosen ethical principles of conscience that are valid for all humanity, regardless of law and social agreement

_____ Ignore people's intentions and focus on fear of authority and avoidance of punishment as reasons for behaving morally

_____ Desire to obey rules because they promote social harmony

_____ Regard laws and rules as flexible and emphasize fair procedures for interpreting and changing the law in order to protect individual rights and the interests of the majority

_____ View right action as flowing from self-interest; reciprocity is understood as equal exchange of favors

1. Punishment and obedience orientation
2. Instrumental purpose orientation
3. "Good boy-good girl" orientation
4. Social-order-maintaining orientation
5. Social contract orientation
6. Universal ethical principle orientation

8. True or False: Longitudinal research suggests that individuals do not move through the stages of moral development in the order in which Kohlberg suggested. (612)

9. True or False: The development of moral understanding is very slow and gradual. (612)

10. Discuss the application of Kohlberg's stages to real-life, as opposed to hypothetical, moral dilemmas. (612-613)

_____

_____

_____

11. Carol Gilligan believes that feminine morality emphasizes an _____ that is devalued in Kohlberg's model. Explain what she meant by this. (613)

_____

_____

_____

12. True or False: Research shows that when given a moral dilemma, females fall behind males in moral development according to Kohlberg's scheme, thus supporting Gilligan's claims. (613)

13. A flexible, _____ approach to new information and experiences is linked to gains in moral reasoning. (614)

14. Describe child-rearing practices that promote gains in moral development during adolescence. (614)

_____

_____

_____

15. True or False: Years of schooling is one of the most powerful predictors of moral maturity. (614)

16. Cite characteristics of peer interaction that promote moral understanding and movement to higher moral stages. (614)

_____

_____

_____

17. True or False: Cross-cultural research shows that individuals in technologically advanced, urban cultures move through Kohlberg's stages more quickly and advance to higher levels of moral reasoning than do individuals in village societies. Based on your response, provide some possible explanations. (614)

_____

_____

_____

18. Kohlberg's theory (does/does not) capture all of the important aspects of moral reasoning in every culture. (615)

19. Kohlberg believed that moral thought and action come together at _____ levels of moral understanding. Is this belief supported by research? _____ (615)

Social Issues: Education — Development of Civic Responsibility

1. Civic responsibility involves _____ of political issues and the means through which citizens can resolve differing views fairly; _____ of attachment to the community, of wanting to make a difference in its welfare, and of trust in others' fairness and helpfulness; and _____ for achieving civic goals. (616)

2. Summarize family, school, and community influences that contribute to adolescents' civic responsibility. (616-617)

Family: _____

_____

School: _____

_____

Community: _____

_____

3. In an investigation of youth in seven countries, adolescents were more likely to regard civic responsibility as an important life goal when (1) their families emphasized _____ and _____; (2) their school engaged in _____ practices, and they felt _____; and (3) they _____ in their community. (617)

Gender Typing

1. What is gender intensification? (616)

   _____

   _____

2. Although it occurs in both sexes, gender intensification is stronger for (boys/girls). (616)

3. Discuss biological, social, and cognitive factors associated with gender intensification. (617-618)

   Biological: _____

   _____

   _____

   Social: _____

   _____

   _____

   Cognitive: _____

   _____

   _____

4. True or False: Androgynous adolescents tend to be psychologically healthier. (618)

The Family

1. Effective parenting strikes a balance between _____ and _____. (619)

2. _____ parenting continues to be the most effective style in adolescence. Discuss at least four specific parenting practices that foster cognitive and social development in adolescence. (619-620)

   A. _____

   _____

   B. _____

   _____

C. _____

_____

D. _____

_____

3. Once teenagers de-_____ their parents, they no longer bend as easily to parental authority as they did at earlier ages. (619)

4. Discuss the life transition that parents may be experiencing as their adolescent children are undergoing their own life transitions, and note how this impacts the parent-child relationship. (620)

_____

_____

_____

_____

5. True or False: Parents who are financially secure, invested in their work, and happy with their marriages find it easier to grant teenagers appropriate autonomy. (621)

6. During adolescence, sibling relationships often become (more/less) intense in both positive and negative feelings. Additionally, adolescents invest (more/less) time in their siblings. Explain how these changes affect the quality of attachment between siblings. (621-622)

_____

_____

Peer Relations

1. Cite the two characteristics of friendship stressed by teenagers. (622-623)

A. _____ B. _____

2. List three changes that result from adolescents' revised view of friendship. (623)

A. _____

B. _____

C. _____

3. Briefly discuss how friendships change during the transition to middle or junior high school. (623)

_____

_____

_____

4. Describe sex differences in friendship during adolescence. (623-624)

_____

_____

_____

_____

5. True or False: Androgynous boys are just as likely as girls to form intimate same-sex ties, whereas boys who identify strongly with the traditional masculine role are less likely to do so. (624)

6. Cite three reasons why friendship is related to psychological health in adolescence. (624)

A. _____

_____

B. _____

_____

C. _____

_____

7. The peer groups of the early teenage years are organized around _____, small groups of five to seven members who are good friends, and therefore, resemble one another in _____, _____, and _____. Describe the main characteristics of this type of peer group. (624-625)

_____

_____

_____

8. Describe the structure of an adolescent crowd, and provide some examples of typical crowds. (625)

_____

_____

_____

_____

9. True or False: Peer group values are often an extension of values learned in the home. (625)

10. Describe the function of mixed-sex cliques in early adolescence. (625)

_____

_____

_____

11. True or False: Crowds decline in importance across the adolescent years. (625)

12. Describe younger and older adolescents' different reasons for dating. (626)

Younger: _____

_____

Older: _____

_____

13. Describe the unique challenges faced by homosexual adolescents in initiating and maintaining romances. (626)

_____

_____

_____

14. In relation to peer pressure and conformity, describe the differing spheres of influence of parents and peers during the adolescent years. (627)

Parents: _____

Peers: _____

15. _____ parenting is related to greater resistance to unfavorable peer pressure. (627)

Problems of Development

1. About _____ to _____ percent of American teenagers have experienced one or more depressive episodes, and _____ to _____ percent are chronically depressed. (628)

2. Summarize consequences of adolescent depression. (628)

   _____

   _____

   _____

3. Explain why adolescent depressive symptoms tend to be overlooked by parents and teachers. (628)

   _____

   _____

4. Explain how biology and experience combine to activate depression among youths. (628-629)

   _____

   _____

   _____

5. List two possible explanations for the higher rate of depression among adolescent girls as compared to boys. (629-630)

   A. _____

   B. _____

6. True or False: Suicide is currently the third leading cause of death among young people. (630)

7. Discuss sex differences in suicidal behavior, noting whether boys or girls are more likely to kill themselves. (630)

_____

_____

_____

8. True or False: Gay, lesbian, and bisexual youth are three times more likely to attempt suicide than are other adolescents. (631)

9. Describe two types of young people who tend to commit suicide. (631)

A. _____

_____

B. _____

_____

10. Cite cognitive changes that contribute to the rise in suicide among adolescents. (631)

_____

_____

11. List at least five warning signs of suicide. (631)

A. _____

B. _____

C. _____

D. _____

E. _____

12. Discuss at least four ways of responding to an adolescent who might be suicidal. (632)

A. _____

_____

B. _____

_____

C. _____

_____

D. _____

_____

13. True or False: Teenage suicides often take place in clusters. (632)

14. Juvenile delinquents are children or adolescents who engage in _____
    acts. (632)

15. Young people under the age of 21 account for _____ percent of police arrests
    in the United States. (632)

16. Explain why delinquency rises during early adolescence, remains high in middle
    adolescence, and then declines into young adulthood. (633)

_____

_____

17. Describe personal, familial, peer, school, and neighborhood factors associated
    with delinquency. (633-634)

Personal: _____

_____

Familial: _____

_____

Peer: _____

_____

School: _____

_____

Neighborhood: _____

_____

18. Prevention of delinquency must start _____ and take place at
    _____. (634)

19. Describe characteristics of treatment programs for delinquents that work best. (635)

_____

_____

_____

Biology and Environment: Two Routes to Adolescent Delinquency

1. Persistent adolescent delinquency follows two paths of development, one with an onset of _____ problems in childhood, the second with an onset in _____. Longitudinal research reveals that the (early/late) onset type is far more likely to lead to a life course pattern of aggression and criminality. (634)

2. True or False: Adolescent-onset delinquent youth show significantly higher levels of serious offenses, involvement with deviant peers, substance abuse, unsafe sex, dangerous driving, and time spent in correctional facilities than do childhood-onset delinquent youth. (634)

3. Describe characteristics that distinguish early-onset from late-onset delinquent youth. (634-635)

Early-onset: _____

_____

_____

Late-onset: _____

_____

_____

410

ASK YOURSELF . . .

REVIEW: Return to the opening of this chapter and review the conversation between Louis and Darryl. Which identity status best characterizes the two boys, and why? What personal and contextual factors may have attributed to their identity progress?

_____

_____

_____

_____

APPLY: At age 13, Jeremy described himself as both "cheerful" and "glum." At age 16, he said, "Sometimes I'm cheerful, at other times I'm glum, so I guess I'm kind of moody." What accounts for this change in Jeremy's self-concept?

_____

_____

_____

_____

CONNECT: Jules is an identity-achieved young person, secure in his self-chosen values and future goals. What have you learned about Franca and Antonio's parenting style in previous chapters that helps explain Jules's adaptive approach to identity formation?

_____

_____

_____

_____

REFLECT: How would you characterize your identity status? Is it the same or different across identity domains of sexuality, vocation, religious beliefs, and political values? Describe the path of identity development you followed, along with factors that may have influenced it.

_____

_____

_____

_____

411

REVIEW: In the discussion of Kohlberg's theory, why were examples of both prostealing and antistealing responses to the Heinz dilemma presented for Stages 1 through 4 but only prostealing responses for Stages 5 and 6?

_____

_____

_____

_____

APPLY: Tam grew up in a small village culture, Lydia in a large industrial city. At age 15, Tam reasons at Kohlberg's Stage 2, Lydia at Stage 4. What factors might account for the difference?

_____

_____

_____

_____

CONNECT: Are environmental influences that foster identity development also likely to promote moral development, and vice versa?

_____

_____

_____

_____

REFLECT: Did you experience gender identification in early adolescence? If so, how was it evident in your attitudes and behavior?

_____

_____

_____

_____

REVIEW: What type of parenting fosters competence in adolescence? Explain why that style of parenting is effective, and cite its many positive outcomes.

_____

_____

_____

_____

APPLY: Phyllis likes her 14-year-old daughter Farrah's friends, but she wonders what Farrah gets out of hanging out at Jakes's Pizza Parlor with them on Friday and Saturday evenings. Explain to Phyllis what Farrah is learning.

_____

_____

_____

_____

CONNECT: How might gender intensification contribute to the shallow quality of early adolescent dating relationships?

_____

_____

_____

_____

REFLECT: To which crowd did you belong in junior high and high school? Did you change crowds? If so, why? How did family experiences influence your crowd membership?

_____

_____

_____

_____

REVIEW: Why are adolescent girls at greater risk for depression, and adolescent boys at greater risk for suicide?

_____

_____

_____

_____

APPLY: Throughout his school years, Mac had difficulty learning, was disobedient, and picked fights with peers. At age 16, he was arrested for burglary. Zeke had been a well-behaved child in elementary school, by around age 13 he started spending time with the "wrong crowd." At age 16, he was arrested for property damage. Which boy is more likely to become a long-term offender, and why?

_____

_____

_____

_____

CONNECT: Return to Chapter 14 and reread the sections on teenage pregnancy and substance abuse. What factors do these programs have in common with adolescent suicide and delinquency? How would you explain the findings that teenagers who experience one of these difficulties are likely to display others?

_____

_____

_____

_____

SUGGESTED STUDENT READINGS

Crockett, L. J., & Silbereisen, R. K. (Eds.). (1999). *Negotiating adolescence in times of social change.* New York: Cambridge University Press. Explores the process through which societal changes affect the course of adolescent development and adolescents' social and psychological adjustment.

Furman, W., Brown, B. B., & Feiring, C. (Eds.). (1999). *The development of romantic relationships during adolescence.* New York: Cambridge University Press. Examines adolescent romantic relationships and general processes and individual differences within the general context of adolescent development.

Graber, J. A., Brooks-Gunn, J., & Petersen, A. C. (Eds.). (1996). *Transitions through adolescence: Interpersonal domains and contexts.* Mahwah, NJ: Erlbaum. Experts contributing chapters to this volume discuss adolescent transitions in three domains: the peer system, the family system, and school and work contexts. Among the topics considered are friendship, child bearing, school transitions, and low-wage employment. In addition to new research, the authors consider intervention strategies and policy implications.

Gullotta, T. P., Adams, G. R., & Montemayor, R. (Eds.). (1998). *Delinquent violent youth.* Thousand Oaks, CA: Sage. Provides an overview of crime among both urban and rural youths. Takes up such issues as how various social factors influence delinquency, treatment for violent behavior, and social policies that prevent crime.

Kroger, J. (1999). *Identity development: Adolescence through adulthood.* Thousand Oaks, CA: Sage Publications. An in-depth analysis of identity formation throughout adolescence and adulthood. Also examines the features of identity that remain stable and those that change across the lifespan.

Taylor, R. W., & Wang, M. C. (Eds.). (1997). *Social and emotional adjustment and family relations in ethnic minority families.* Mahwah, NJ: Erlbaum. Each chapter in this book considers the impact of family context on emotional and social adjustment of ethnic minority adolescents. Questions addressed include: How do parents' experiences in the labor market affect family functioning and adolescent adjustment? What impact do neighborhoods and communities have on parenting practices and adolescents' well-being? Do particular ethnic groups have unique parenting styles, and how are they related to adolescents' competence?

PUZZLE TERM REVIEW

Puzzle 16

Across

7. Kohlberg's highest level of moral development, morality is defined in terms of abstract principles and values that apply to all situations and societies
10. A well-organized conception of the self made up of values, beliefs, and goals to which the individual is solidly committed
13. Identity constructed by adolescents who explore and adopt values from both their subculture and the dominant culture
16. Identity versus identity _____: Erikson's psychological conflict of adolescence
17. A large, loosely organized group consisting of several cliques; membership is based on reputation and stereotype

Down

1. _____ morality: Piaget's first stage of moral development; children view moral rules as permanent, unchangeable features of the external world
2. Kohlberg's first level of moral development; moral understanding is based on rewards, punishments, and the power of authority figures
3. Gender _____: Increased gender stereotyping of attitudes and behavior
4. Identity status of individuals who have accepted ready-made values and goals that authority figures have chosen for them
5. Kohlberg's second level of moral development; moral understanding is based on conforming to social rules to ensure positive relationships and social order
6. Identity status of individuals who are exploring alternatives in an effort to find values and goals to guide their life
8. Identity status of individuals who have explored and committed themselves to self- chosen values and goals
9. _____ identity: Aspect of self that includes sense of ethnic group membership and Attitudes associated with that membership
11. Identity status of individuals who have no commitments to values and goals and are not actively trying to reach them
12. _____ morality: Piaget's second stage of moral development; children view rules as flexible, socially-agreed upon principles that can be revised
14. Sense of self as a separate, self-governing individual
15. Small group of 5 to 7 members who are good friends

SELF-TEST

1. Erikson was the first to recognize the formation of a(n) _____ as the major personality achievement in adolescence. (600)

   a. self-concept
   b. identity
   c. moral understanding
   d. gender schema

2. Compared to school-age children, adolescents place more emphasis on _____ in their self-descriptions. (602)

   a. physical appearance
   b. favorite activities
   c. social virtues
   d. school performance

3. All of the following are dimensions added to the self-evaluation of adolescents EXCEPT: (602)

   a. moral behavior.
   b. close friendship.
   c. romantic appeal.
   d. job competence.

4. Which of the following is NOT true? (603)

   a. Most adolescents show a rise in self-esteem.
   b. Girls are more likely than are boys to show declines in self-esteem during adolescence.
   c. African-American adolescents tend to have lower self-esteem than Caucasian adolescents.
   d. Cross-cultural research suggests that patterns of adolescent self-esteem are similar in industrialized nations throughout the world.

5. Kieran has followed the religious path of his family without exploring alternatives and tends to be defensive when his teenage friends bring up the subject. Kieran is: (603)

   a. identity foreclosed.
   b. identity diffused.
   c. in moratorium.
   d. identity achieved.

6. Adolescents who lack confidence in the prospect of ever knowing anything with certainty and who report low levels of warm, open communication in the home are likely to have which identity status? (605)

   a. identity achievement
   b. moratorium
   c. identity foreclosure
   d. identity diffusion

7. In Piaget's heteronomous stage: (608)

   a. an act's wrongness is judged on the basis of intent to do harm.
   b. moral rules are viewed as permanent, unchangeable features of the external world.
   c. rules are regarded as socially-agreed-upon principles that can be revised.
   d. a standard of fairness called reciprocity is used.

8. According to Kohlberg, which is more important in determining the maturity of responses to moral dilemmas? (609)

   a. reasoning rather than content
   b. content rather than reasoning
   c. reasoning rather than emotion
   d. emotion rather than reasoning

9. When an individual's moral reasoning stems from self-interest, which stage of Kohlberg's theory would best characterize his or her level of moral understanding? (610)

   a. Stage 2: The instrumental purpose orientation
   b. Stage 3: The "good boy-good girl" orientation
   c. Stage 4: The social-order-maintaining orientation
   d. Stage 6: The universal ethical principle orientation

10. When individuals are faced with real-life, as opposed to hypothetical, moral dilemmas, their moral reasoning tends to: (612)

    a. become more mature.
    b. become less mature.
    c. remain at the same level of maturity.
    d. follow no predictable pattern.

11. Research shows that: (613)

    a. females show less mature moral reasoning than do males.
    b. females show more mature moral reasoning than do males.
    c. females and males reason about moral issues differently, with females tending to emphasize an "ethic of care", while males tend to emphasize justice or to use justice and care equally.
    d. males and females do not differ in the level or content of their moral reasoning.

12. Which of the following is NOT associated with advanced moral reasoning? (614)

    a. authoritative parenting
    b. completion of more years of schooling
    c. emotionally intense peer discussion
    d. membership in a small, collectivist community

13. During early adolescence, gender intensification is: (616)

    a. stronger for boys.
    b. stronger for girls.
    c. the same for girls and boys.
    d. not yet an important issue.

14. Which of the following is true of the parent-child relationship during adolescence? (620)

    a. Parents and adolescents need to focus less on their attachment relationship and should begin to focus entirely on issues of separation.
    b. Adolescents tend to idealize their parents and are more compliant with parental authority than they were at earlier ages.
    c. Both adolescents and parents are undergoing major life transitions, and the pressures of each generation often oppose the other.
    d. Positive parent-child interaction declines in late adolescence as teenagers start to drive, hold part-time jobs, and stay out late.

15. During adolescence, siblings: (622)

    a. have a more unequal relationship, with younger siblings showing greater willingness to accept direction from older siblings.
    b. devote more time to each other.
    c. have less intense interactions.
    d. experience a decline in the quality of their relationship.

16. Teenagers in the United States spend more time together outside the classroom than do teenagers in Asian countries. The difference is primarily due to: (622)

    a. less demanding academic standards in the United States.
    b. higher rates of maternal employment in the United States.
    c. differences in peer group structures between the countries.
    d. differences in parenting styles between the countries.

17. Which of the following is NOT true of adolescent friendships? (623)

    a. Adolescent friendships are fairly stable except during the transition to middle or junior high school.
    b. Teens of both sexes avoid forming friendships with aggressive boys.
    c. Girls' friendships are based largely on emotional closeness, whereas boys' friendships tend to be grounded in shared activities.
    d. In early adolescence, young people who are either very popular or very unpopular are more likely to have other-sex friends than are "average" young people.

18. Adolescent crowds: (625)

    a. are more intimate than cliques.
    b. become increasingly important across adolescence.
    c. are typically small groups of about five to seven members who are close friends.
    d. are based on reputation and stereotype.

19. In early adolescence, dating: (626)

    a. is done for recreational purposes, as well as to achieve status among agemates.
    b. is focused on psychological intimacy, shared interests, and the search for a good permanent partner.
    c. fosters social maturity.
    d. allows girls to gain status among same-sex peers, as well as strengthening friendship ties.

419

20. Peers would be most likely to influence one another's: (627)

    a. religious values.
    b. choice of college.
    c. choice of clothes.
    d. career plans.

21. Adolescent depression: (628)

    a. occurs more often in boys than in girls.
    b. is usually recognized quickly by parents and teachers.
    c. can be entirely attributed to biological causes.
    d. prevents young people from mastering important developmental tasks, including identity development.

22. Which of the following is true? (630)

    a. Suicide rates have been steadily declining over the past 30 years.
    b. Boys are 4 to 5 times more likely to kill themselves than are girls.
    c. Ethnic minority adolescents have higher suicide rates than Caucasian-American adolescents.
    d. Adolescent suicide rates are similar in all industrialized nations.

23. Which of the following factors contributes to the sharp rise in suicide from childhood to adolescence? (631)

    a. adolescent impulsiveness
    b. belief in the personal fable
    c. increased emotional distance between parent and child
    d. impersonal school environments

24. Youth crime: (632)

    a. has declined over the past decade.
    b. accounts for a minimal proportion of police arrests-less than 5 percent.
    c. is most often serious in nature.
    d. forecasts a long-term pattern of anti-social behavior for most adolescents.

25. All of the following are factors associated with juvenile delinquency EXCEPT: (633-634)

    a. parental divorce and remarriage
    b. inconsistent discipline and low monitoring
    c. acceptance by a conventional peer group
    d. poor school performance

ANSWERS TO PUZZLES

Puzzle 1a

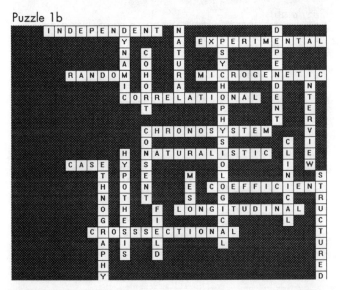

Puzzle 1b

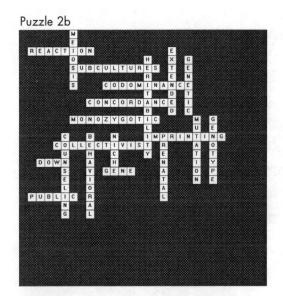

Puzzle 2b

Puzzle 2a

Puzzle 3

ANSWERS TO PUZZLES

Puzzle 5a

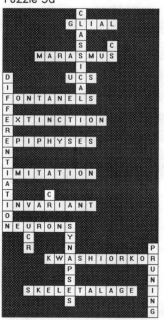

Puzzle 4a

Puzzle 4b

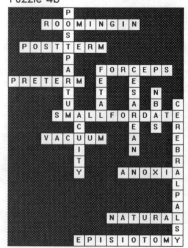

Puzzle 5b

Puzzle 6a

ANSWERS TO PUZZLES

Puzzle 6b

Puzzle 7a

Puzzle 8

Puzzle 7b

Puzzle 9a

ANSWERS TO PUZZLES

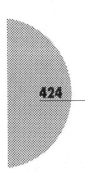

Puzzle 10b

Puzzle 9b

Puzzle 11

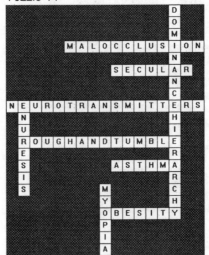

Puzzle 10a

Puzzle 12a

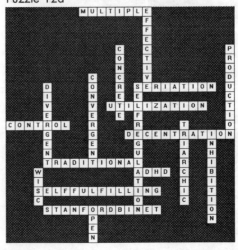

ANSWERS TO PUZZLES

Puzzle 12b

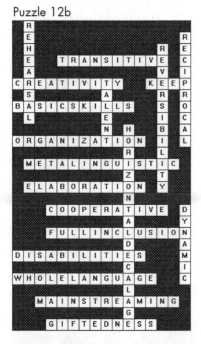

Puzzle 13a

Puzzle 13b

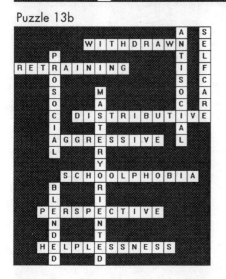

Puzzle 14

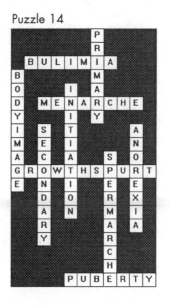

425

Puzzle 15

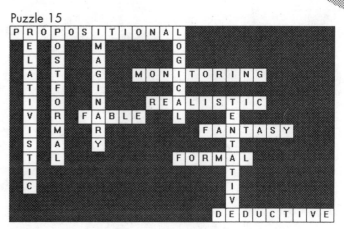

Puzzle 16

ANSWERS TO SELF-TESTS

Chapter 1

1. c	2. c	3. b	4. b	5. a
6. c	7. d	8. d	9. c	10. b
11. d	12. d	13. b	14. c	15. a
16. b	17. c	18. a	19. b	20. a
21. c	22. b	23. d	24. c	25. d

Chapter 2

1. b	2. d	3. a	4. c	5. a
6. c	7. c	8. b	9. d	10. a
11. d	12. b	13. a	14. b	15. b
16. d	17. a	18. d	19. d	20. c
21. b	22. a	23. d	24. a	25. c

Chapter 3

1. b	2. a	3. c	4. a	5. d
6. c	7. d	8. b	9. c	10. b
11. d	12. a	13. c	14. a	15. c
16. d	17. b	18. c	19. a	20. a
21. d	22. d	23. b	24. c	25. b

Chapter 4

1. a	2. c	3. b	4. a	5. d
6. a	7. c	8. c	9. c	10. c
11. a	12. b	13. c	14. c	15. d
16. a	17. d	18. b	19. a	20. c
21. b	22. c	23. d	24. b	25. a

Chapter 5

1. c	2. b	3. b	4. a	5. d
6. b	7. b	8. a	9. d	10. b
11. a	12. c	13. d	14. a	15. c
16. b	17. b	18. a	19. c	20. a
21. d	22. b	23. d	24. a	25. b

Chapter 6

1. a	2. b	3. a	4. c	5. c
6. d	7. c	8. b	9. a	10. c
11. a	12. d	13. c	14. b	15. d
16. c	17. a	18. b	19. d	20. d
21. a	22. c	23. a	24. b	25. d

Chapter 7

1. a	2. c	3. a	4. d	5. a
6. b	7. b	8. d	9. c	10. a
11. c	12. b	13. b	14. c	15. c
16. d	17. c	18. b	19. d	20. a
21. c	22. a	23. b	24. d	25. b

Chapter 8

1. d	2. c	3. b	4. c	5. a
6. a	7. b	8. c	9. d	10. c
11. a	12. b	13. d	14. a	15. b
16. c	17. c	18. d	19. b	20. b
21. a	22. d	23. d	24. a	25. a

Chapter 9

1. c	2. b	3. a	4. a	5. d
6. c	7. b	8. a	9. d	10. d
11. a	12. b	13. b	14. c	15. a
16. b	17. a	18. d	19. b	20. a
21. b	22. c	23. a	24. c	25. d

Chapter 10

1. c	2. c	3. a	4. a	5. b
6. c	7. b	8. a	9. d	10. d
11. b	12. c	13. c	14. b	15. c
16. c	17. a	18. a	19. b	20. c
21. d	22. a	23. c	24. b	25. d

Chapter 11

1. a	2. b	3. a	4. d	5. b
6. c	7. a	8. d	9. d	10. b
11. c	12. a	13. b	14. d	15. c
16. b	17. a	18. d	19. b	20. c
21. a	22. c	23. b	24. a	25. d

Chapter 12

1. c	2. b	3. c	4. a	5. b
6. d	7. c	8. a	9. d	10. b
11. d	12. b	13. b	14. c	15. a
16. c	17. d	18. c	19. a	20. d
21. b	22. c	23. d	24. b	25. b

Chapter 13

1. d	2. b	3. c	4. a	5. b
6. c	7. d	8. a	9. c	10. b
11. d	12. b	13. b	14. c	15. b
16. b	17. d	18. b	19. b	20. a
21. b	22. c	23. d	24. d	25. a

Chapter 14

1. d	2. c	3. c	4. b	5. c
6. a	7. d	8. b	9. a	10. d
11. c	12. c	13. a	14. b	15. d
16. a	17. c	18. c	19. d	20. c
21. b	22. b	23. d	24. c	25. b

Chapter 15

1. a	2. c	3. b	4. b	5. d
6. b	7. a	8. a	9. b	10. d
11. c	12. c	13. a	14. c	15. a
16. c	17. b	18. d	19. a	20. b
21. c	22. b	23. d	24. b	25. c

Chapter 16

1. b	2. c	3. a	4. c	5. a
6. d	7. b	8. a	9. a	10. b
11. c	12. d	13. b	14. c	15. c
16. a	17. b	18. d	19. a	20. c
21. d	22. b	23. b	24. a	25. c

NOTES

NOTES

NOTES

NOTES

NOTES

NOTES

NOTES

NOTES

NOTES

NOTES

NOTES

NOTES